The Complete Idiot's Guide to Gardening Reference Card

Tool Tips

➤ Start by buying a steel-tempered spade, spading fork, hoe, trowel, pruning shears, and hat. The rest you can pick up later.

➤ Keep all your tools clean; keep sharp-edged tools both clean and sharp.

➤ Bring tools indoors when not in use.

➤ Drain water from hoses and store indoors for winter.

What to Do When You See Plant Trouble

➤ Always wait until you see the signs of bugs before you treat the plant. The correct diagnosis is the key to success.

➤ Get to know the "good bugs" in the garden. Natural predators that are helpful in the garden include toads, earwigs, ladybugs, and praying mantises.

➤ If a plant loses its vigor or does not recover rapidly after treatment, discard it.

Tips for Digging the Bed

➤ Remove all weeds and grass before you do anything to your new garden bed.

➤ Invest in heavy-duty tools—they'll pay for themselves over time.

➤ Use tools for exactly what they were designed for and use them properly.

➤ Pay attention to your body for signs of dehydration, fatigue, or sun poisoning.

➤ Don't hurt your back! Be careful carrying heavy loads.

Tips for Container Planting

➤ Don't overwater! More plants are killed this way than any other. The soil should be dry between waterings.

➤ Potting soils (or potting mediums, as they are called), are a soilless mix. You can buy potting soils at the garden center or, if you are feeling ambitious, you can make your own potting medium.

➤ If your plant is top-heavy, or your plant's container is small, add weight to the bottom of the container with crushed rocks or chips of broken clay pots.

➤ Never allow roots to stick out of the pot—they need protection from the drying winds and sun.

Good Gardening: All-Time Favorite Tips for Healthy Plants

➤ However easy some annuals are to grow, watch any growing plant to be sure it's healthy and doing well.

➤ Deadhead and prune plants to stimulate new growth.

➤ Taller perennials on single stems and plants with heavy flowers, like peonies, need to be staked.

➤ Divide perennials only in the spring or fall, when the soil temperature is cool.

➤ Learn how your vine grows so you can train and support it.

alpha
books

Easiest Annuals You'll Ever Grow

This list includes the "0" maintenance plants listed in Chapter 7. The common name is first, followed by genus name in parenthesis.

Cockscombe *(Celosia)*   Candytuft *(Iberis)*   Portulaca *(Portulaca)*

Trailing Lobelia *(Lobelia)*   Sweet Alyssum *(Lobularis)*   Nasturtium *(Tropaeolum)*

Easiest Self-Sowing Annuals

The common name is first, followed by genus name in parenthesis.

Spider Flower *(Cleome)*   Sunflower *(Helianthus)*

Flowering Tobacco *(Nicotiana)*   Forget-me-Not *(Myosotis)*

Poppy *(Papaver)*

Ten Easiest Perennials to Grow and Maintain

Achillea	*Hemerocallis*	*Lysimachia*
Alchemilla	*Hosta*	*Phlox*
Astilbe	*Iris*	*Sedum*
Chrysanthemum		

Easiest Self-Sowing Perennials

Alchemilla	*Coreopsis grandiflora*	*Linum*
Baptisia	*Digitalis*	*Malva*
Chrysanthemum parthenium	*Echinacea*	*Viola*

Shrub Shortlist

➤ Shrubs with nice, round shapes: *Berberis, Caryopteris, Choisya, Deutzia, Daphne, Ilex, Potentilla, Pinus mugo, Spiraea Japonica*

➤ Shrubs with wonderful fragrance: *Clethra, Choisya, Daphne, Fothergilla, Gardenia, Malus, Philadelphus, Syringea, Viburnum*

➤ Shrubs with arching or weeping stems: *Buddleia, Forsythia (unpruned), Hydrangea paniculata, Kolkwitzia, Spiraea thunbergii, Weigela*

➤ Shrubs that tolerate seashore conditions: *Berberis, Buddleia, Caryopteris, Chamaecyparis, Clethra, Cornus, Cytisus, Forsythia, Hydrangea, Juniperus, Kolkwitzia, Potentilla, Prunus, Spiraea, Syringea, Taxus, Viburnum, Weigela*

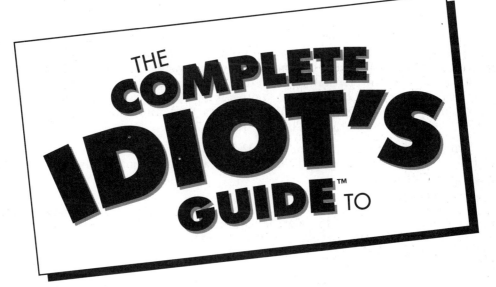

THE COMPLETE IDIOT'S GUIDE™ TO

Gardening
Second Edition

by Jane O'Connor and Emma Sweeney

alpha books

A Division of Macmillan General Reference
A Simon & Schuster Macmillan Company
1633 Broadway, New York, NY 10019-6785

International Standard Book Number: 0-02-862767-9
Library of Congress Catalog Card Number: The catalogue record is available from the Library of Congress.

00 99 98   8 7 6 5 4 3 2 1

Interpretation of the printing code: the rightmost number of the first series of numbers is the year of the book's printing; the rightmost number of the second series of numbers is the number of the book's printing. For example, a printing code of 98-1 shows that the first printing occurred in 1998.

Printed in the United States of America

Alpha Development Team

Publisher
Kathy Nebenhaus

Editorial Director
Gary M. Krebs

Managing Editor
Bob Shuman

Associate Gardening Editor
Barbara Berger

Marketing Brand Manager
Felice Primeau

Senior Editor
Nancy Mikhail

Editorial Assistant
Maureen Horn

Production Team

Production Editor
Mark Enochs

Cover Designer
Mike Freeland

Photo Editor
Barbara Berger

Illustrators
Susan MacNeil
Jody P. Shaeffer

Photographers
David Cavagnaro
Gregory Piatrowski

Designer
Glenn Larsen

Indexer
Carol Sheehan, Lisa Stumpf

Layout
Melissa Auciello-Brogan

Contents at a Glance

Contents

Part 4: Putting It on Paper

13 Measuring Up: Putting Plans on Paper

14 Easy Garden Plans

Part 6: Making the Bed 229

16 Don't Shoot the Messenger 231

Foreword

So you've caught the gardening bug; well, congratulations and welcome to one of the oldest, largest, and most diverse "clubs" around. In fact, in the United States alone, gardening is more popular than tennis and golf combined. While serious horticulturists consider gardening high science, most of the rest of us garden as a leisure activity. And well we should, because gardening is a whole lot of fun, and anyone of any age or sex can join in. It is a great way to relax, extremely rewarding, and puts us in touch with our roots—literally! With all the hustle and bustle we face each day, spending time in the garden gives us a much needed break; it connects us with nature and gives us a sense of peace and satisfaction so desperately needed in these fast-paced times. And how many other activities utilize all of our senses? We get to put our hands in the earth and feel all of the interesting textures of different plants. We inhale the heady fragrance of flowers. We savor fresh sun-ripe, just-picked produce. We delight in the visual feast of colors while hearing the soft rustle of leaves in the breeze and chirping of birds as they frolic among the foliage. The feeling of accomplishment and daily pleasure that comes with gardening really can't be beat.

This excellent guide will become indispensable as you venture into your garden. Authors Jane O'Connor and Emma Sweeney have culled an astonishing amount of information in one comprehensive compendium, answering nearly any question you may have in a handy reference that's as easy to follow as it is fun to read. Helpful tips accompany each chapter, and all the nitty-gritty details you'll need when choosing plants—such as the common and Latin names, height and spread, where it grows best and in what type of soil—are included. And everything is broken down into specific chapters so it's easy to look up just what you need, whether it's planting bulbs, how to design the perfect bed, or weeding. It's all presented in an encouraging, motivating way that will have you raring to go.

You'll find it's easy to get started gardening, but once you have you'll quickly realize it becomes tough to stop. All it takes is one plant and one pot, and soon you'll be hooked—that's how I started, and now my lawn is shrinking to near non-existence as I keep replacing long stretches of it with new garden beds. I've spent many an evening fussing over my flowers until well past dusk; my neighbors may think I'm nuts, but the results are clearly worth it when I see them admiring my handiwork come daylight. Tending tender plants you've nurtured from tiny seedlings is so spiritually fulfilling, especially when they come to full bloom. Noting with fascination the garden's daily progression—as tiny buds appear overnight through the foliage, then burst open almost before your eyes—you, too, may find it becomes a passion that almost borders on obsession.

Before you make that first trip to the nursery, spend a little bit of time planning ahead. Leaf through this book to help determine what to tackle first and how to approach it. Think about the colors you love, the shapes and textures that you find appealing. Do you want cut flowers to decorate your home, herbs or vegetables you can cook with, or some privacy from next-door-neighbors? A great way to help decide what to plant is to take a walk around your neighborhood and see what other people have put in their gardens. And don't be afraid to ask questions; gardeners are a friendly lot who love to share their tips, experiences, and even plants if you're lucky. It's best to take tiny steps before tackling your whole yard; perhaps start first with a container—a clay pot or a windowbox—then graduate to a small bed or border. And when planning these, remember to include trees and shrubs in the mix; these become the "bones" of your garden, adding focal points, backdrops, and winter interest.

Don't be discouraged by failures in your garden, because these are ultimately the best lessons. Finding out what works under which conditions, or which plants just don't do well no matter where you place them or what you feed them, is half the fun of the process. Even the most experienced gardeners have serious flops; this is what makes gardening so challenging and rewarding, and a constant learning experience.

Gardening is an activity the whole family can participate in. Kids revel in watching nature unfold, and you'll feel like a kid again, too, once you've got your hands in the dirt (remember how much fun it was making mud pies?). While gardening is chore-oriented, always keep a positive attitude about it; otherwise it's not worth doing in the first place. While weeding or watering, allow your mind to wander and wallow in the Zen-like euphoria that inevitably takes over. Enjoy the peacefulness of the garden, and the precious few moments away from the hectic outside world. And remind yourself that you are getting a great workout (you'll find you've used muscles you never knew you had!) and plenty of fresh air to boot. Seeing how beautiful your grounds look as the seasons evolve is worth every bit of effort you've put in.

Whether you're tending a small pot or an extensive plot, gardening is a terrific way to express yourself. It utilizes your creativity, brings you closer to nature, and is something you can do by yourself or with your loved ones. You get so much more than you give in a garden—pleasure, beauty, knowlege, exercise—it even increases the value of your home. What more could you ask for?

—Diana Gold Murphy, Editor, *Country Living Gardener*

Country Living Gardener is a bimonthly lifestyle publication devoted to gardening enthusiasts from the novice to the expert who manifest their passion for gardening both indoors and out. Advice from the country's leading horticulture experts and lavishly photographed gardens supported by plenty of hands-on, how-to information are accompanied by features on all the natural offshoots of gardening including decorating, travel, cooking, crafts, health and beauty, and the environment.

Country Living Gardener has met with unparalleled success in the garden magazine genre; the magazine was founded as an annual in 1993, was published as a biannual in 1994, went quarterly in 1995, and bimonthly in 1996. It remains the leading gardening publication on the newsstand.

Introduction

This is a garden primer, designed to introduce you, the beginner gardener, to the wonderful world of gardening. Growing ornamental plants, whether annuals, perennials, bulbs, or even shrubs is immensely satisfying, and the reward for the time and effort you spend growing and caring for your plants pays off beautifully in flowers!

In *The Complete Idiot's Guide to Gardening, Second Edition* we provide you with all the information you need to start your first garden. You'll learn how to garden one step at a time. We've structured the book into nine neatly organized parts, so you can learn what you need to know as you are building your first garden. It's organized around the seasons of the year, beginning in winter, when you dream about and plan the gardens you'll build, through spring planting, summer maintenance (and coping with bugs, diseases, and weeds), through the fall, when you eventually put the garden to bed (but not without a fall planting!).

Let's run through the average year of the gardener and the chapters in the book.

We begin with Part 1, "Green Thoughts, Black Thumbs." Think about the garden you want, ideally over the winter. Start small and make your first garden manageable. You'll get an overview of popular garden terms and a chapter on finding your garden "style."

Part 2, "Just the Facts," is the nitty gritty—all about climate considerations, soil, sun, and water. All of these factors are extremely important, and you'll want to carefully read all of the facts in these chapters.

Part 3, "The Idiot's Guide to the Best Plants," has six chapters full of the easiest plants to grow. There are chapters on the easiest annuals, perennials, shrubs, vines, herbs, and bulbs. In the chapter on annuals, you'll find each annual coded: "0" maintenance (no work); "10 minutes" (just that—ten minutes per week); and "low" maintenance (you'll have to do some very basic pinching and trimming to keep the plant looking neat).

Part 4, "Putting It on Paper," shows you how exactly to plan a garden on paper. It requires some work, but that work pays off in spades—less use of spades, that is. Bonus: It's all here for you! This chapter has 14 easy garden plans that you can follow.

Part 5, "Shopping Sprees!," is the shortest part in the book, with just one chapter, but definitely the most fun chapter if you like to shop. Everything you need for both your garden and yourself is in this chapter.

Part 6, "Making the Bed," puts you in the garden, showing and telling you exactly how to make your first garden bed. It's hard work making a bed—digging soil, lifting rocks and sod and weeds, but you've got to do it (or hire some strong backs!). You'll also learn how to improve the soil with the use of organic and inorganic fertilizers.

Part 7, "Into the Garden," outlines exactly what to do on planting day, whether your plants are going into beds or pots.

When you get to Part 8, "Water, Weed, Feed, and Don't Forget to Mulch," you should be enjoying the fruits of your labor. Flowers are coming, plants are growing. This part is about keeping the weeds in the garden down, the flowers up, and includes some troubleshooting tips on identifying diseases and insects in the garden.

Part 9, "Putting It All Together," is all about fall cleanup, and we offer more ideas for planting. Fall is a great time to plant poppies, peonies, and tall-bearded irises. You'll be putting the bed to bed in the fall, and it's a good time to think about those new gardens you want to start the following spring. Order some gardening catalogs to see you through the winter.

By the time you finish this book you should feel more confident as a gardener, and more capable of creating the gardens of your dreams. And that's what the best garden is—even if the garden is simply two pots on a terrace—a place you dreamed of first, then made a reality. You're on your way!

Extras

We've used some special boxed notes throughout the book to help you learn. These include:

Green Meany
These sidebars alert you to important gardening facts and caution you against making mistakes that could harm you or your garden.

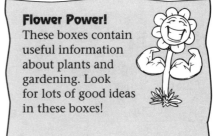

Flower Power!
These boxes contain useful information about plants and gardening. Look for lots of good ideas in these boxes!

Garden Talk
These are definitions or terms you may be unfamiliar with.

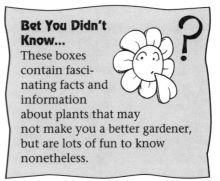

Bet You Didn't Know...
These boxes contain fascinating facts and information about plants that may not make you a better gardener, but are lots of fun to know nonetheless.

Acknowledgments

From Jane O'Connor:

Thank you to the team at Macmillan for all your hard work in getting this book into production. I would also like to thank Richard Parks, my agent, who has the happiest disposition I've ever had the pleasure to meet and work with. Thank you to Laurie S. Barnett, our editor, for making this job seem so easy. And my deepest thanks to Susan McNeil for all the beautiful artwork she provided for this book.

I particularly thank Emma Sweeney for coming to me with this project and the opportunity to write this book together. We did it!! Who would have thought?

And thanks to all my active friends and family who still call and try to get me away from the typewriter long enough to get the usual answer, "Sorry, I can't today." And special thanks to my love of my life for buying me my very first computer.

From Emma Sweeney:

I'm grateful to the people who have made writing this book a pleasure: Richard Parks; our editors, Laurie S. Barnett, Megan Newman, and Lynn Northrup; Jane O'Connor; Susan McNeil; my favorite "gardening idiot" Janice Potter; Julia Sweeney; and Mac McDermott, who inspired me to garden when he told me I looked sexy gardening. We now have five gardens.

Dedication

To the memory of my mother, whose love of gardening and life is always with me. (Emma Sweeney)

Part 1
Green Thoughts, Black Thumbs

You'd love to start a garden, but when it comes to growing plants, you're all thumbs— and none of them are green! Relax. This part of the book starts you off by introducing you to some Latin lingo (Latin nomenclature, that is), as well as the definitions of annuals, perennials, bulbs, herbs, vines, and shrubs.

To build the garden of your dreams, you need to figure out what garden best suits your needs and your landscape. You'll learn about garden "styles" and how to create the look you want for your garden. You'll also learn how to use color, shape, and texture in the garden.

Getting Started

Gardening for the beginner is often overwhelming. There are hundreds of thousands of flowering plants, shrubs, and trees, each with subdivisions of varieties, cultivars, and species. As a result, many of the plants' Latin names are daunting to pronounce and impossible to remember.

Then there's the little matter of the actual plants. Planting, watering, feeding. What if they wilt? Turn brown? Turn yellow? Die? At first, gardening can be intimidating.

All you need is a little guidance and confidence. Before long, you'll actually begin to have a lot of fun. And you'll quickly find that gardening isn't the least overwhelming. Gardening is a real joy. It's great exercise (all that bending and lifting!), and the best part is you're in charge. It's your garden—not your grandmother's garden or your neighbor's garden. So enjoy.

Start with an Idea

Every garden begins, like any creative endeavor, with an idea. Start to imagine your own ideal garden. Is it filled with your favorite colors? Or are you drawn to a single-color garden, all white, for instance? You may want to create a garden that blooms in the spring, or in the fall, or in the summer, depending on the time of year you are most likely to enjoy your garden. You may want a cottage garden or a formal garden, a low mainte- nance shrub border, or a highly structured herb garden. The choice is yours.

Start Small and Use Easy, Reliable Plants

You'll quickly gain gardening confidence if you start with a small garden and use plants that are easy to grow. It's a sensible (and economical) approach. You'll find a lot of great ideas for gardens in later chapters, and Part 3 is devoted entirely to the plants best suited for the beginner gardener.

Keep the Garden Under 50 Square Feet

The size of your first garden should be no bigger than 50 square feet. This is plenty of room for any of the gardens mentioned earlier, and it's manageable.

Use Plants That Work for You

Get your feet wet with plants that are easy to care for. Chances are, if you get used to gardening with plants like these, you'll want to continue using these easy plants even when you're a seasoned gardener. At any rate, you'll have plenty of time later to take on temperamental delphiniums or finicky hybrid roses.

Try a Garden of Daylilies

A daylily garden is a wonderful first garden and will provide a number of options as well. Your garden could be limited to daylilies of the same variety—yellow, for instance— which would give your garden a "tied together" look. Or you could have many different varieties of daylilies, providing a rainbow of colors and a long bloom season. Either way, your garden will have a pleasant feeling of unity, as all the daylilies have the same straplike foliage.

Daylily (Hemerocallis).

One Garden "Room" at a Time

Think of each garden you add to your front- and backyards as separate "rooms." If you put in a 50-square-foot garden this year, next year add another "room" to a different area of the yard. You may want to go back to the garden you did the year before and expand it (if space allows) or rearrange it.

Green Meany

Avoid major landscaping: Don't start a big landscaping project unless you've allowed for it in your budget. Major landscaping renovations are expensive, time-consuming, and can often fall into that "someday I'll finish that project" trap.

Where to Put the Garden

To assign a good place for your first garden, take the time now to learn what you don't already know about your property. Walk around the outside your house. Think about how you use your property and what your priorities are. Do you and your family spend a great deal of time outside in the summer months? Do you do much entertaining outdoors? Do you need privacy for your home?

Not on My Lawn!

If you have a lawn where the kids play ball, you probably don't want a garden in the middle of their playing field. High-traffic areas are not suitable places for gardens.

Put Your Garden Where You'll Most Enjoy It

If space is limited, consider using property lines for borders or placing a garden against the house. It's wonderful to have a fragrant garden just outside a window—near the kitchen or a big picture window—where you can enjoy the color and fragrance of the flowers. A white garden on a terrace is lovely because white flowers can be seen and enjoyed at night. This is called a "moon garden."

Work with What You Have

If your property is heavily wooded, think about creating a naturalistic woodland garden. If you've recently added a deck or if your new house is scantily landscaped, consider softening the lines with some planters and potted plants.

Another garden idea is the shrub border, which makes an excellent screen and is very effective in the front of the property because it will muffle street traffic noises.

Flower Power!

Screens of flowering shrubs placed along the sides of your property are attractive and provide privacy from neighbors.

All It Takes Is Time and Money

How much time will you spend in the garden? What does your budget allow for plants and materials? These are two big factors to consider when thinking about your new garden.

If you expect to spend about 20 minutes a week on your new garden, you can't expect miracles right away. But if you choose the right plants—long-living, low-maintenance perennials and shrubs—and plant them correctly in the right locations, you might be surprised to see how well they will fare with minimum care. Don't be surprised if you get the gardening bug, however, and wind up spending hours on end in the garden. The point is to be realistic at the outset about your time constraints so you don't get overburdened with gardening chores.

The Investment of a Lifetime: Your Home

It's hard to ignore budget constraints. But when you consider how landscaping can enhance the value of your property, it makes sense to think of each garden you build as an investment in one of your biggest assets—your house. Many plants will go on looking good long after the plaster on the walls has fallen.

We know that trees can live long lives, and the same is true for many shrubs and perennials. Rhododendrons, yews, and hydrangeas are just a few examples of shrubs that can live 60 years and longer. Peonies, a beautiful perennial known for its showy blossoms, can live virtually forever.

But Can You Take Your Garden with You?

Although you can amortize your garden costs effectively in the long run, what if you rent or want a garden for a summer home? In either case, you may want to put your plants in containers or use easy-to-grow annuals: snapdragons, zinnias, sunflowers, and marigolds, to name just a few, require very little care and are inexpensive and beautiful flowers. You'll learn what annuals are in the next chapter.

Know Your Property

You need to take a thorough look at your property, including a complete inspection of pipes, underground lines, and cables. First, locate your outside water faucet. You'll want to place your garden no more than 40 feet from this water source.

Dig Up Blueprints of Electrical and Gas Lines Before You Dig at All

If you're thinking of planting around the foundation of your house, be sure you know where all underground electrical and cable lines are. Make sure you've either obtained a blueprint of all underground cables or have solid knowledge of their locations. If you have a well, you'll need to know where your septic system is. Water lines can be easily damaged. If you rent your home, first ask your landlord about installing a garden. Chances are he or she will be thrilled that you want to improve the property and gladly provide you with the necessary information.

Watering Problems for High-Rise Dwellers

Green Meany
If you have a ground-floor garden apartment, beware of mice eating your bulbs!

If your potential garden is on a terrace in a high-rise building, be aware of potential watering problems. For instance, some buildings have strict rules regarding the use of water on terraces. If watering your plants means watering your downstairs neighbor's terrace, this could be a problem! Generally, a terrace garden will have fewer in-ground impediments.

Plan Your Garden When You Can't Plant

The best time to think about a new garden is when you can't plant, like during the winter months when the ground is frozen. There is considerable planning that needs to be done, and it's better to plan your garden when leafless trees under gray skies show you the "structure" of your landscape. (You'll learn in Chapter 3 about creating structure and "backbones" in gardens, but first know what you're working with and what your needs are.)

Another good time to plan your garden is during the hottest days of summer. No matter where you live, you won't want to be outdoors planting when the ground is simply too hot and the soil too dry. Who wants to dig holes in the dog days of August?

Green Meany

If you've never gardened before and suddenly have spring gardening fever, try to avoid buying plants and hoping to find a home for them in your as-yet-unmade garden. This is a big mistake. A good garden is well planned; a good garden bed prepared well.

Start a Garden Notebook

The only thing you should buy now is a notebook. First orders of entry are the following:

➤ *The dimensions of your house.* Record your house's dimensions—its length, width, distance from the street, and property lines. If you're considering foundation plants, go outside and measure the height of your windows from ground to the bottom of the window sill.

➤ *Existing trees and shrubs.* Make notes of all existing trees and shrubs on your property. By incorporating them into your garden, they can add backbone and give the feeling that the garden has been there for years. You may want to make note of trees and shrubs that appear unsightly or ill, and then consider that they just may need some TLC in the form of a good pruning.

Flower Power!

Keep as many of your trees and shrubs as possible. For those that have gotten out of hand over the years, consider giving them a good pruning. You can read about pruning in Chapter 21.

➤ *The sun's movement.* Note the sun's movement over your house, or, if you live in an apartment, note the direction your terrace faces. Keep in mind that the winter sun stays low in the sky and the sun is highest in midsummer.

➤ *Names and descriptions of plants that appeal to you.* Look through nursery catalogs (you'll find a good list in Chapter 27), and look at plants everywhere—in garden centers or your neighbor's garden—to get a good idea what colors, shapes, and foliage appeal to you. Gather information and record names and descriptions of plants you like in your gardening notebook.

➤ *Your green thoughts.* Don't forget to jot down the ideas you have for your garden. As we said at the start of this chapter, every garden begins with an idea.

The Least You Need to Know

➤ Make your first garden no larger than 50 square feet.

➤ Use plants that are easy to care for (listed in Part 3).

➤ Know your time and budget constraints.

➤ Know where the electrical and water lines are on your property.

Chapter 2

A Gardener's Lexicon

In This Chapter

➤ Plant names: botanical and common

➤ What exactly are annuals, biennials, perennials, shrubs, vines, herbs, and bulbs?

➤ Where these plants are used

New gardeners often find the distinctions between annuals and perennials confusing, not to mention all the tongue-twisting Latin plant names. But you'll get the hang of it, and sooner than you think.

What's in a Name?

A plant is known by at least two different names. One name, a two-word scientific name for a plant (or an animal), is assigned by the Latin binomial system, which is the internationally accepted method for naming plants. The other name is the plant's common name. It's a good idea to acquaint yourself with both names. You'll often see both names, like this:

Baby's breath *(Gypsophila paniculata)*

The first name is the common name and the second, in parentheses and italics, is the Latin name. The common name sometimes describes a plant, like the common sunflower *(Helianthus annuus)*, with its big, sunlike flowers; or a spider flower *(Cleome spinosa)*, whose long, thin seed pods resemble spider legs. Just as often, the common name is pretty, if not descriptive, as in baby's breath.

Picking Up a Little Latin

In the Latin binomial system, each plant has a generic name that tells you the plant's *genus* (meaning "type" or "gender") and the plant's *species*. In the earlier example, the genus name is *Gypsophila*; the species name is *paniculata*. A genus may have more than one subdivision or species within it. The species name follows the genus name. Within the species there could be more subdivisions or varieties.

In some parts of this book, you'll find the names of *cultivars* listed after the genus and the species. Cultivar names are always enclosed in single quotation marks (' '). The name of a cultivar is usually given by the person who propagated the plant, and it is often registered. Here's an example:

> *Aquilegia x hybrida* 'Jane's White' (as in Jane O'Connor)

A final note on the Latin binomial: Sometimes you'll see an *x* following the genus name. This identifies *hybrids*, which is the crossing of two genera, species, or cultivars. *Aquilegia* in the example above is a hybrid.

A Deep Appreciation of Botanical Names

You'll find that all these names actually make a lot of sense. Botanical names accurately describe the plant, which is important when you have a specific plant in mind. Let's say you wanted to buy a Hydrangea. This is a huge genus! "Hydrangea" won't indicate the flower color (blue? pink? white?) or the shape you want (tree? shrub? vine?). But if you know you want the oak-leaved Hydrangea, whose Latin name is *Hydrangea quercifolia* (*querci* = oak, *folia* = leaves), you'll get exactly the plant you want.

Common Names

Common names are the names plants have acquired through common usage. You may not be able to depend on these names to tell you anything about the plant, but sometimes they do tell you something, and they make sense, as in "sunflower." More often, common names make no sense at all, as in the plant names "lungwort," "Cupid's dart," and "beard tongue." (You have to admit the names are fun, though!)

Flower Power!

The American Horticultural Society provides suggestions for pronouncing these Latin names, but there are no hard and fast rules. In some cases, proper pronunciation goes to the "you say po-*tay*-to, I say po-*tah*-to" argument. Try using the Latin names as often as you can to get the hang of it, and don't worry if your pronunciation is corrected.

Defining Plants

The following sections give you brief definitions of annuals, biennials, shrubs, etc. As you'll see, the rule of thumb is that plants are divided into categories according to the length of their life-cycles. Part 3 of the book is devoted entirely to foolproof plants in each category.

What Are Annuals?

Annuals are plants that flower, set seed, and die in one-year cycles. Because their life span is short, most of the plant's energy goes into producing colorful flowers instead of roots.

These quick-growing plants are ideal for the gardener who wants instant gratification. They will bloom the same year you plant them (perhaps even for the entire growing season!), reach their peak size that same year, and die when the winter cold comes.

When Do Annuals Bloom?

Annuals will bloom for most of the growing season, usually until the first frost. When you see pretty annuals in bloom, you can be sure that the plants will continue to produce flowers until the first frost, provided you take good care of the plants!

How Do Annuals "Self-Sow?"

Some annuals "self-sow," which means that the seeds will sow themselves into the ground. You can plant an annual, such as spider flower (*Cleome spinosa*), and the following year and every year after that you get the same big blooms for free!

Spider flower
(Cleome spinosa).

Where Will Annuals Grow Best?

Annuals are great in many places, whether it's a sunny or shady spot, which is why an annual bed garden is one of the easiest and most satisfying gardens to grow (see Chapter 14). With a little deadheading, your flowers will bloom all summer! *Deadheading* simply means cutting off the old flowers.

Cutting Gardens

Cutting gardens are grown specifically for cut flowers, so you would want to plant annuals that make the best cut flowers, such as snapdragons, cosmos, and zinnias, as well as everlastings like statice. With annuals, the more you cut, the more they flower. What could be better?

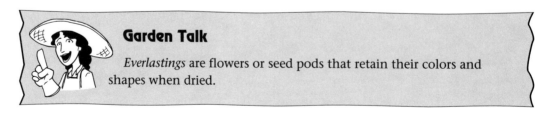

Garden Talk

Everlastings are flowers or seed pods that retain their colors and shapes when dried.

Other Places for Annuals

Another place to plant annuals is with other plants—under shrubs or between perennials. Annuals add continuous color to any garden. Pile up your annuals together as much as you can to make your garden appear rich and abundant.

What Are Biennials?

Biennials take two years to complete their life-cycles. The first year you usually won't see flowers, but the plant is growing. The second year the plant flowers. While the plant you bought will then die, having completed its life-cycle, it may self-sow, in which case the seedlings will grow into mature plants and continue the cycle.

Some Popular Biennials

While biennials make up a fairly small group of plants, there are some popular ones you may want to try. One great biennial is hollyhocks (*Althaea*). Another is foxgloves (*Digitalis*). Both of these plants will self-sow, so you may find more of these plants in your garden each spring. You'll find these plants, and a few other biennials, listed as short-lived perennials in Chapter 8.

What Are Perennials?

Perennials make up a huge category of plants. These are plants that continue to flower and seed year after year. Some perennials live longer than others; some, like peonies, may live longer than any of us. Others, like feverfew (*Chrysanthemum parthenium*), are short-lived.

You'll often see the word *herbaceous* (meaning "nonwoody") before "perennial." Shrubs and trees have woody stems and trunks; herbaceous perennials with their nonwoody stems will die back to the ground in the winter.

Perennials are important and necessary plants. And they can be expensive: A one-gallon plant from a nursery may cost as much as $10. But remember that when you buy perennials, you are building up your stock in that plant. Whether the plant self-sows or you divide the plant many times over, the investment in that first perennial will seem small in comparison to its value.

When Do Perennials Bloom?

Perennials bloom during the growing season, generally for a few weeks, like hostas, but some will bloom for longer. Lavenders, for example, will bloom for up to a month. You can also deadhead to get the plants to bloom again. Tickweed (*Coreopsis*), for instance, will bloom again after deadheading.

The exact time of bloom for each perennial will vary depending on the climate. Spring comes much earlier to the South, so a spring-blooming perennial growing there might bloom as early as February, while in most Northern gardens the same perennial may not bloom until May.

When Do Perennials Reach Their Full Height?

Perennials will spend their first years in your garden establishing their roots, and you may not actually see much growth above ground. Don't be discouraged. By the second year, the perennials will bloom and attain their proper heights.

Flower Power!
Plant annuals in a garden's bare spots to fill in the spaces until the perennials reach full height.

In a few years, you may want to move your plants around. You might decide a plant would look better in a different spot, or you may just want to dig and divide your perennials for more stock. Feel free to dig up your plants, divide them, or move them to new locations. Just be sure to do this in the spring or the fall when the soil and outdoor temperatures are cool. It's not wise to move perennials in the heat of summer—conditions are too stressful. You'll read more about digging and dividing in Chapter 25.

Where Do Perennials Work Best?

There are so many perennials, and the category is so vast, that you can literally find a perennial to suit any spot, whether it's dry, wet, shady, or sunny. Versatility is just one of the perennial's many charms. You'll fall in love with them for lots of reasons, and especially because so many of them are the most beautiful flowering plants.

Perennials are at home in any garden, from the formal to the informal—in beds, borders, islands, cottage gardens, woodland gardens, herb gardens, and rock gardens.

Flower Power!

"To grow it is to know it": Always work with plants that work for you. If sedum was a success in your first garden, use more sedum in your next garden. Dig and divide the plant to create more stock. You'll not only have more plants, you'll know what your soil likes and add unity to your garden by repeating the plants.

A Word About Tender Perennials

Tender perennials are perennials that are not hardy enough to survive in cold climates. We may grow them in colder climates, but we do so by treating them like annuals. With just about any tender perennial, as with most annuals, the plant can be brought indoors before the first frost, wintered over, and taken back outside in the spring after the last frost date.

Where Vines Fit In

Some vines are annuals, some are biennials, and some are perennials. It's not the length of their life-cycles that distinguishes them, but rather their habit of growth. Vines grow in one of three ways: by twining; by clinging with the use of suction discs; or by growing tendrils or leaf stalks.

Some Vines Are Annuals

Remember: Annuals flower, set seed, and die in the same year; biannuals take two years to complete their life-cycles; perennials can take many years to complete their life-cycles. An annual vine like morning glory (*Ipomoea purpurea*) is a wonderful climber and will cover whatever you want covered with flowers and foliage the same year you plant it.

Some Vines Are Perennials

Perennial vines, on the other hand, may be slower to establish, but once established, will return every year to your garden. A beautiful vine is trumpet creeper (*Campsis radicans*), which has orange, red, or yellow flowers in summer. This vine starts slow in its early years but will eventually reach 30 feet.

Trumpet creeper (Campsis radicans).

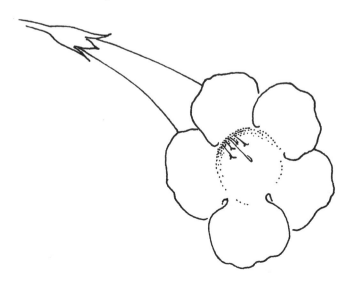

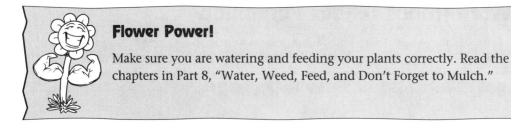

Flower Power!

Make sure you are watering and feeding your plants correctly. Read the chapters in Part 8, "Water, Weed, Feed, and Don't Forget to Mulch."

Where Can I Use Vines?

Vines that climb by twining or tendrils can be used anywhere there is support for them. If they are clinging vines, they will need a structure they can climb—a trellis, chimney, side of building, mailbox, unsightly chain link fence, or container with wire support. Anywhere. Just keep in mind how the vine grows and whether it needs support.

Green Meany

Don't allow vines that grow by suction cups or lateral roots to climb up wood structures as they can damage the wood by causing it to rot. Either grow them on other materials (brick, cement, stone) or install a trellis.

How Tall Will a Vine Grow?

When reading about the heights of vines, keep in mind that the heights given are the average. Remember, too, that perennials and annuals grow differently: Morning glory (*Ipomoea purpurea*), the popular annual vine, may grow as much as 10 feet in one year. Trumpet creeper (*Campsis radicans*), a perennial, may only grow 2 to 3 feet each year but will eventually reach a height of 30 feet.

What Are Herbs?

Herbs, like vines, can be annual, biennial, or perennial. These are wonderfully versatile plants with many uses. Herbs such as parsley and thyme are well-loved and used for flavoring food; other herbs like lavender (*Lavendula*) are grown for their fragrance. Herbs also provide a delicious fragrance to the garden, with scents like pungent rosemary (*Rosmarinus officinalis*) and tangy basil (*Ocimum basilicum*). Herbs make any garden a pleasure to walk through, picking bits of leaves and crushing them between our fingers to release the plants' scents.

Where Can I Grow Herbs?

Most herbs prefer a sunny site and thrive in just about any garden, from a kitchen garden placed just outside your back door (and listed in Chapter 14) to garden beds with flowering perennials and annuals. Many herbs also make terrific container plants.

What Are Shrubs?

Besides being the last thing on your mind as you contemplate your new garden, shrubs are woody plants, either deciduous or evergreen, branching from the ground, usually under 15 feet. Shrubs include everything from a low grower like creeping juniper (*Junipers horizontalis*) to a tall one such as camelia (*Camelia japonica*). The camelia bush gets as big as 25 feet and seems to have nothing in common with the evergreen juniper.

> **Flower Power!**
> Help yourself to your growing herbs when you are cooking—you'll keep the plant in control and your meals will be more nutritious and taste better than ever!

> **Garden Talk**
> *Deciduous* shrubs and trees shed their foliage in the autumn; *evergreen* shrubs and trees keep their green leaves year-round.

The Beauty of Shrubs

Shrubs are one of the few plants that can give your home and property four seasons of color. In addition to flowers, shrubs also provide berries and fruits. Evergreen shrubs provide their green color in the winter, and deciduous shrubs often provide brilliant leaf color in the fall.

Shrubs and Their Flowers

While spring is the season we usually associate with shrubs, when rhododendron, azaleas, prunus, forsythia, cherry trees, and lilac come into bloom, you can also have flowering shrubs in the summer and fall.

Where the Shrubs Are

Shrubs are so varied that the real question is not finding the right location, but finding the right shrub for the location you have in mind. Much depends on the shrub's shape, size, and its requirements in terms of sun and soil. Shrubs can work as foundation plants, as hedges, in their own garden, or in a garden with flowering perennials and annuals.

Even if you don't plant any shrubs your first year, you will want to include them in future gardens and certainly use them in your landscaping. These are the plants that can really tie your landscape together.

What About Bulbs, Corms, Rhizomes, and Tubers?

Bulbs, technically speaking, are storage organs consisting of fleshy scales and swollen, modified leaf bases on a much reduced stem. Corms, rhizomes, and tubers also have these common storage organs, which are usually underground. It's easiest to group all plants with these storage organs under the heading "bulbs."

Bulbs in Bloom

Early spring bloomers like daffodils and crocus are much beloved plants, especially since they usher in spring with their bright and glorious colors. But bulbs also bloom in summer, including most of the plants in the lily genus, as well as in fall.

Some Bulbs Are Hardy, Some Are Tender

Bulbs, like perennials, fall into two groups: those that are *hardy* (such as daffodils), meaning they can withstand freezing temperatures, and those that are *tender* (such as begonias), meaning they must be brought inside before temperatures drop below freezing.

Where to Best Grow Bulbs

Traditionally, bulbs like tulips have gone in beds and borders—they can have a formal look to them—and daffodils are naturalized in lawns and fields. But there are no rights and wrongs, so feel free to put them where you think they look best.

Flower Power!

A great place for bulbs is in containers where many of them do quite well, which is especially appealing to those of you who rent and want to take your garden with you!

The Least You Need to Know

➤ Always try to use the Latin name of a plant—it gets easier over time, and you'll be glad you know it so you can get the plant you want.

➤ Annuals grow, set seed, and die in one-year cycles; perennials live longer than a year.

➤ Vines can make great screens for a small landscape.

➤ Shrubs can make great screens for large landscapes.

➤ Many bulbs do well in containers.

Chapter 3

Finding Your Bliss

In This Chapter

➤ Garden designs: formal or informal?

➤ Finding the right garden to suit you and your house

➤ Gardens in the right places: climate, sun, and soil

➤ Designing your garden: using shapes and textures

➤ Working with color in flowers and foliage

Now that you have a general sense of what you want your garden to do for you and your property, as well as some ideas about plants that appeal to you, you'll want to figure out what kind of garden best suits you and your property. In this chapter, you'll also learn about garden design and how to use color, shapes, and textures to enhance the beauty of your garden.

Finding Your Garden Style

The ideal garden design will reflect your own personal style and complement your property. If you already have a strong sense of your own style, you're ahead of the game. But there are still basic elements of garden design: What makes a garden formal or informal? What does the shape of a garden do for the landscape? How does the choice of plants affect the garden's look? Once you know the basics of garden design, you can find the design that's right for you.

What's Your Style?

The way you live can be a good indication as to whether you want a formal or informal design in your garden. If you're not sure whether your taste runs to formal or informal, it's easy to find out. Think about and answer the following questions. If the questions don't apply, think about how you would answer them if they did.

Take the Style Quiz! (There Are No Wrong Answers)

1. Do you position furniture in your living room at right angles? Do you prefer to place chairs at odd angles?

2. If you have a wood floor, does it have a glossy look and a dark stain? Or is the floor lightly treated or untreated pine?

3. Are your dining room furnishings of dark wood?

4. Where do you and your family usually have dinner, in the dining room or the kitchen?

5. Would you consider yourself eclectic, enjoying a wide assortment of art, furnishings, and styles? Or is your taste more specific?

Your answers to these questions will tell you a lot about your garden style. If you're more comfortable with formal design, you probably have chairs at right angles, dark floors, and a formal dining room where you like to eat. If you prefer a more relaxed way of living—chairs at odd angles, lightly treated floors, eclectic furnishings, and so on, then let your informal style come through in your garden.

Creating a Formal Garden

A formal garden has an overall look of neatness and tidiness about it. Its design is based on the same principles that bring a feeling of formality into the home.

A well-manicured hedge often surrounds the formal garden and the plants that edge the garden are clipped and neat. If there are paths through the garden, they are straight or at right angles to each other. The idea is to give a sense of order to the garden, and the first step toward this goal is to create the boundaries that separate the wild and untamed world on the outside and the neat, orderly, civilized world within the boundaries. Well-maintained edges can do this.

Formal Gardens, Formal Plants

The use of a certain type of plant, both in the hedge and in the garden itself, is important in the formal garden. These gardens work best with plants that have what we call "neat habits of growth." These plants naturally grow in rounded shapes or tight mounds. They do not sprawl.

Boxwood (*Buxus*), for instance, is a familiar hedge in the formal garden. This evergreen shrub is ideal as a small hedge around a garden bed. Just about any plant with compact growth can be kept neat and thus find a place in the formal bed. Lavender (*Lavendula*), is always great in formal gardens, either as an edging plant or planted in the garden. Also, plants in the geranium genus work well in formal gardens because they form pretty mounds.

Creating an Informal Garden

An informal garden, on the other hand, uses curved lines both in the shape of the garden itself and in the plants chosen for the garden. This garden doesn't have a formal hedge around it, and may not have anything separating it from the outside world but the plants that are falling over the borders.

Plants That Work in Informal Beds

The plants here tend to have a relaxed and unshaped habit about them. They often have daisylike flowers or feathery plumes. Some plants that are at home in the informal garden are cosmos and perovskia. Their long, graceful stems bend in the wind and give these plants a relaxed feeling. A big clump of tall black-eyed Susans (*Rudbeckia*), which are in the daisy family, would also catch the wind and tend to create movement in the garden.

Merging Plants

Plants in informal gardens also tend to merge into one another, so that you can't tell where one plant begins and another ends. Edging plants often spill out of the garden. An herb garden is an informal garden, for example—it's often placed near the kitchen door where the oregano is spilling over the walkway and mixing with the thyme.

Coordinating House and Garden

If your garden is close to your house, try to let the garden complement the house. If your garden is at a distance from the house, feel free to experiment, but don't let these considerations get in the way of having the garden you want.

Gardens for Traditional Homes

Formal gardens work best with traditional homes, where symmetry is important. These houses usually have a kind of "boxy" architecture, such as the familiar Georgian architecture. Other houses with formal touches, such as those with round or square pillars in the front, dictate the need for similar treatment in the landscape.

Gardens for Relaxed Homes

Informal gardens work well with houses that are more relaxed, such as Capes and bungalows. When a house's architecture is based on a rambling design, or a design that is modest and understated (such as a beach cottage), you'll want to continue that theme into the garden, especially if the garden is close to the house.

New Neighborhoods

If your house is in a new development and the personality of the house and neighborhood are not so pronounced, you'll find some clues around you to help you out. Using the basic guidelines discussed earlier—straight lines, symmetry, and right angles for a formal design; curved lines and odd angles for an informal feeling—go with the feeling you get from the house and its neighborhood. For instance, a newer ranch-style house could go either way—formal or informal—depending on the neighborhood and the house itself.

Flower Power!

One idea for a garden away from an informal house is a formal rose garden; an idea for a garden away from a formal house is daffodils in a meadow.

Using Color, Shape, and Texture

Colors create moods in gardens, and while you want to avoid obvious clashes like fiery red with hot pink, keep in mind that colors are very personal things: What appeals to one person may not appeal to the next.

Shape and texture also contribute greatly to the overall picture of a garden. Earlier in this chapter, you learned how the plant itself makes a statement, whether it's a low-growing evergreen perennial like boxwood or a tall sunflower. The shapes and textures of a plant's foliage and flowers also give a garden its overall feeling.

What Gives Color Its Color?

A color is only as good as the light it is seen in. For instance, colors in temperate climates will look different than colors in climates closer to the equator. Think of the cool, soft pinks, blues, and grays in an English border garden, and try to picture the same garden in the south of Spain. It would look out of place, or at least different, where the light is different.

Remember, too, the influences a backdrop will have on your garden. A dark row of evergreens behind your garden will give it one feeling, while the brick or granite walls of a town garden will give it another—and an open split-rail fence yet another.

Running Hot...

When you use hot colors like reds, yellows, and oranges, you create a bright and eye-opening effect. A garden filled with these colors brings to the garden the feelings associated with them: passion, excitement, immediacy, and energy.

...and Cold

On the other side of the color spectrum are the cool colors: blue, green, purple, and silver. These colors have a relaxing, calming effect, and when used in the garden, can create a peaceful, tranquil, and soothing atmosphere. Soft colors like these can increase the sense of space and are particularly wonderful in small gardens.

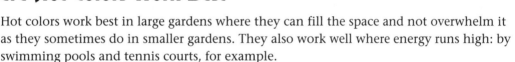

Bet You Didn't Know... The color red is said to raise your blood pressure.

Flower Power! For gardeners with small spaces: Use cool colors to create the illusion of more space.

Where Hot Colors Work Best

Hot colors work best in large gardens where they can fill the space and not overwhelm it as they sometimes do in smaller gardens. They also work well where energy runs high: by swimming pools and tennis courts, for example.

Playing It Cool

Cool colors create the kind of calm and peaceful gardens where you will want to relax. These colors also work well in gardens that are placed at some distance from the house, because they recede, making them seem farther away than they really are.

Working with White

When white is added to a hot color, it mutes it or tones it down. For instance, when white is added to red you get pink, a much softer color than red. With white, purples become lavenders, yellows become mellow, and even orange can be transformed into a soft apricot color.

White, itself, is a very useful color in the garden. White flowers can appear luminous by moonlight. When repeated throughout the garden, white can give the garden a feeling of unity and repetition. White will also brighten a shady nook.

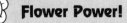

Flower Power!

Try to stay within a two-color range in your first garden and add a liberal dose of white. This way you'll create a sense of unity and tie the garden together with the white.

Harmonize or Contrast?

Colors that harmonize sit next to each other on the color wheel, and colors that contrast are directly opposite each other on the color wheel. Picture a blue flower surrounded by green foliage: These colors intermingle for a harmonious look. Think of the same blue flower next to an orange flower. These contrasting colors make a strong statement.

Whether you combine colors to harmonize or contrast, both concepts work well in the garden. Remember the sayings: "Like attracts like" and the equally important "Opposites attract." Go either way to create the mood you want in your garden.

Color wheel (primary and secondary colors).

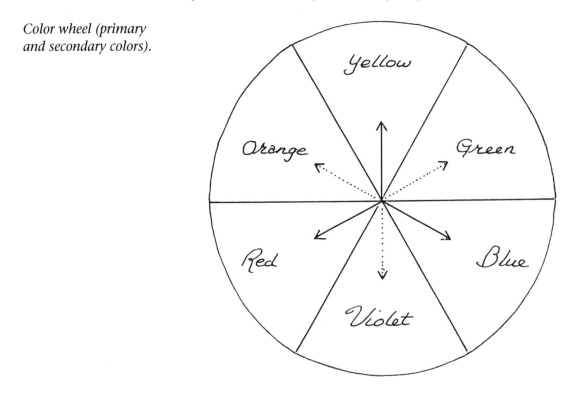

Driving the Green

Green is certainly the one given color in any garden. If you can't immediately think of how valuable green is to flowers, think about the green, fernlike leaves that always accompany flower arrangements. Without the green backdrop to set them off, the flowers are much less vibrant and colorful.

Shades of Green

Green foliage and its shades will modify any plant placed in front of it, and as you become acquainted with plants, you'll find many wonderful and interesting colors in foliage—from bluish-greens to silvers to grays. Some foliage is *variegated*, meaning it is dappled or streaked with various colors. Many of the hosta plants, for instance, have interesting variegated foliage. Variegated leaves are spotted, striped, or veined with various colors.

Flower Power!
By using the right combinations of plants, your garden can be hot in July with reds, yellows, and orange flowering plants in bloom, and cool in early fall, with pinks, blues, and grays.

Spread Color Around

When working with color, your garden will look larger if you spread color around. For instance, if your blue-flowering geranium did well in a particular spot, the following year weave some more of that same geranium throughout the garden. This way the blue color will be repeated, tying the garden together and making it look larger at the same time.

The Shape of Things

You know how the shape of a plant can influence the feeling of a garden, and the shape of its flowers and the texture of a plant's foliage also make statements in the garden.

Flower shapes can vary widely from one plant to another. Along with the familiar daisylike flower, which you can probably recognize, take a look at the following five figures that show some common flower shapes.

Umbel: A rounded or flat-topped flower cluster where flower stalks arise from a central point.

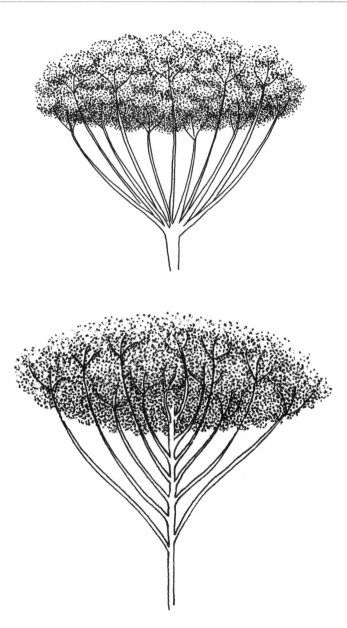

Corymb: A rounded or flat-topped head.

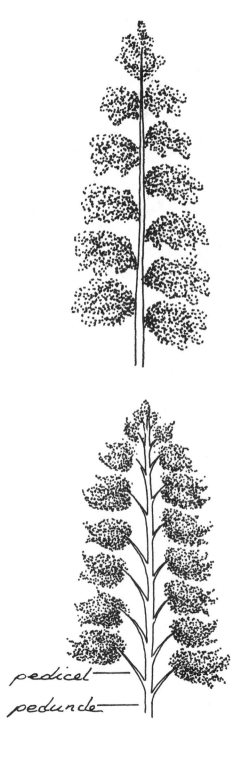

Spike: A flower cluster with several unstalked flowers borne along a common axis.

Raceme: An unbranched flower cluster with many flowers borne singly along a main axis.

pedicel

peduncle

Panicle: A branched raceme.

Flower Shapes and Designing a Garden

Flower shapes play a large role in the overall garden design. For instance, a plant with light and airy flowers will stand out in the garden when placed next to a plant whose flowers are bold, like a daisy's. The daisylike flowers will enhance the other plant's flowers. When plants are used in this way, to their best ability, they give a garden definition.

Foliage Shapes and Textures

As mentioned earlier, there can be many different colors in a plant's foliage, and many different shapes and textures—from the big, bold leaves of a hosta plant to the airy fronds of a fern. There are fine, lacy, feathery leaves, sword-shaped leaves, spiky leaves, rough and smooth leaves, dull and shiny leaves, wide and narrow leaves, even woolly leaves.

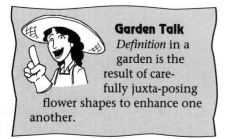

Garden Talk
Definition in a garden is the result of carefully juxta-posing flower shapes to enhance one another.

Some plants, like hostas and ferns, are often used in gardens because of their unusual and interesting shapes and textures. Let your artist's eye be your guide when selecting plants for texture and foliage, and have fun.

What Your Environment Will Tell You

You'll hear much more about climate, soil, and light in later chapters, but it's important to keep them in mind when deciding where to place your garden. You can use just about any plant for your garden, but unless you can provide the plant with the right environment in terms of climate, sun, and soil, you'll be waging an uphill battle.

Climate

Climate will tell you a lot about the kinds of plants you can grow successfully in your area, especially if your climate is extremely hot or extremely cold. Other climatic considerations are wind and air quality. For instance, if you live by the ocean, the salt air and wind are big factors. Desert conditions—high winds and dry, arid weather—are also obvious considerations.

Pollution

If your new garden will be in or around a major city, take into consideration that air pollution can be a problem. Luckily, there are many plants that have adapted well to these strenuous conditions. The star magnolia (*Magnolia stellata*) tree, for instance, can withstand poor air quality.

Soil

Your soil plays a big role. You'll learn in Chapter 5 that most soils can be amended to accommodate the plants you want to use, but that it's often better to work with what you have. Gardeners today are much more conscious of environmental conservation and try to use plants that can adapt to an area. For instance, if you have a rocky slope with unsightly weeds, instead of clearing it completely—rocks and all—work with it to create a rock garden filled with low-growing, drought-tolerant plants such as alyssum, crocus, and sedum.

Sun

Available sunlight is yet another thing to think about in terms of your landscape. (You'll hear more about sun considerations in Chapter 8.) Basically, you use a plant that needs full sun in an area that receives at least six hours of direct sun, and a shade garden where tree limbs, walls, or buildings provide shade for the garden. If trees are shading your plants, you may want to cut back some of the tree's lower branches to allow more light to reach the plants.

Flower Power!

In a heavily wooded area, you may need to carefully select the trees you want to keep and then remove unwanted, spindly trees, as well as some of the underbrush in the area.

Wherever you are, whether it's the desert, seashore, inner city, or suburbs, keep in mind your environment when choosing your garden style.

The Least You Need to Know

➤ Your personal style often determines the kind of garden that's best for you.

➤ Formal houses look best with formal gardens close by, and informal houses look best when informal gardens are planted near the house.

➤ White flowers are some of the most useful: They can brighten up a shady area, appear luminous under moonlight, and, when repeated throughout the garden, give the garden a feeling of unity and repetition.

➤ Think about a plant's shape and texture when considering it for your garden.

➤ Use the plants that are best suited to your climate, sun, and soil.

Part 2
Just the Facts

There are some basic facts about your climate, the soil you have, and the sun that you need to learn. In Part 2 you'll find out the nitty gritty of hardiness zones, the dirt on soil, and how to measure the sun in your garden.

In addition to learning about your own soil, we'll teach you how to properly water plants in the ground and in containers. If you're going to grow plants in containers, you need to know about potting soil (it ain't soil!).

Chapter 4

Zoning In on Zones

Now that you've got a sense of what gardening is from the creative standpoint—using color in the garden, finding the plants and flowers that appeal to you, and working with plants that reflect your "garden style"—it's time to get an understanding of some basic facts about using plants in your climate.

Take the time to learn a little about hardiness zones in this chapter. You'll save a lot of time and money in the long run because you'll avoid investing in plants that are not hardy in your area.

What Are "Hardiness Zones"?

The following USDA Hardiness Zone Map breaks up the continental map of the United States into ten zones—from the coldest, zone 1, to the warmest zone in the South, which is zone 10. The zones are divided according to annual minimum temperatures.

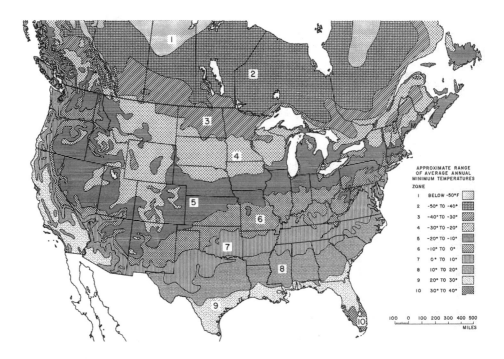

Find your zone on the map. For example, if you live in northwest Connecticut, you're in zone 5. To the north is zone 4, which is colder, and to the south is zone 6, which is warmer. By looking at the map's legend, you can see the annual minimum temperatures for your region. Of course, these numbers are general; to get a more accurate picture of your region's temperatures, frost dates, and other climatic conditions, contact your county Extension Agent or State Cooperative Extension Service.

Garden Talk
Some catalogs, books, and nursery centers use another zone map, called the Arnold Arboretum Zone Map, and there are slight differences between the USDA and the Arnold Arboretum maps, so make sure you know which zone map you are using.

Plants and the Hardiness Zones

You need to know about hardiness zones in order to know which plants will be reliably hardy in your area. Let's say you live in zone 6, and you want to grow a plant that is hardy to zone 3. This means that the plant will survive winter cold in zone 3, where average annual minimum temperatures are –30 or –40 degrees, and yes, it will be hardy in your climate. Another plant may be listed as "hardy in zones 3–7," which tells you that the plant will survive the cold in zone 3 to the summer heat of zone 7 in the south. This also means that the plant can't grow in zones 8 to 10 and that it may require a dormant period and some cold in order to survive.

How "Microclimates" Affect Zones

Even though your zone is generally the zone listed on the USDA Hardiness Map, changes in the topography of your property (or even your small terrace!) will influence the climate of a particular area. We call these areas that cause the temperatures to be colder or warmer *microclimates*.

The biggest influences creating microclimates are topography, water, reflected light, and heat. Local topography such as banks, small hills, exposed flatlands, and bodies of water can cause temperatures to be cooler or warmer by as much as 5 degrees.

The Lay of the Land

Temperatures will vary depending on whether you live on top of a hill or at the bottom of a valley. Local climates or microclimates are created by such hills and valleys. While flatlands—large, open, and exposed areas—are prone to collect cold air, the rule of thumb is that the higher the altitude, the cooler it gets.

> **Flower Power!**
> The higher up your terrace, the cooler the temperature is. Terraces above the ninth floor drop a whole climate zone!

Another topographical factor is banks, which can have a pronounced effect. Water will drain to the bottom of the bank, keeping the top of the bank dry and the bottom moist where the water collects.

It's Cooler by Water

Temperatures will be cooler for gardens that are in shade, with northern exposures, or close to water (streams, lakes, oceans, and so on). Warmer areas are places exposed to southern and western sun, areas that are protected from winds, and areas that receive reflected light.

Reflections of Light and Heat

The reflected light and heat off a building may create a warm microclimate. Because it will be warmer here, a plant that may not be as hardy out in an open, unprotected perennial bed may survive the winter if protected by the warmth of the building and the reflected light and heat it provides.

> **Flower Power!**
> If you are uncertain whether a plant is hardy in your zone, plant it next to your house, which is always a warm microclimate.

Think about the various microclimates you may have on your property. If you find, in your walks around your property, that you have hills, banks, exposed flatlands, or areas that are exposed to windy conditions, keep in mind how these conditions can influence the temperature. When you know how to work with these conditions, you can use the plants best suited for those areas.

Creating Microclimates: Working with Windbreaks

Some garden environments need to have protection from winds (particularly north winds). Screens and hedges, placed to protect the garden, are called *windbreaks*.

Screens and Hedges

Screens and hedges reduce the speed of wind by allowing air to filter through the open spaces. These open spaces help to prevent turbulence. Plants that are downwind receive shelter from the screen or hedge. In fact, hedges will reduce the wind's velocity as much as 30 times their height.

Walls, on the other hand, are solid structures and don't reduce the speed of wind, but deflect it, causing it to gather speed as it heads down and away from the wall. It's worth thinking about installing a hedge or screen if you think your potential garden may suffer from cold east or north winds, or from wind that comes off any large body of water such as an ocean or lake.

Making a Small Windbreak

If you decide to build a windbreak for your garden, you don't have to plant a straight row of shrubs across the whole length of the garden. By placing two or three sturdy shrubs in the right place you'll get the effect you want.

Create a windbreak with shrubs.

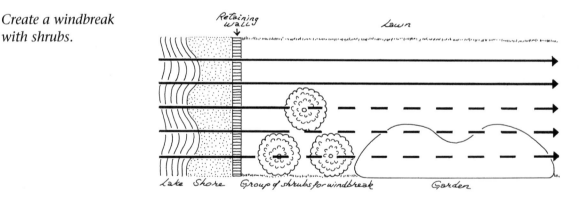

For instance, a garden exposed to winds that come off the lake in this picture can be protected by placing a few shrubs in the corner. Now the garden is not exposed to all the wind that comes off the lake, just a part of it.

Choose Plants That Like What You Have

Knowing which plants will tolerate your particular climatic conditions may be difficult at first, but with a little common sense and gardening knowledge, you'll soon get the hang of it.

Some Common Sense Goes a Long Way

It may not seem obvious to you now, but a tall sunflower planted at the top of a windy hill isn't a good idea—the plant may snap at the stem. On the other hand, a short and compact plant would work fine there. It wouldn't need any protection. Some good plants that fit this description are alyssum *(Aurinia)* and garden pinks *(Dianthus)*.

Plants for Seaside Conditions

Seaside conditions, where the wind and salt sprays are big factors, can present problems because plants often lose a great deal of water through evaporation.

However, there are plants that are ideal for these conditions. The shrubs in the *Viburnum* genus, for instance, have coarse leaves with little hairs on them. Most viburnums are dense shrubs, so they can double as wonderful windbreaks for coastal regions (or any exposed site). Another good windbreak plant that is also very dense is *Taxus*, also known as a "yew." These plants are evergreen.

Making Plants Work That Are Not Hardy in Your Climate

When you find that the plant you want is not hardy in your zone, whether your zone is too cool or too warm, you may be able to work around the situation.

Some (Plants) Like It Hot

In colder climates, tender plants unable to survive cold winters can be brought in before the cold hits. Depending on the plant and your indoor environment, you can either keep the plant in a sunny window as a houseplant, or let it go dormant, which means you cut it back and provide it with a cool, dry location.

Some (Plants) Like It Cool

Gardeners in the South who want to grow plants that like it cool may have to provide the plant with a summer mulch to keep the roots of the plant cool, or place the plant in an area that gets afternoon shade.

Another way for Southern gardeners to have plants more suited to Northern temperatures is to dig up the plant or bulb in the fall, bring it indoors, and provide it with a cooling period.

Experiment, have fun, become familiar with hardiness zones, and learn about climatic considerations in your zone. You'll be a more successful gardener for it and have a wider variety of plants to work with.

The Least You Need to Know

➤ Find out what zone you live in.

➤ Check your property for natural windbreaks and to find out if you need to construct some.

➤ Screens and hedges are effective in reducing wind and sheltering downwind plants. In fact, hedges will greatly reduce the wind's velocity.

➤ Always use plants that are hardy in your area.

Chapter 5

The Dirt on Soil

In This Chapter

➤ Modifying soil textures

➤ What pH balance means and how to change it

➤ Nutrients in the soil

➤ The best soil for container plants

You probably chose the house you live in for many different reasons (or maybe just one—location, location, location). But now you're stuck with the soil that came with your property. Whether your lot is no more than a thicket of brambles and weeds or barren because the house is a new construction, you have to learn something about soil before you can get that garden underway.

Not to worry—there are ways to improve just about every situation. In this chapter you learn how to identify the kind of soil you have and the various ways you can modify and improve it. If your new garden will be on a terrace, read on to learn about using potting soils and some important facts about container gardening.

Know Your Local Soil

There are a couple of reasons why it's important to know what kind of soil you have. The most important reason to become familiar with your soil is so you'll know how to improve it. Another reason is that this knowledge will tell you about the kinds of plants you can grow. For instance, certain plants—blueberries, azaleas, hemlocks, mountain laurel, and rhododendron among them—do best in an acid soil, while balsam, clover, grapes, and poppies prefer a slightly alkaline soil. Acidity and alkaline levels in the soil are measured in the pH ratio, which you'll read about later in this chapter.

What Is Soil?

Soil is a rich and aromatic mixture of weathered rock and mineral particles broken down over hundreds of thousands of years, resulting in organic matter teeming with helpful microorganisms, water, and air.

Garden Talk

You'll also hear the term *topsoil*, which refers to the top layer of soil—the first few inches. You can purchase quality topsoil by the bag at a local nursery or garden center.

The diagram on the following page shows the relative composition of soil with good structure.

➤ Air (±25 percent)

➤ Water (±25 percent)

➤ Organic matter (±5 percent)

➤ Mineral matter (±50 percent)

Minerals Matter Most

The largest component in soil is rock mineral particles, and soil scientists categorize textures of soil based on the size of these particles. Rock particles in sand are the biggest; on the other end of spectrum is clay, which has the smallest—even microscopic—rock particles.

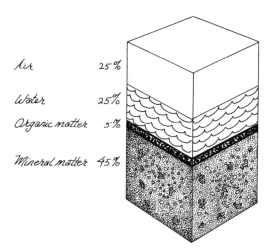

Air   25%
Water   25%
Organic matter 5%
Mineral matter 45%

Approximate ratios of air, water, organic, and mineral matter in soil.

Sandy Soil

Soil with a sandy texture is generally not very fertile because nutrients drain through too quickly. To find out if your soil is sandy, take the following soil ball test: Dig a hole that's two inches deep (your first clue to sandy soil is that it's very easy to dig a hole). Take some soil from the hole and squeeze it in your hand. If the soil falls down between your fingers without forming a ball, you have sandy soil.

There are some advantages to sandy soil: Plant roots spread easily through the light soil, drainage is good, and sandy soil warms up faster in the spring. The desert and the seashore are two places where you'll find the extremes of sandy soil.

Clay Soil

Clay soil is heavy; if you dig a hole (and this would be quite difficult) and try to form a ball, you will either get a wet ball that is sticky and gummy, or if the soil is dry, the soil will be as hard as a brick. Clay soil, because it has extremely fine-textured particles, holds in moisture and takes all the air out of the soil. Drainage is characteristically poor and plants' roots have a hard time establishing themselves. On the plus side, clay soil is often rich with nutrients.

Ah, Loam!

The happy balance of rock particles of both sizes, plenty of organic matter, and humus is called *loam*. A loamy soil holds moisture and nutrients in the ground. It's well-aerated, meaning the supply of air in the soil is just right. When you take the soil ball test, loam will form a nice ball, and if you tap the ball with your finger a few times, the ball will crumble. The texture of good loam is like the topping of an apple crumb cake.

What Is Organic Matter?

Although organic matter accounts for only 5 percent of the soil's composition, it's an important element. Depending on the type of soil you have, you can build up its structure with organic matter. You'll read about different kinds of organic matter in later chapters.

Adding Organic Matter to Soil

When organic matter is added to soil, it alters the structure of the soil. Organic matter such as peat moss and sawdust added to clay soils lightens up the heavy soil and makes it easier to break up. In sandy soil, organic matter in the form of peat moss and manure mix helps regulate the amount of moisture and increase the availability of nutrients in soil.

What Is "pH Balance"?

You're probably familiar with the term *pH balance*, but you may not know that pH is "the symbol for the logarithm of the reciprocal of hydrogen ion concentration in gram atoms per liter." Lucky for us we don't need four years of chemistry to understand the role pH plays in gardening.

The pH scale is the level of acidity or alkaline in the soil. The scale runs from "0" at the bottom, meaning extremely acid or "sour," to 14, meaning extremely alkaline or "sweet." Between these two extremes is neutral pH, located in the center of the graph at 7.0.

A pH scale.

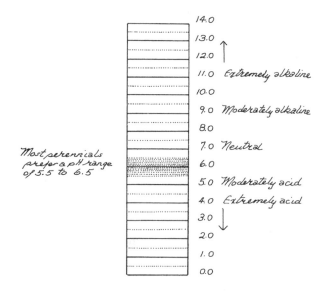

14.0
13.0
12.0
11.0 *Extremely alkaline*
10.0
9.0 *Moderately alkaline*
8.0
7.0 *Neutral*
6.0
5.0 *Moderately acid*
4.0 *Extremely acid*
3.0
2.0
1.0
0.0

Most perennials prefer a pH range of 5.5 to 6.5

Why a Neutral Level of pH Is Important

A neutral level of pH is always desirable because under these conditions the minerals present in the soil are available to the plant. When the pH reaction is too high or too low, nutrients in the soil can't reach the plant. The other reason plants do better when the pH is close to neutral is that bacteria, which breaks down organic matter, performs better. While it's important and useful to know the pH balance in your soil, you'll only need to modify your soil pH if it's extremely acidic or alkaline.

Look for Clues in the Plants Around You

There are easier ways to find out what your soil's pH level is. In fact, clues to your area's soil type can be found in the kinds of plants and trees you see growing around you. In primarily acidic soils, you'll find the kinds of trees and plants mentioned earlier in this chapter: oak trees, wild blueberries, azaleas, and rhododendron. In alkaline soils, you'll find beech trees, olive trees, cherry trees, and rosemary.

Testing Your Soil for its pH Balance

If you want to have your soil's pH level tested—perhaps you've been told your area's soil is heavily acidic or alkaline—call your local Extension Service, located at the college nearest you, and tell them you want your soil analyzed. Some Extension Services will provide this service for free; others may charge a small fee.

They will explain how to take a soil sample (the best time of year for a sample is mid-June) and where to send it. It's a good idea to let them know what plants you want to grow. When the soil test comes back, it will tell you the pH reaction in your soil and the quantities of other nutrients in your soil. One method you can use to find out a soil's pH is one old-time gardeners used: Taste the soil. Acidic soils have a sour taste; alkaline soils taste sweet. We don't recommend this method!

The Do-It-Yourself Way

Another way to test your soil is to purchase a soil kit at your local hardware or general supply store. The soil kit's meter reads your pH. The kit also provides charts to help you read the meter and to tell you how much lime or sulfur to add to the soil to correct the pH balance.

The "Ask-Your-Friendly-Gardener-Neighbor" Way

You could, of course, ask your friendly neighbor gardener about the soil in the area, although that may not necessarily be the most accurate method. Or ask someone at the nursery nearest your home. At any rate, you'll know more than you did before.

Changing Your Soil's pH

If you've received the results on your soil test and found you have extremely alkaline or acidic soil, you'll want to correct the balance. Most likely your soil is slightly one way or the other, and you won't need to change your soil's pH. But if you live in an area where the soil is extremely acidic or alkaline, you can add either limestone or sulfur to lower or raise the pH reading.

Correcting the pH Balance: When and How?

The best time to add these elements is late fall or early spring; don't use them in the summer during the growing season or in the winter when the ground is frozen.

Sulfur changes an alkaline soil. Use iron sulfate or ground sulfur. Iron sulfate acts more immediately to change the pH, and the iron encourages a rich, dark-green foliage. However, iron sulfate leeches out of the ground quickly. Ground sulfur, on the other hand, acts more slowly and stays in the ground for years. One other way to lower the pH is to add organic matter such as peat moss or sawdust.

Flower Power!
If you have a fireplace or a wood stove, save the ashes and keep them dry. Spread them in the garden in the spring to raise the pH.

All About Lime

Lime is not a fertilizer, as some people think, but is used to correct an extremely acidic soil. It brings soil to a neutral level and improves the soil structure by providing calcium. The safest form of lime is ground limestone—it's slow acting and works for years. Slaked or hydrated lime works more quickly than ground limestone, but be careful—it's very strong and twice the strength of ground limestone.

Three Major Elements: Nitrogen, Phosphorus, and Potassium

The most important nutrients in the soil are nitrogen, phosphorus, and potassium. Each of these elements contributes to the plant's overall health, and the combination of all of them in the soil makes the soil fertile.

If you've ever looked at a bag of fertilizer, you've probably noticed three numbers listed on the front label, such as "10–10–10." These numbers refer to nitrogen, phosphorus, and potassium, and tell you that the fertilizer contains 10 percent nitrogen, 10 percent phosphorus, and 10 percent potassium. What about the other 70 percent? This percentage is made up of a mixing agent that simply allows the fertilizer to be spread evenly in the soil.

Nitrogen develops the plant's green color in the foliage and stems. It should only be applied in the spring when you want new growth to start. Phosphorus is very important in developing flowers, seeds, and fruit production. It also helps in root development and aids the plant in disease resistance. Potassium helps in the overall growth of the plant and makes the plant's stems strong and healthy. The stronger a plant is, the better able it is to resist diseases.

Other elements in the soil include magnesium, iron, sulfur, and calcium. Trace elements include boron and zinc, both of which are used in plant development. Most chemical fertilizers have traces of these elements already mixed into them.

The Difference Between Garden Soil and Potting Soil

Garden soil and potting soil are two very different things. Garden soil doesn't belong in a pot for a number of reasons. One is that if you were to bring the pot indoors at any time (over the winter, for instance), the warm conditions in a house would create a haven for disease and insects. Also, garden soil alone in a pot would have poor drainage qualities and cause the plant's roots to rot.

What Is Potting Soil?

Potting soils (or *potting mediums*, as they are called), are a soilless mix. You can buy potting soils at the garden center, or if you're feeling ambitious, you can make your own potting medium.

Flower Power!

An easy recipe for potting soil is two parts peat moss, one part vermiculite, and one part perlite. Peat moss gives the soil its body, vermiculite holds the water in, and perlite aids in the drainage and keeps the mix lightweight. Because this soil has no fertility, you must add fertilizers either in organic or inorganic form. Fertilizers can be added in dry or liquid form.

Other Mediums for Potting Soils

There are other mediums you can add to your mix, such as charcoal, lime, sand, or composted bark. Charcoal in your soilless mix helps filter out any toxic elements in the soil, lime helps regulate the soil's pH, and composted bark contributes to the composition of organic matter. If you do add composted bark, make sure it's of a fine texture and smaller than the bark you use for mulch.

Mixing Potting Soil

It's important that all the ingredients of the soilless mix are dry when you mix them. But before you add the plant to the pot with the potting soil, add water, moisten the soil well, and let it sit for 30 minutes. Then mix it again. Now you're ready to pot up the plant. A helpful hint: If you have many pots to fill, mix the ingredients in a wheelbarrow.

Add Organic Compost to Your Potting Mix

If you decide to use organic compost in your mix, you'll need to sterilize it before putting it in a container. Unfortunately, sterilizing it yourself involves cooking the soil at 180 degrees for a half-hour and enduring the disagreeable and lingering odor of strong manure in the kitchen. Store-bought sterilized mix is the way to go.

Potting Soils for Outdoor Containers

If you plan to leave your potted plants outside, some soil from your garden will work fine with the potting mix. Remember that potting soil is lightweight, and if your plant is top-heavy or your plant's container is small, you'll need to weight the bottom of the container with a layer of crushed rocks or chips of broken clay pots. Add crushed rocks to large containers that are going to be staying outside for long periods of time. They add extra drainage and prevent the soil from passing through the drainage hole.

Sand is a wonderful drainage medium, but it's heavy. Perlite is also a good drainage medium and it's light, so you may prefer this (who wants to lift heavy pots?). It's a good idea to add superphosphate and lime (read the packages and remember, less is better) at the time you're making up this potting soil. Mix well, water, and let it sit for a half an hour (take a break), then pot up the plant.

> **Flower Power!**
> An easy recipe for potting soil for perennials in containers is two parts topsoil, one part peat moss, one part sand or perlite, and a few handfuls of organic matter.

> **Flower Power!**
> If you're using a large container, use Styrofoam™ peanuts instead of rocks and stones at the bottom of the pot so you can pick it up more easily.

Getting the Most from Store-Bought Potting Soils

When you buy potting soil, be sure to check what the potting soil contains. Since most potting soils are made up of equal parts peat moss, vermiculite, and perlite, you should add organic mix to the potting soil. Use it in a ratio of one part organic mix to two parts potting soil. Often you'll find that fertilizers and lime have already been added to the mix, so you won't have to fertilize for a while.

Different plants often have very different requirements, and ready-made potting soils accommodate these specific plants. For instance, African violets require a soil with more compost in it, whereas cacti need more sand for drainage. You can find specific potting soils for each. If you need a small bag of compost, use potting soil made especially for African violets; it's very rich.

There are also soilless mixes specifically for starting seeds that are extremely lightweight and allow for good drainage. As you garden, you'll learn how to mix and match various soils to get the right one for you and your needs.

The Least You Need to Know

➤ Know your soil type: sandy or clay. You can modify your soil type to grow happier and healthier plants.

➤ Organic matter regulates the amount of moisture and availability of nutrients.

➤ Only in extreme cases do you need to change the soil's pH.

➤ Lime is not a fertilizer. It's applied on acidic soils to bring the soil to a neutral level so more nutrients are available to the plants.

➤ Be sure your containers have holes for good drainage. Large containers need drainage mediums as well.

➤ Apply nitrogen to plants only in the spring when you want new growth.

Chapter 6

Sun and Water

Sun and water are vital to growing plants. Without sun, plants can't make food; without water, plants die. In this chapter, you learn how to avoid making the two most costly mistakes in gardening: giving plants too much or too little sun and water.

By now you should know where you'll put your garden. So before you set your heart on any particular plants, take the time to learn what you absolutely need to know about sun and water.

You need to be certain of the amount of sun your potential garden will receive before you do anything, and you can do this by measuring available sunlight at different times of the day. (You learn how to do this later in the chapter.) Even if you think you know how much sunlight the area receives, until you measure the available sunlight, you're only guessing at the hours of sunlight it actually receives.

Urban gardeners in high-rise buildings might want to pay particularly close attention to this chapter, since plants on high-rise terraces are often exposed to extremely windy conditions that can cause plants to dry out quickly. Plants on terraces need special attention to watering, as do all container plants. Proper watering for container plants is also explained in this chapter.

Sun, Water, and a Little Thing Called Photosynthesis

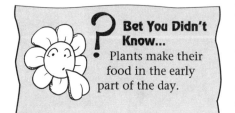

Bet You Didn't Know…
Plants make their food in the early part of the day.

Remember learning about *photosynthesis* in high school? This is the process by which plants make their "food"—in other words, the green leaves convert chemical substances with the aid of light and water into carbohydrates. Photosynthesis is more complicated than this, involving carbon dioxide, oxygen, and chlorophyll. But it's enough to know that without sunlight or water, photosynthesis won't occur.

Light Consequences

Plants require certain light conditions to carry on food production. They can't have too much or too little. A sun-loving plant needs enough sun to carry on its flower production and reach its proper height. By the same token, a shade-loving plant needs a certain amount of shade. Too much sun for a shade-loving plant can result in scorched leaves and prevent the plant from creating enough food to continue its life-cycle.

Proper Amounts of Sunlight for Plants

When you read about a plant's sun requirements, you'll see that plants require light in one of the three following amounts:

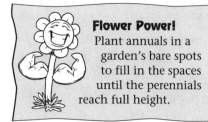

Flower Power!
Plant annuals in a garden's bare spots to fill in the spaces until the perennials reach full height.

1. *Full sun (six hours of direct sun between the hours of 9 A.M. to 5 P.M.).* A full-sun garden may also be shaded during these hours, either in the early morning or afternoon. Plants that receive sun from 9 A.M. to 3 P.M., and then shade from 3 P.M. on, get the best of both sun and shade, particularly in southern gardens. Afternoon shade is very good for plants, allowing them to take a break from the hot sun.

2. *Partial sun or partial shade.* Partial sun, also known as partial shade, is sun half the day (about four hours) and shade half the day (about four hours), again using the

time table of 9 A.M. to 5 P.M. It can also mean filtered or dappled light, which is the shade created by the branches of trees.

You may also hear the term "bright shade," which refers to reflected light, such as that from a white wall or building.

3. *Shade.* Fewer than four hours of direct sunlight. You'll find this kind of shade in north-facing gardens, dense woodlands, and areas with low branches overhead. Plants that survive deep shade like these are usually labeled "shade tolerant."

Flower Power!
Plant spring-flowering bulbs under deciduous trees. The trees' bare limbs in early spring make these sunny spots.

How to Measure the Sun in Your Garden

Here's an exercise to find out how much sun your garden will receive. You'll have to go outside to your potential garden, and take just a few minutes. You'll want to take notes in your gardening notebook. Be sure to note the day and month in your notebook and keep in mind that any areas shaded by deciduous trees will have more shade in the summer months, when the trees get their leaves.

Mark the Potential Garden

Begin by marking the potential garden with four sticks in the four corners of the garden. Draw its corresponding shape three times in your notebook. Label the three drawings "morning," "noon," and "afternoon."

Morning Light

In the morning, between 7 and 9 A.M., watch the sun's movement. You don't need to spend two hours doing this, just enough (perhaps ten minutes) to get a sense of it. Record in your notebook whether your garden gets sun, partial sun, or shade by marking a circle for sun, a half-darkened circle for partial shade, and a fully darkened circle for shade.

High Noon and Afternoon Light

Do the same thing around noon to 1 P.M., and record your findings under "noon," then do the same thing between 3 and 5 P.M., and record findings under "afternoon." If you come up with sun for all three times, your garden is in full sun. Partial sun would be sun and shade divided fairly (though not absolutely) equally, such as sun in the morning, and shade at noon and between 3 and 5 P.M. A garden in shade would have direct sunlight for fewer than three hours.

*Sun movement
in the yard.*

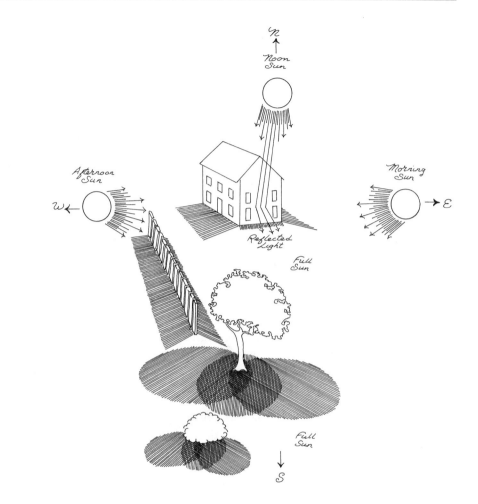

This exercise need not be time-consuming, and you don't have to take all three measurements in the same day. Take the measurements when you can—you'll appreciate that you did when you set off to buy plants and get the right ones for your garden.

What You Need to Know About Water

You know that plants need water for photosynthesis to occur. Deficient or excessive amounts of water in the soil decreases the rate of photosynthesis. But it's also important that plants are watered properly. Proper watering ensures that the water is reaching a plant's roots.

When to Water

The rule of thumb is to water in cool, early mornings or similar evenings. Don't water in the middle of the day when plants, because of the sun, temperature, wind, and relative humidity, are transpiring. Transpiring is akin to our perspiring; it's the plant's way of doing basically the same thing. A plant wilts when it loses too much water through transpiring, and the wilting indicates a water deficiency.

Green Meany

Never water at high noon! Plants are "transpiring" at this time, which is their way of perspiring and dealing with the sun, temperature, wind, and relative humidity. Most of the water you give the plant, at this time, will evaporate before the plant can use it.

Water Properly, or Don't Water At All

There's actually a nicer way to put it, but you get the message. They say "Water as deeply as the root tips and a touch more for tomorrow's growth."

You must water deeply to encourage the plant roots to dig deeply. Don't sprinkle a little water here and there, or the plant's roots will only grow close to the surface, where the soil is the hottest.

The deeper the roots penetrate the soil, where it is cool, the better able the plant will be to withstand heat and drought.

How Much Water Is Right for My Garden?

You want to get the water to the root tips, but, of course, you can't know for certain how deeply the water is penetrating. Soil type and climate influence how much water it can retain, so use your own judgment, and keep in mind what you picked up in the chapter on soils (see Chapter 5).

Flower Power!
An estimated one inch of water will keep soil moist for a week or two.

Sandy soils dry out fastest, so they will need to be watered more frequently than loamy or clay ones. Hot climates need water more often than cool ones.

Water in Your Area

If you want to find out what the average rainfall is for your area, write or call your local Extension Service. You'll find the number in the blue pages of your telephone book. If you don't have blue pages, look under the name of your closest college or university.

Flower Power!

Get in the habit of listening to the local weather on the news. Forewarned is forearmed, and if you know a storm or high winds are coming, you can plan accordingly. Knowing the general weather patterns in your area will help you plan your gardening chores.

Watering and Your Plant's Age

A young plant needs more water than an older one, so treat your young plants well: Water them and check on them regularly to get them off to a healthy start.

What You Need to Know About Plants in Containers

Potted plants are easy to overwater. In fact, drowning is the #1 cause of death among container plants! To avoid the mistake of overwatering container plants, use the same watering techniques as those for garden plants.

When to Water

Flower Power!
Keep a record of your watering times in your garden notebook, to remind you when to water and to also help you establish a watering pattern.

Plants in containers should be watered in the morning, so that the plant can absorb the water during the day. Be sure to soak the plant thoroughly. Allow the water to catch in a drip pan beneath the pot. In the evening, look at the drip pan to see if there is still water in it. If there is, empty it. Never allow a plant to sit in water for long periods of time or the root tips will rot, causing the plant to wilt because its roots will no longer receive water.

Consider these factors that influence how much water container plants need:

➤ *The type of container you use.* Clay pots are porous, and will dry out faster than plastic ones.

➤ *The size of the container.* Small containers will need more frequent watering than larger ones.

➤ *The location of the container.* Sun dries out plants. Wind also dries out plants and is a factor if your containers are, for instance, on a terrace with windy exposures.

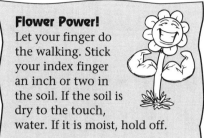

Flower Power!
Let your finger do the walking. Stick your index finger an inch or two in the soil. If the soil is dry to the touch, water. If it is moist, hold off.

The Least You Need to Know

➤ Most plants like the sun, but there are plants that need shade to grow to their prime.

➤ If your plant wilts for a day, water it—it should come back within a few hours.

➤ Don't let a plant lose too much water. If you see your foliage crisp up, you've lost your plant.

➤ Water deeply and less frequently.

➤ Don't overwater potted plants!

Part 3
The Idiot's Guide to the Best Plants

There are literally hundreds of thousands of flowering plants to choose from, but we've made the difficult process of selecting plants much easier for you with lists of the easiest and most reliable annuals, perennials, shrubs, vines, herbs, and bulbs. Each chapter in this part is devoted to a plant group, and in addition to descriptions of the easiest plants, you'll also get specific care instructions on each plant and suggestions on where to grow it.

Annuals are categorized according to their degree of difficulty. You'll find some annuals require no maintenance (no lie!), while others require about 20 minutes a week. In the perennials chapter, you'll find suggestions for combining perennials for the best color effects. Herbs, bulbs, vines, and shrubs also get their own chapters, each with all the information you'll need to grow them in your garden.

Chapter 7

The Idiot's Guide to the Easiest Annuals

> ## In This Chapter
>
> ➤ The easiest annuals you'll ever grow
>
> ➤ Descriptions (color, height, shape) of plants
>
> ➤ The best places to grow these annuals
>
> ➤ Special! Annuals rated for maintenance levels: no maintenance (*no*), low maintenance (*low*), and ten minutes a week (*10*)

In Chapter 2 you learned what annuals are; in this chapter you'll get a foolproof list of 32 easy and reliable annuals that you'll want to grow in all your gardens.

What Are Annuals?

As we have learned, annuals grow to full height, flower, set seed, and die in the same year. They put on a great show of flowers the same year you plant them and are very easy to grow.

Using Annuals in Gardens

Annuals are popular everywhere, from a cutting garden (see Chapter 14 for easy garden plans) to container gardens filled with annuals. You can always plant annuals to use as "filler" plants in your new garden where the bigger plants (perennials and shrubs) are still young and small.

Flower Power!
Avoid planting annuals in straight lines, and don't skimp.

The key to success when working with annuals is to use a lot of the same annual; it will give you a strong visual effect. For instance, if you want to add annuals as filler plants in between ground-covering perennials or shrubs, pick one annual, sweet alyssum, for instance, and plant it throughout the garden in groups. If you still have open areas, pick another annual, maybe impatiens, and plant it in groups. Plant as many as will fit, according to the spacing guidelines listed with each plant here.

Start Annuals from Seeds or Seedlings?

This is an important question. To grow an annual from seed, you must provide it with the proper conditions for germination (that is, for the seed to become a seedling and eventually a healthy plant). In some cases, seeds are fairly easy to sow outdoors where they will stay throughout the summer.

We recommend that you buy seedlings for plants where seeds are better started indoors and transplanted to the garden. Let the nursery do the work of starting the seeds. Then all you have to do is pick out the seedling. The only exception to this is the marigold, which is so easy to start indoors that you should have no problem. These annuals are mentioned in the text and include: cleome, helianthus, nicotiana, myosotis, and papaver.

What to Look for in a Healthy Seedling Plant

Let's describe what a healthy seedling plant is by what it is not:

➤ It's not leggy; in other words, it does not consist of one long, tall stem, which would indicate that the plant was not properly "pinched" in its earliest stages to get it to bush out.

➤ The bottom-most leaves show no signs of yellowing, which would indicate that the plant is suffering from being in a pot that is too small.

➤ The plant is not "root bound," meaning that you can see many roots growing out of the drainage holes on the bottom of the pot.

➤ The plant is not wilting, brown, or otherwise suffering from lack or excess of water or disease.

Cut Off the Flowers

A final word on purchasing seedlings of annuals: If the annual you buy has flowers, that's fine, because you are assured of the color you want. However, you must cut off the flower a week or two after you plant! This way the plant will have time to build healthy root systems and grow into a nice, bushy plant.

Annuals Are So Easy to Grow

We've divided the list into three categories, based on their maintenance needs:

Flower Power!
Make sure you are watering and feeding correctly. The chapters in Part 8 tell you everything you need to know.

1. *The no-maintenance annual.* Some annuals, like celosia, nasturtium, and portulaca, require no garden care whatsoever. In fact, these annuals thrive on neglect! With these plants, and others like them in this category, the key to success is no water, no food, no attention.

2. *The low-maintenance annual.* These annuals require just the basics: food and water. With impatiens, limonium, and nicotiana among them, they require no care beyond regular watering and fertilizing. There are many annuals that fall into this category, and with basic garden care they'll give you no trouble at all.

3. *The 10-minute maintenance annual.* These annuals require some care, but certainly should not be avoided. The work is minimal—you'll spend maybe ten minutes a week deadheading or cutting flowers—but it'll be worth it. You'll love the deliciously fragrant heliotrope blossoms. Grow zinnias for a cut-flower garden and—get this—your chore is cutting the flowers to enjoy indoors! Trailing petunias are also in this category. Whatever the chores involved with these annuals, their beauty will far outweigh them.

What Information Is Included on the Annuals List?

You'll find the following information listed with each annual, and what you can expect from the categories.

Genus/Common Name

Annuals are listed here with their genus name and common name and are alphabetized according to their genus name. To find a plant by its common name, refer to the index. In some cases, a species name follows a genus name for reasons of specificity. For more information about plant names, refer to Chapter 2.

Flower

Tells you the color or color range of annuals.

Height

Gives you the average height for the plant. Both dwarfs or miniatures and taller varieties of annuals will grow to their full height in the same year.

Sun

Tells you how much sun the annual requires—full, partial, or shade.

Spacing

Indicates the planting distance between this plant and the plants around it. For instance, if it says one foot then plant the annual one foot apart from other plants in all directions.

Self-Sows

Tells you whether the plant will naturally self-sow. Remember that a self-sowing plant needs to be happy and doing well in order to self-sow. Self-sowing annuals get a "yes" in this category; plants that don't self-sow get a "no" here.

Maintenance

The Idiot's rating system: "0" means no maintenance, "Low" means low maintenance, and "10" means ten minutes of maintenance a week.

The Idiot's Guide to the Easiest Annuals

GENUS/COMMON NAME: *Ageratum*/Ageratum
FLOWER: pastels (blue, pink, white)
HEIGHT: 6"
SUN: full
SPACING: 6"
SELF-SOWS: yes
MAINTENANCE: 10

Ageratum's small, fluffy flowers on little branchlets come in a range of nice pastel colors. The heart-shaped leaves are often hard to find under the cover of the flowers. Ageratum is a great plant for the front of a border or as an edging plant in a container. It blooms from summer until first frost.

Deadhead throughout the season for continuous bloom.

GENUS/COMMON NAME: *Antirrhinum*/Snapdragon
FLOWER: yellow, red, white, purple, orange, pink

HEIGHT: 6–36"
SUN: full
SPACING: 8–12"
SELF-SOWS: yes
MAINTENANCE: 10

Snapdragons come in just about every color but blue. The flowers are borne along a long stem and open from the bottom upward, making this a very long-blooming flower. Some snapdragon varieties are tall, intermediate, dwarf, and trailing. The tall size is best for cutting and is often used in flower arrangements. The intermediate and dwarf sizes are great for containers or for the front of a border. The trailing group is the least common and may be hard to find.

If your plant gets too leggy (see figure), cut it back by one-third or so, and the plant will rejuvenate and bloom again. Where winters are mild, snapdragons are best planted in the fall for continuous winter color. They'll bloom beautifully in the cool weather until the summer heat hits them.

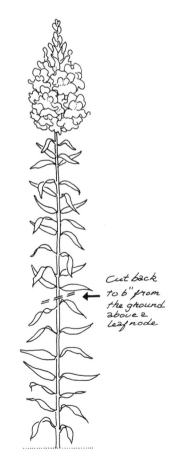

How to cut back a leggy snapdragon.

Cut back to 6" from the ground above a leaf node

GENUS/COMMON NAME: *Begonia semperflorens*/Wax Begonia
FLOWER: purple, red, white
HEIGHT: 6–18"
SUN: shade
SPACING: 6–8"
SELF-SOWS: no
MAINTENANCE: low

Wax begonias' single- and double-form flowers look like miniature rose petals and the foliage on these plants is attractive by itself when the flowers are not in bloom. Leaves are shiny and round in greenish or reddish hues and are about 2 to 4 inches wide. Begonias' preference for shade makes it a valuable plant for the shade garden. They will withstand some sun if the soil stays rich and moist and are great for window boxes as well as in the front of the garden. Or you can group them together as a whole garden.

Begonias can be brought indoors to be used as a houseplant for the winter months.

GENUS/COMMON NAME: *Browallia*/Browallia
FLOWER: blue, white
HEIGHT: 12–15"
SUN: full or partial
SPACING: 6–12"
SELF-SOWS: no
MAINTENANCE: low

One of the best blue annuals, browallia flowers are velvety-textured and last a long time in the garden. They trail up to 15 inches so are perfect for baskets and window boxes. They prefer a moist soil, even in the shade.

If you like, bring the plant in for the winter before the first frost. Cut the plant back by one half, pot it up in good potting soil, and place it in sunny window.

GENUS/COMMON NAME: *Celosia*/Cockscombe
FLOWER: white, red, orange, purple, pink
HEIGHT: 12–42"
SUN: full
SPACING: 1'
SELF-SOWS: no
MAINTENANCE: 0

Cockscombe grow in two very different forms. One is a feathery plume and the other tight velvet curls that barely resemble flowers. The plume varieties are a nice accent in pots; one flower head will last two months before fading. Cockscombe will tolerate dry conditions and loves the sun and heat. Both forms make fine dried flowers. Cut the flowers at their peaks and hang them upside down in a dry and airy place.

GENUS/COMMON NAME: *Centaurea*/Bachelor's Button, Cornflower
FLOWER: blue, mauve, rosy pink, white, crimson red
HEIGHT: 12–36"
SUN: full
SPACING: 6–12"
SELF-SOWS: yes
MAINTENANCE: 10

These ragged, button-shaped flowers are 2 inches across and come in beautiful shades and colors. They will flower throughout the summer.

Centaurea is easily sown outdoors in the spring or fall. While it is not a native American plant, it grows wild along roadsides and in fields and meadows. Some people think this makes it a weed, but beauty is in the eye of the beholder. Try it in a mass in the middle or back of the border.

Flower Power!
Definition of a weed: A misplaced plant.

GENUS/COMMON NAME: *Cleome spinosa*/Spider Flower
FLOWER: pink, white, purple
HEIGHT: 3–5'
SUN: full
SPACING: 6–12"
SELF-SOWS: yes
MAINTENANCE: low

Cleome is a tall, graceful plant with large 6- to 8-inch flower heads. Though big, the flowers are light and airy and produce long, thin seed pods that dance under the new flowers, making this plant seem like it is always in bloom. Be careful of cleome's spines at the base of each leaf: the sharp point can hurt. Cleome has a pungent smell you may or may not like. Only your nose knows. Try cleome at the back of the border or along a fence. Cleome is easy to grow from seed and readily self-sows. It likes hot and dry conditions.

GENUS/COMMON NAME: *Coleus blumei*/Coleus
FLOWER: insignificant, but foliage is chartreuse, apricot, copper, and bronze
HEIGHT: 30"
SUN: partial/shade
SPACING: 12"
SELF-SOWS: no
MAINTENANCE: low

Coleus are grown for their colorful leaves that appear in interesting patterns. Their flowers are second to the foliage; in fact, it's better to disbud the flowers so all the plant's energy goes into the foliage. Coleus work well in pots or as edging for a bed. It also makes quite a show when massed in a border.

Coleus are easy to propagate: Just put a stem in the water and it will root. It's a good plant to bring in for the winter (see Chapter 5 about bringing garden soil into the house).

GENUS/COMMON NAME: *Cosmos*/Cosmos
FLOWER: pink, red, white, yellow, orange
HEIGHT: 30–60"
SUN: full/partial
SPACING: 1'
SELF-SOWS: yes
MAINTENANCE: 10

Cosmos is a tall plant with a fine, airy habit—its foliage is fine and feathery—that gives it a nice touch in the garden. The daisylike flowers with yellow centers are either single or double forms and are about three inches wide. The taller cosmos are perfect for the back of the border, the shorter varieties work well in containers. Cosmos also makes a great cut flower.

Cosmos can be sown directly in the ground when dangers of frost are gone. They prefer to be on the dry side and will tolerate partial shade. Pinch plants back when young (see Part 8) to create a bushy plant.

GENUS/COMMON NAME: *Delphinium ajacia*/Larkspur
FLOWER: pink, white, blue, purple
HEIGHT: 12–36"
SUN: full
SPACING: 1'
SELF-SOWS: no
MAINTENANCE: 10

Larkspur has dwarf forms (12-inch) as well as taller varieties, both of which have tall spikes of papery flowers. The flowers grow along one large stem of the "hyacinth-flowering" variety. Other varieties have branching stems. The larkspur foliage is a bright green. The taller varieties of larkspur may require staking.

Sow seeds outdoors in the early spring or in the fall if you live in the South or, better yet, start with seedlings.

GENUS/COMMON NAME: *Gomphrena globosa*/Globe Amaranth
FLOWER: purple, white, pink, orange
HEIGHT: 18"
SUN: full

SPACING: 6–12"
SELF-SOWS: no
MAINTENANCE: low

Gomphrena's bright, 1-inch wide, globelike flowers bloom in late summer and do well in the garden or in containers. Gomphrena tolerate the heat, love the sun, and they don't mind windy conditions.

Gomphrena make great dried flowers. To dry, cut the flower just before it opens up and hang to dry in a dark, airy location. They also make a nice cut flower.

GENUS/COMMON NAME: *Helianthus*/Sunflower
FLOWER: yellow, orange, white, gold, reddish
HEIGHT: 2–10'
SUN: full
SPACING: 2–3'
SELF-SOWS: yes
MAINTENANCE: low

The wide range of heights and colors available for sunflowers, including pure yellow, orange and white, two-toned golden, red, and even bronzes, make sunflowers one of the most versatile annuals to grow. Varieties are multistemmed and single-stemmed varieties. The short varieties are great for containers and the taller varieties work anywhere but on a windy hill where the stems may break. Sunflowers make great cut flowers.

Flower Power!
If you have children, put them in charge of growing the sunflowers.

Sow the seeds where you want them to grow. Sunflowers grow very quickly. Everyone loves sunflowers!

GENUS/COMMON NAME: *Helichrysum*/Strawflower
FLOWER: white, red, yellow, orange
HEIGHT: 12–30"
SUN: full
SPACING: 1'
SELF-SOWS: no
MAINTENANCE: low

Strawflowers are one of the most popular dried flowers with their single or double daisylike flowers, each about 2 inches wide. They can also be used as cut flowers. They love the sun and would prefer a dry soil to a wet one.

The best time to cut the flowers for drying is when the center of the flower is just beginning to open. Then hang the flowers upside down in a dark, dry area. If you should miss cutting the flowers at the perfect blooming time, try this trick: When the petals are fully open, cut the flower head off and stick a thin wire through the flower head, turn the flower upside down, and make a small hook at the end of the wire. Pull the wire through until it catches on the flowerhead and you can't see it. This way you use the flower upside down and no one will know the difference.

GENUS/COMMON NAME: *Heliotropium*/Heliotrope
FLOWER: blue, white, violet
HEIGHT: 24"
SUN: full
SPACING: 1–2'
SELF-SOWS: no
MAINTENANCE: 10

Flower Power!
Ask your local garden center as early as February if they carry heliotrope, and if so, ask them to set aside as many plants as you can use.

Heliotrope's delicious, vanilla-scented flowers make this plant ideal for a window box or in pots placed by doorways. The blue flowers are more fragrant than the white or violet, and the large heliotrope can smell almost like a narcissus. It is great in the garden. Give it a rich soil, lots of sun and, if you live in the South, some afternoon shade.

It's easiest to start with heliotrope seedlings in the early spring.

GENUS/COMMON NAME: *Iberis*/Candytuft
FLOWER: white, pink, red, violet
HEIGHT: 18"
SUN: full
SPACING: 1'
SELF-SOWS: yes
MAINTENANCE: 0

There are two types of candytuft; both have different flowers. The "hyacinth-flowering" variety, which resembles the plant *hyacinth*, are tall with 1-inch long white flower heads. The other type is "globe" candytuft. It is shorter and its flower heads are flat clusters of tiny flowers. The globe candytuft makes an excellent plant for the front of the border or rock garden. The taller varieties make wonderful cut flowers. The bloom lasts a long time.

GENUS/COMMON NAME: *Impatiens balsamina*/Garden Balsam
FLOWER: red, pink, white, purple, salmon
HEIGHT: 2–2$^{1}/_{2}$'
SUN: shade; partial shade

SPACING: 1'
SELF-SOWS: no
MAINTENANCE: low

Impatiens are colorful and get along fine with very little sun, making them popular plants for the shade. Their flowers come in single, semidouble, and double forms. Flower sizes will vary. New Guinea impatiens are the tallest at 2 feet tall, and can tolerate more sun than the other varieties. Keep all impatiens' soil moist.

Impatiens root easily in water. Take a cutting and try it.

GENUS/COMMON NAME: *Limonium*/Statice
FLOWER: yellow, blue, purple, pink, white
HEIGHT: 24"
SUN: full
SPACING: 1'
SELF-SOWS: no
MAINTENANCE: low

Statice's paper-textured flowers are popular dried flowers and can also be used as cut flowers. They love the seashore and tolerate hot and dry conditions. They need a well-drained soil in a sunny location.

Start with seedlings. If you wish to dry statice, cut the flowers during peak bloom and hang upside down in a dry, airy location.

GENUS/COMMON NAME: *Lobelia*/Trailing Lobelia
FLOWER: blue, white, pink
HEIGHT: 3–6"
SUN: full/partial
SPACING: 6"
SELF-SOWS: no
MAINTENANCE: 0

One of the best annuals to grow for its trailing habit over pots and window boxes, lobelia can also be used for a summer ground cover to fill an empty spot. The blues are all spectacular. Lobelias are popular and sell quickly, so look for the seedlings early in garden centers.

GENUS/COMMON NAME: *Lobularis*/Sweet Alyssum
FLOWER: white, pink, lavender
HEIGHT: 4"
SUN: full
SPACING: 6"
SELF-SOWS: yes
MAINTENANCE: 0

Flower Power!
Put seedlings in the cracks of walkways for easy color.

These gems begin to bloom in the spring and continue all summer into the fall. The tiny flowers form a round cluster, and the white varieties have a sweet smell. Alyssum is great when used as an edging plant around walkways, the garden bed, in window boxes, containers, or in hanging baskets.

Sow seeds directly in the ground or a pot in early spring in cool regions, and in the fall where winters are mild. Transplant seedlings any time during growing season.

GENUS/COMMON NAME: *Mathiola*/Stock
FLOWER: pink, white, lavender, rose, purple
HEIGHT: 12–30"
SUN: full/partial
SPACING: 6–12"
SELF-SOWS: no
MAINTENANCE: 10

Stock have tall flowering spikes and a wonderful, old-fashioned fragrance. The soft colors are all very easy to work with and look great in all containers and gardens. They like a moist, rich soil and the sun. In southern areas they will need afternoon shade.

GENUS/COMMON NAME: *Myosotis*/Forget-me-Nots
FLOWER: blue, white, pink
HEIGHT: 9–12"
SUN: full/shade
SPACING: 6"
SELF-SOWS: yes
MAINTENANCE: low

These springtime bloomers will self-sow where the soil is moist; the woodlands are their natural setting. Forget-me-nots like the cool weather and continue blooming until the heat of summer. Some will rebloom in the fall. As a cut flower, it will last a long time in water. Forget-me-nots are easy to sow directly in the ground. Sow forget-me-nots in the fall when you plant bulbs. This way your bulbs will have lovely flowers underneath them when they come up in the spring.

GENUS/COMMON NAME: *Nicotiana*/Flowering Tobacco
FLOWER: white, greenish-yellow, red, pink, lavender
HEIGHT: 18–24"
SUN: full/partial
SPACING: 18–20"
SELF-SOWS: yes
MAINTENANCE: low

Nicotiana is related to the commercial tobacco but nothing about this plant will tell you that. Its tubular-shaped flowers are in full bloom at night, which is when the delicious fragrance of Nicotiana is most pungent. The white flowers seem to be the most fragrant.

Plant it near a doorway or in containers on patios and decks where you spend summer evenings. Use the shorter varieties in pots and the taller ones for the back of the border.

Nicotiana grows well in average soil, in sun or light shade, and even does well on north-facing terraces or gardens. They make an excellent cut flower. It's best to start with seedlings.

GENUS/COMMON NAME: *Nigella*/Love-in-a-Mist
FLOWER: blue, pink, white
HEIGHT: 18–24"
SUN: full
SPACING: 6"
SELF-SOWS: yes
MAINTENANCE: 10

The Nigella flower.

Nigella's finely cut foliage is bright green with flowers that dance above the threadlike bracts. The foliage makes a great backdrop for the flowers.

A great filler plant in the border, nigella also makes a wonderful cut flower. Cut them in their globe stage, and hang them upside down in a dark, dry place until the stems are dry.

The flowers are short-lived, and because of this, two or three sowings would extend the growing season. They are easy to grow by seed—sow in the garden bed. They do not like to be transplanted.

GENUS/COMMON NAME: *Papaver*/Poppy
FLOWER: red, pink, oranges, white, yellow
HEIGHT: 12–24"
SUN: full
SPACING: 6–12"
SELF-SOWS: yes
MAINTENANCE: 10

Flower Power!
Add new seed every year to a poppy patch to rejuvenate it.

Poppies come in many colors, solid or striped, and their foliage ranges from a grayish to a bluish green. Flowers are single or semi-double. While these beauties only bloom once, they are easy to grow from seed and some varieties, such as Shirley poppies, will self-sow.

Plant a poppy patch in the rock garden or mass them in a sunny garden for a real show.

Sow poppy seeds directly in place in the fall for warm climates and in the early spring elsewhere.

If you want to use poppies as a cut flower, sear the stem of the plant so it doesn't lose its moisture. Place a match or candle flame at the freshly cut end of the stem and hold it there briefly, no more than 5 seconds. Or place the end of the stem in boiling water, making sure the steam doesn't touch the flower.

GENUS/COMMON NAME: *Petunia*/Petunia
FLOWER: blue, pink, white, red, purples, yellows
HEIGHT: 6–24"
SUN: full/partial
SPACING: 6–12"
SELF-SOWS: yes
MAINTENANCE: 10

Petunias are one of the most popular bedding plants around. They come in all colors, single and double forms, ruffled or fringed edges, solids and stripes, dwarfs at 6 inches or taller 24-inch varieties. Some petunias are even fragrant at night. There are also trailing varieties that are delightful in planters or window boxes.

It's best to buy plants that have already started so you can see the flower's color and form. At summer's end, bring the plants in for the winter, cut back the plant to a couple of inches, and pot up for the winter. Place the pots in a sunny window. Keep the plants on the moist side.

GENUS/COMMON NAME: *Portulaca*/Portulaca
FLOWER: rose, pink, yellows, oranges, white
HEIGHT: 6"
SUN: full
SPACING: none
SELF-SOWS: yes
MAINTENANCE: 0

Portulaca is a plant that will grow where no other plant will: in full and hot sun, in dry or poor soil. The plant's needlelike, succulent foliage and brightly colored flowers identify it as a plant accustomed to dry and arid conditions.

Portulaca will do well in a container if you forget to water and feed it. Use this plant along the driveway, pool, patio, or on dry, south-facing slopes or banks.

These plants object to being transplanted, so sow your seeds directly in soil. Mix a little sand with the seeds for even distribution. No need to cover the seeds with soil. Portulaca will self-sow so you can have color every year. The seedling may not come up the color you wanted, but this is portulaca's only downfall.

GENUS/COMMON NAME: *Salvia*/Salvia
FLOWER: red, white, blue
HEIGHT: 24–36"
SUN: full
SPACING: 1–1$^{1}/_{2}$'
SELF-SOWS: yes
MAINTENANCE: 10

Salvia is a huge genus and includes annuals, perennials, and "tender perennials," which means they are hardy in the United States to zone 9 and elsewhere are treated like annuals.

Blue is a wonderful color in the salvia. Use the plants, depending on their variety and height, to fill in those empty spots in the garden.

Here are three salvias species to try:

➤ Scarlet Sage *(S. splendens)* has brightly colored flowers (reds, pinks, whites, and sometimes purple) and grows from 10 to 30 inches.

➤ Gentian Sage *(S. patens)* is a deep blue salvia that grows about 2 feet tall and branches nicely. *S. petens* flowers late in the summer.

➤ Mealycup Sage *(S. farinacea),* has flowers that are long and slender, giving it an airy feeling. The lavender flowers look dusted with powder.

All salvias like a well-drained soil and should be fertilized a couple of times throughout the growing season.

GENUS/COMMON NAME: *Tagetes*/Marigold
FLOWER: yellow, orange, red
HEIGHT: 4–24"
SUN: full
SPACING: 6–12"
SELF-SOWS: yes
MAINTENANCE: 10

Marigolds are a must. This popular flower has a color range from solids to combinations of yellows, oranges, and reds, with every shade of color in between. They are great in pots, on terraces, or in the garden. The bright colors last, and the flowers don't seem to mind heavy rain or strong winds. Some varieties have a pungent smell. Marigolds grow in any kind of soil and love the sun.

There are two types of marigolds: one is the African marigold, the other is the French marigold.

The African types have larger flowers and look something like a chrysanthemum or a carnation flower. Their sizes range from 2 to 5 inches across. The plant itself is larger and can grow up to 3 feet in optimum conditions.

The French marigold's flowers are smaller and come in single and double forms, from 1 to 2 inches wide, and their heights range from 6 to 18 inches. There are dwarf varieties that are even shorter.

These plants are easy to grow by seed: sow inside, or directly outside. Try it either way—marigolds are one of the easiest plants you will ever grow.

GENUS/COMMON NAME: *Tropaeolum*/Nasturtium
FLOWER: shades of red, white, yellow, orange
HEIGHT: 6–30"
SUN: full
SPACING: 6–12"
SELF-SOWS: no
MAINTENANCE: 0

Nasturtiums either grow as bushy mounds, 6 to 12 inches tall, or as trailing vines that can reach 6 to 8 feet. They come in wonderful shades, including creams, apricot, salmon, and deep mahogany colors. Leaves are round and light green to blue-green; some varieties are variegated. They work well in hanging baskets or trailing out of window boxes.

Flower Power!
Both flowers and leaves are edible; use in salads or to decorate cakes.

If you water and fertilize these plants, you will get beautiful round foliage, but no flowers. The seeds are easy to sow directly in the ground where you want them to grow; they don't like to be transplanted. Sow nasturtium seeds in fall where winters are mild, throughout spring in cooler regions. They can be planted in light shade in hot climates.

GENUS/COMMON NAME: *Verbena*/Verbena
FLOWER: pink, white, purple
HEIGHT: 6–24"
SUN: full
SPACING: 1'
SELF-SOWS: no
MAINTENANCE: low

Verbena flower and foliage.

Verbena's sprawling flowers, in terminal clusters from 1 to 3 inches across, grow vigorously from spring until frost. The lance-shaped leaves are round, toothed, and about 3 inches long. It makes a wonderful ground cover or edging plant. Or use in a hanging basket or trailing in a planter.

It is best to start with seedlings. Verbena like fertile soil and can take some light shade in the heat of the South.

> GENUS/COMMON NAME: *Viola*/Pansy
> FLOWER: blue, white, purple, yellow, red
> HEIGHT: 6–12"
> SUN: full/shade
> SPACING: 6–12"
> SELF-SOWS: yes
> MAINTENANCE: 10

Violas come in a wide array of colors, from solids to combinations of colors with blotches or stripes.

Viola tricolor are low-growing—they stay low to the ground, and spread out to form a mat. Leaves are oval and about 6 inches wide. They are wonderful plants for pots and window boxes and also good for edging a border of the garden. In hot climates, violas need afternoon shade. The more flowers you pick, the more flowers you have. If the plant gets too leggy in appearance, cut it back by one-half. Violas love a moist soil and need fertilizer.

The seedlings of pansies are best planted in spring in cooler climates (these are some of the first annuals you will see at your local nursery) and in fall where winters are mild. Pansies do self-sow, but you may not like the color of the seedling that comes up.

> GENUS/COMMON NAME: *Zinnia*/Zinnia
> FLOWER: pink, red, white, yellow, orange
> HEIGHT: 12–36"
> SUN: full
> SPACING: 6–12"
> SELF-SOWS: no
> MAINTENANCE: 10

Zinnias are available in the bold colors for which they are well known, as well as in many pretty pastel colors. They come in solids or stripes and as many different sizes of flower heads as you have room for. The more you cut of this plant, the more flowers you get. Great as cut flowers, zinnias will last a long time in water. They like the heat, and average garden soil is fine.

Choose your color, choose your height, and sow directly in the ground when night temperatures stay above 50 degrees (F). Cut flower gardens would not be complete without zinnias.

The Least You Need to Know

> ➤ Easiest annuals to sow directly into the ground: helianthus, cleome, iberis, nigella, papaver, tropaeolum, and zinnia.

> ➤ The more you cut, the more you get flowers: antirrhinum, cosmos, heliotrope, nicotiana, tagetes, verbena, and viola.

> ➤ Shade-lovers: begonias, coleus, impatiens, and some violas.

> ➤ Easiest self-sowers: cleome, helianthus, nicotiana, myosotis, and papaver.

Chapter 8

The Idiot's Guide to the Easiest Perennials

In This Chapter

➤ The easiest perennials to grow

➤ Descriptions (color, height, shape) of plants

➤ The best places to grow the plants

Perennials, as you'll recall from Chapter 2, are plants whose life-cycles last more than one year. Unlike shrubs and trees that last from year to year, and have woody stems and trunks, most perennials are "herbaceous," which means their stems aren't woody. In late fall and winter, the stems of your perennials will "die back." The plant will continue living, but because its stems will be bare you may think the plant is dead. Then, miraculously, in the spring, new green shoots will emerge from the center of the plant. The plant's alive! It's always a thrilling sight.

Putting Perennials in Their Places

There are so many perennials, you'll be able to find one to suit any spot, whether it's dry, wet, shady, or sunny. Their versatility is just one of the perennials' many charms. You'll fall in love with perennials for lots of reasons, and undoubtedly find the ones you like best.

Perennials in Gardens

Perennials are at home in any garden, from the formal to the informal garden—in beds, borders, islands, cottage gardens, woodland gardens, herb gardens, and rock gardens.

You'll find wonderful garden plans for perennials in Chapter 14. Use one of the plans, and become acquainted with the perennials in your first garden.

The Keys to Success

Beginning gardeners can be intimidated by the vast array of perennial choices. Here are a few guidelines to keep you on track when planning to use perennials:

➤ Always plant in threes and fives: uneven numbers make plant groupings aesthetically pleasing.

➤ Try limiting your first garden to only two or three colors, and make white one of the colors. White flowers work to neutralize the other colors and will tie your garden together.

➤ Work with the shades and hues of the colors you choose. If you choose yellow and blue, complementing these colors will be flowers in *shades* of yellow or blue; doing this will also tie the garden together.

Flower Power!

Continue working with the perennials you like best. Dig and divide in later years for more plants. You'll accomplish three things by continuing to work with plants you know: You'll know what plants work well in your soil and climate, you'll increase your stock with perennials you dig and divide, and you'll create a sense of unity in your landscape by repetition of the same plant.

Perennials in Bloom

Perennials bloom at specific times in the spring, summer, or fall. The exact time of bloom for each perennial will vary depending on your climate. Southern parts of the United States warm up more quickly than northern areas.

Deadhead for Second Bloom

To deadhead or not varies from plant to plant, and perennials that bloom again with deadheading are indicated with each plant on our list in this chapter. Perennials like coreopsis, campanula, and gaillardia can bloom for up to a month. The usual length of time for a perennial to remain in bloom is about two to three weeks.

Perennials for Life

Some perennials have short lives, like feverfew (*Chrysanthemum parthenium*), while others, like hemerocallis and baptisia, live very long lives. Many of the short-lived perennials will "self-sow" each year, which means that even though your plant will die, you'll have its offspring—its seedlings continue on.

To help your perennials have a long life, you need to space the perennials correctly when planting. For instance, *1'* would tell you that you should plant this perennial one foot apart in every direction from the plants around it.

Keeping Perennials Healthy

One way to keep perennial plants healthy is by digging them up and dividing them every couple of years, either in the spring or the fall. When you divide your perennials, you not only rejuvenate the plants' root systems but you also increase your stock for free. You can read more about "digging and dividing" in Chapter 21.

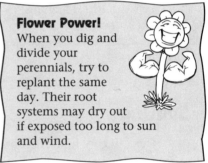

Flower Power!
When you dig and divide your perennials, try to replant the same day. Their root systems may dry out if exposed too long to sun and wind.

What Information Is Included on the Perennials List?

You'll find the following information listed with each perennial, and what you can expect from the categories.

Genus/Common Name

This category gives you both names by which a plant is known—its *genus* name, which is Latin, and its common name, which is simply the name the plant has acquired through the ages.

Bet You Didn't Know...
A plant may be known by more than one common name, but it only has one genus name.

Flower

This category indicates both the color of the flower and the window of time when the flower will bloom. For example, a spring-blooming perennial that blooms as early as February in the South may bloom as late as May in the North. It will be listed as "March–May." These are the average times this genus blooms in the middle zones, 5–6.

Height

Perennials need approximately two to three years to reach their full height. Keep this in mind when you buy young plants. It's a good idea to use annuals to fill spaces in your garden that are bare until the perennials mature.

Flower Power!
Check the zone map for your zone before you continue reading this chapter!

Zone

This category tells you the plant's hardiness zone. (For more information on zones, please refer to Chapter 4.)

Sun

This category tells you whether the plant requires full sun, partial sun, or shade—or some combination of the three. Read more about plants and sun in Chapter 6.

Spacing

This category indicates how far apart to space the perennials when planting.

The Idiot's Guide to the Easiest Perennials

GENUS/COMMON NAME: *Achillea*/Yarrow
FLOWER: yellow, white, pink, red in June–September
HEIGHT: 1–4'
ZONE: 3–9
SUN: full
SOIL: dry
SPACING: 1'

Yarrow (Achillea).

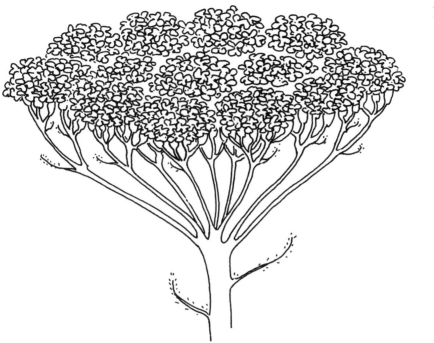

Yarrow's fernlike foliage forms a mound at the base of the plant, and the flowers atop the 1-foot stem are flattened heads. The first burst of color is quite a show. Deadhead soon after the first show, and you may get a second bloom.

Cut the plant back, just above the mound of foliage, in the fall. When the mounds gets too large, dig and divide in spring or fall. With a sharp knife, cut the center of the plant into quarters. You now have four plants.

Yarrow is very hardy, needs no winter protection, and withstands drought periods. It's great as a cut or dried flower.

GENUS/COMMON NAME: *Ajuga*/Bugle Weed
FLOWER: blue or white in May–June
HEIGHT: $^1/_4$–$^1/_2$"
ZONE: 3–9
SUN: partial shade/shade
SOIL: average
SPACING: 1'

Ajuga is a creeping perennial that likes the shade and makes great ground cover. The blue or white flowers are very pretty. The foliage is either a dark green or a variegated form with burgundy and a hint of white.

Plant ajuga where grass won't grow, or let it take off on a shady slope.

The only thing ajuga requires is space to grow. Divide in spring or fall to make more.

> GENUS/COMMON NAME: *Alchemilla*/Lady's Mantle
> FLOWER: yellow in June–August
> HEIGHT: 12–18"
> ZONE: 3–7
> SUN: full/partial
> SOIL: average/dry
> SPACING: 12–18"

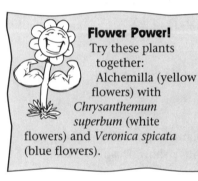

Flower Power!
Try these plants together: Alchemilla (yellow flowers) with *Chrysanthemum superbum* (white flowers) and *Veronica spicata* (blue flowers).

Alchemilla's flowers are light and airy in a beautiful chartreuse color. The plant's attractive grayish-green foliage keep it looking good even when the flowers are gone. They work well in floral arrangements—a nice alternative to baby's breath.

Cut back the foliage in the late summer about 4 inches from the ground. The new foliage you see growing will be next season's growth. Dig and divide every 4 or 5 years in the spring.

> GENUS/COMMON NAME: *Althaea*/Hollyhock
> FLOWER: pink, red, white, or yellow in June–August
> HEIGHT: 4–6'
> ZONE: 4–8
> SUN: full
> SOIL: average
> SPACING: 2'

Hollyhocks are great for the country cottage garden. If you're lucky enough to have an old barn, plant a stand of hollyhocks along the sunny side of the barn. The flowers—single or double—grow along a tall stem and at the base of the plant is a cluster of leaves.

Hollyhocks are a short-lived perennial but will self-sow readily. Cut back after the seed pods have opened. Lay the stems with seeds on the ground behind the old althaeas to keep the seeds in the back of the garden.

GENUS/COMMON NAME: *Artemisia*/Wormwood
FLOWER: silver foliage in July–September
HEIGHT: 6"–3$\frac{1}{2}$'
ZONE: 3–9
SUN: full
SOIL: dry
SPACING: 1–2'

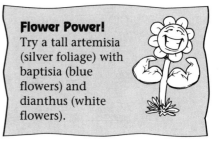

Flower Power!
Try a tall artemisia (silver foliage) with baptisia (blue flowers) and dianthus (white flowers).

After learning this plant's common name, wormwood, you may want to use its Latin name, *Artemisia*. These plants are known for their beautiful silvery gray foliage, which is a great filler next to blue or white flowering plants. The heights of the plants in this genus will differ greatly, and some varieties can spread a little too much at times.

A. 'Silver Mound' stays in a nice, neat mound provided you cut off the little flower stems as they come up. You'll recognize the flower stems by the little balls climbing up them. If the flowers are kept on, the weight will cause the mound to split. A. 'Silver Mound' is a charming plant that can look great in the front of any border until a hard frost.

Cut back to the ground in late fall; you'll see next year's growth in the tiny woolly buds.

For all other taller varieties of artemisia, don't cut back in the fall unless you want to neaten up the plant.

GENUS/COMMON NAME: *Aruncus*/Goat's Beard
FLOWER: white in May–July
HEIGHT: 1–5'
ZONE: 3–8
SUN: partial/shade
SOIL: average/moist
SPACING: 1–3'

A. *dioicious* is the most popular of the aruncus. Their 5-foot height provides a wonderful backdrop to the shade garden. The plume-shaped flowers of aruncus are open and airy.

You can also find smaller varieties that work well in the front of the border, such as the dwarf variety *A. aethusifolius.*

For fall cleanup, cut back to ground-level when the foliage has turned brown.

GENUS/COMMON NAME: *Asclepias*/Milkweed
FLOWER: orange, red in June–September
HEIGHT: 2–2$\frac{1}{2}$'
ZONE: 3–9
SUN: full
SOIL: well-drained, dry
SPACING: 1'

Garden Talk
A "butterfly border" is a garden filled with plants that attract butterflies.

Asclepias is a familiar meadow plant and easy to grow in the garden. It's a must-have if you're creating a butterfly border. It will self-sow. This is a very showy flower that lasts a long time in the garden and can be used as a cut flower. The foliage and stems have a milky juice and can be poisonous to some animals.

Asclepias has a long tap root, so be sure when you dig and divide this plant in the spring that you take the time to dig up a big clump of roots.

GENUS/COMMON NAME: *Aster*/Michaelmas Daisy
FLOWER: white, red, pink, blue, or purples in June–October
HEIGHT: 1–4'
ZONE: 3–8
SUN: full
SOIL: average
SPACING: 1–2'

Asters provide great color to a garden in both summer and fall. It's a huge genus. Here are a couple of good species to choose from, both of which have small, daisylike flowers: *A. novi-belgii* is a short, compact variety for the front of the border; *A. novae-angliae* is a taller hybrid that prefers moister conditions, so be sure to water during dry spells.

Dig and divide asters every two or three years: You'll increase your stock and help prevent any potential diseases.

Tall asters require this special treatment: They should be pinched in the early spring to create a bushier plant with more flowers.

> GENUS/COMMON NAME: *Astilbe*/Garden Spirea
> FLOWER: white, red, or pink in June–July
> HEIGHT: 1¹/₂ to 4'
> ZONE: 3–9
> SUN: partial/shade
> SOIL: average/wet
> SPACING: 1–2'

Astilbe is one of the most useful plants for the shade garden. The flowers' plumes will either be stiff or arching, depending on the variety of plant. Their heights include short hybrids that work well in the rock gardens to tall showbusters that are great for the shade garden.

Flower Power!
Try astilbe (pink flowers) with convallaria (white flowers) and hosta (white flowers).

Astilbe doesn't like the heat of the summer and may go dormant at this time. If this happens, cut back the foliage, and in the following year, water more during the growing season.

Dig and divide astilbe in the spring or fall every two to three years if you want to increase your stock, otherwise leave well enough alone—astilbes are a long-lived perennial. When dividing, use a sharp knife as the center of these plants are tough.

Astilbes make wonderful cut and dried flowers. Reds are the best for drying. Astilbes look great in the garden, even in winter. Cut back the old foliage and leave the dried flowers on the plant for winter gardens.

> GENUS/COMMON NAME: *Aurinia*/Alyssum, Basket-of-Gold
> FLOWER: yellow, gold, or white in May–June
> HEIGHT: 1'
> ZONE: 4–9
> SUN: full
> SOIL: dry
> SPACING: 1'

Aurinia is a very low-growing, spreading habit perennial. It's a wonderful plant to use as an edging for a border, in the rock garden, or to let spill over a stone wall.

Plant aurinia in the spring to establish a good root system. Trim back plant to keep in shape.

> GENUS/COMMON NAME: *Baptisia*/False Indigo
> FLOWER: blue or white in June
> HEIGHT: 3–4'
> ZONE: 3–9
> SUN: full/partial
> SOIL: average
> SPACING: $2^1/_2$–3'

Baptisia's attractive foliage is gray-green and clover-shaped. The flowers look like little sweet-pea flowers on a stem. Baptisia has a shrubby habit that makes it great for the back of the border or used as a summer hedge. After baptisia flowers, seed pods form that are also very pretty.

These plants have long root systems that make them hard to dig and move, so it's best not to move them. They do self-sow and the seedlings can be easily moved in the spring when young. Cut back to the ground for fall cleanup.

> GENUS/COMMON NAME: *Campanula*/Bellflower
> FLOWER: blue or white in May–September (depends on variety)
> HEIGHT: 6" to 3'
> ZONE: 4–8
> SUN: full/partial
> SOIL: average
> SPACING: 1–2'

Campanulas are a staple in the perennial border. Most campanulas have bell-shaped flowers that hang down, while others have flowers opening upward. In hot climates, campanulas will need some shade in the day.

Campanula habits vary. *C. capatica* are low, round mounds of foliage with stems that only reach a foot. *C. lactiflora* can reach 3 to 4 feet and may need staking.

Divide campanulas in the spring if you want to make more plants. Species like *C. persicifolia* will self-sow. Cut back old flower stems and clean up foliage for fall. Deadhead when needed—it can promote a second bloom.

GENUS/COMMON NAME: *Chrysanthemum*/Daisy
FLOWER: every color but blue in June–October
HEIGHT: 6" to 3'
ZONE: 3–9
SUN: full
SOIL: average/moist
SPACING: 1–2'

This is a huge genus with many species and many varieties within each species. The popular fall mum is also in this genus. Mums come in many different shapes and sizes. Cushion mums are only 12 to 15 inches tall; Spider mums are 2 feet tall with flowers 3 to 4 inches wide.

A summer-flowering chrysanthemum is *C. coccineum*, also known as "He loves me, he loves me not" or "painted daisy." There are also Shasta daisies, called *C. x superbum*, which bloom summer through fall. Feverfew (*C. parthenium*) have tiny, daisylike flowers. This short-lived perennial will self-sow everywhere. *C. x rubellium* blooms late in the summer.

> **Flower Power!**
> Try a fall-blooming chrysanthemum (yellow flower) with *Iris germanica* (blue flowers) and alyssum (pale yellow).

Be sure to plant fall mums in the spring and continue to pinch back the plant until early July. Gardeners in the south may want to keep pinching back until the end of July. This practice promotes a healthy root system and creates a large, bushy plant for the fall. Each spring thereafter, dig, divide, and make more. Dividing at this time is as necessary as planting in the spring. For fall cleanup, trim plant to the ground.

GENUS/COMMON NAME: *Convallaria*/Lily-of-the-Valley
FLOWER: white or pink in May–June
HEIGHT: 1'
ZONE: 2–7
SUN: partial shade
SOIL: average/moist
SPACING: 3–6"

Lily-of-the-valley is well known for its wonderful scent and is a great plant for the shade or woodland garden. Two large, oval-shaped leaves hold the fragrant bell-shaped flowers. It will make a nice ground cover if it has a moist home.

When you buy Convallaria, you'll probably get "pips," the eye and the roots. To plant the pips, dig a wide but shallow hole and spread the roots out horizontally in the soil. Add rich humus. The foliage may die back in the late summer. If so, just cut it back to the ground to neaten appearance.

> GENUS/COMMON NAME: *Coreopsis*/Tickseed
> FLOWER: yellow, pink in June–September
> HEIGHT: 1–2'
> ZONE: 4–9
> SUN: full
> SOIL: average/dry
> SPACING: 1'

Coreopsis are small, daisylike flowers. They vary from species to species. The foliage on *C. verticillata* is light and airy, and the flowers appear to dance on top of fine foliage. *C. grandiflora's* flowers are larger. Some are doubles. With regular deadheading, both plants will bloom into the fall. *C. grandiflora* will self-sow easily so leave some flowers on the plant to go to seed.

All coreopsis are easy to dig and divide in the spring or fall. This practice will keep the plant healthy and in good shape. Cut back to the ground for fall cleanup.

> GENUS/COMMON NAME: *Dianthus*/Garden Pinks
> FLOWER: white, pink, or red in April–August
> HEIGHT: $^1/_2$–1'
> ZONE: 4–8
> SUN: full/ partial
> SOIL: average/dry
> SPACING: 1'

Do you love the smell of carnations? Well, here they are. Dianthus are charming, low-growing perennials. They come in single and double forms and spread above the ground in thick mounds of gray-green or blue-green, grasslike clumps. Dianthus are at home anywhere: the rock garden, the front of a perennial bed, or in a cottage garden. You can never have too many Dianthus.

Deadhead after the first show of flowers, and they will repeat blooming all summer. A well-drained soil (sandy loam) is best for dianthus. Leave the foliage alone for winter, and if the winters where you live are hard, you may want to cover with ever-green boughs. This will protect the plant without causing the foliage to rot.

Spring planting is recommended so that the plants' root systems are strong for the winter.

GENUS/COMMON NAME: *Dicentra*/Bleeding Heart
FLOWER: white, pink, or red in May–August
HEIGHT: 1–3'
ZONE: 2–9
SUN: partial/shade
SOIL: average
SPACING: 1–2'

Bleeding heart (Dicentre spectabilis).

There are two very popular types of dicentras. The first is *D. eximea*, a low-growing plant in a compact mound. Its heart-shaped flowers are on stems above the fernlike foliage. It's a nice plant for the shade or woodland gardens. These dicentra will bloom all summer and they readily self-sow.

Flower Power!
Try *Dicentra eximia* (pink flowers) with *Phlox divaricata* (blue flowers) and *Digitalis ambigua* (yellow flowers).

The second is *D. spectabilis*, which grows 2 to 3 feet early in the spring. The graceful, arching flower stems are eye-catchers. The foliage on this plant isn't as fine-toothed as the *D. eximia's*. The larger *D. spectabilis* will die back to the ground in the heat of the summer. Don't be alarmed when this happens; it's natural.

In the South, keep these gems in the shade. Try planting a leafy hosta in front of dicentra and a large fern behind it to fill in the empty space. Dicentras don't like their feet to stand in water. But they should have a humus-loam to grow in. Cut back to the ground in the fall.

GENUS/COMMON NAME: *Digitalis*/Foxglove
FLOWER: white, yellow, pink, or red in May–July
HEIGHT: 1$\frac{1}{2}$ to 3'
ZONE: 4–9
SUN: full/partial
SOIL: average/moist
SPACING: 1–2'

These tubular-shaped flowers grow along a multistemmed plant and have the perfect country cottage garden look. If deadheaded, digitalis blooms into the fall. It also self-sows readily, so leave some seeds on the plant in the fall.

The short species, *D. ambigua*, is about 6 inches tall. Two taller species, *D. purpurea* (which is actually a biennial) and *D. x mertonensis* (a short-lived perennial) are very tall with colorful, showy flowers. They are both great for the back of the border and make good cut flowers.

Cut back flower stems to just above the foliage for fall cleanup.

GENUS/COMMON NAME: *Echinacea*/Coneflower
FLOWER: white or rose/purple in June–October
HEIGHT: 2$\frac{1}{2}$–4'
ZONE: 3–8

SUN: full/partial
SOIL: average/dry
SPACING: 2'

Echinacea resemble black-eyed Susans in their daisylike flower shapes. Their flower colors won't fade as quickly in partial shade as in full sun, but plants in the shade won't grow as tall as those in the sun. Echinacea's flowers are long-lasting in the garden and make wonderful cut or dried flowers. You can try them in a windy area—they can handle it.

Echinacea's raggedy foliage often gives the plant a straggly and unkempt appearance, but you can hide the foliage if you place it in the back of the border. Butterflies love echinacea.

Dig and divide to make more plants in the spring. Echinacea will also self-sow.

Cut flower stems to the ground and trim up basal foliage for fall cleanup.

GENUS/COMMON NAME: *Gaillardia*/Blanketflower
FLOWER: yellow, orange, or red in June–September
HEIGHT: 1–2'
ZONE: 2–10
SUN: full
SOIL: dry
SPACING: 1'

> **Flower Power!**
> There are many annuals of gaillardia, so look at the hardiness zone to see if your plant is a perennial.

The gaillardia flowers are bright bands of red and yellow or solid colors of gold and burgundy. This plant survives drought very well and is perfect for the sunny border. Gaillardia is a wonderful plant for the cut flower garden.

Gaillardia doesn't have to be deadheaded; it will keep blooming naturally. New shoots will appear in the spring when the middle of the plant dies out. Dig up the new shoots and replant them in a new location. You could dig out the old plant and add fresh soil to the hole, and replant the gaillardia in the same spot.

GENUS/COMMON NAME: *Geranium*/Crane's Bill, Hardy Geranium
FLOWER: white, blue, shade of pink, lavender, or magenta in May–August
HEIGHT: 1'
ZONE: 5–8

SUN: full/partial
SOIL: average/dry
SPACING: 1'

These geraniums don't resemble the familiar plants we see all summer with the same name (the Latin name for those plants is actually *Pelargonium*). These geraniums are usually low-growing mounds of beautiful green foliage (some have a spicy scent) with

Flower Power!
Try a pink-flowering geranium with *Iris sibirica* (purple flowers) and a low-growing artemisia (silver foliage).

simple flowers that come in an interesting range of colors and vary in height depending on the variety. In very hot locations, you may want to plant in partial shade, but in cooler regions full sun is fine unless noted by the variety.

Deadhead after blooming. The best way to deadhead geraniums is to lace your fingers through the stems, with your palms up, and gently pull up. If the spent blooms come away from the plant easily, continue. If not, gather up the plant with one hand and cut the plant's blooms with the other. Leave the foliage all winter.

GENUS/COMMON NAME: *Gypsophila*/Baby's Breath
FLOWER: pink or white in June–August
HEIGHT: $1^1/_2$–3'
ZONE: 3–9
SUN: full
SOIL: average/dry
SPACING: 1–2'

Baby's breath are a feather-light cloud of light pink or white tiny flowers on tall-branched stems that can reach 3 feet tall. These plants are a staple in the cutting garden and can be used fresh or dried. The small varieties are like ground cover with the same tiny flowers, but stems that reach only a foot high.

Gypsophila do best in a very well-drained area (try them on a slope). It's important that the crowns of the plant not rest in a moist situation. Plant gypsophila close to other plants so that they can lean against the other plants for support, and so the neighboring plants will conceal the gypsophila's leaves after it flowers.

Once planted, gypsophila shouldn't be transplanted because it has a very long tap root and resists being moved. Basal foliage should be left alone for the winter; just cut off the old flower stems for fall cleanup.

> GENUS/COMMON NAME: *Heliopsis*/False Sunflower
> FLOWER: yellow, orange in July–September
> HEIGHT: $3^1/_2$–4'
> ZONE: 4–9
> SUN: full
> SOIL: average/dry
> SPACING: 1–2'

Heliopsis are easy to work into the garden because of their height and long blooming period. Although they are tall and carry many flowers, none of these forms require staking. The more you cut of heliopsis, the more it blooms. This is another wonderful plant to use for cut flowers.

Dig and divide these plants in spring or fall to make more. If, after a few years, the plants seems to be flowering less, dig and divide to help rejuvenate the plant. For fall cleanup, cut back to the ground (you'll need pruners for the thick stems) after the foliage has turned brown.

> GENUS/COMMON NAME: *Hemerocallis*/Daylily
> FLOWER: yellow, red, orange, purple in May–September
> HEIGHT: 1–5'
> ZONE: 3–9
> SUN: full/partial
> SOIL: average
> SPACING: 1–2'

Many people make the mistake of confusing hemerocallis with lillium, which is a bulb. While plants in both genera have trumpet-shaped flowers, the foliage is very different for each genus. Keep in mind this distinction when shopping for daylilies.

Daylilies are called "day" lilies because each flower opens for just one day. The grasslike foliage grows in clumps and looks attractive even when the flowers aren't in bloom.

There are hundreds of daylilies to choose from in just about every shade and color. Depending on the variety, the flower shapes and sizes will differ as well. Some have more ruffles along the edges and others have curved petals. These differences are slight—the main thing is to get the color and the height you want.

Dwarfs look great in front of the border or rock garden. The taller, 3-foot hemerocallis is perfect for the middle of the border. Then there are the 5-foot daylilies (*H. altissima*) that look great in a field of tall grass.

All daylilies prefer full sun but can grow in partial shade—they may not produce as many flowering buds, but the colors will seem deeper. Daylilies can be planted in either spring or fall; divide after the clump is established, about three to four years.

Cut back flower stems when they turn brown, and cut back the foliage an inch from the ground when the plant no longer looks good. Water deeply if your area goes through a drought.

> GENUS/COMMON NAME: *Heuchera*/Coralbells
> FLOWER: red, pink, white in May–August
> HEIGHT: 1–2'
> ZONE: 3–8
> SUN: full/partial
> SOIL: average
> SPACING: 1'

Flower Power!
Try heuchera (red flowers) with lavendula (blue flowers) and *Chrysanthemum parthenium* (white flowers).

Heuchera is a dainty-looking plant with slender stems that produce small, bell-shaped flowers. The round leaves form a nice clump. Heuchera is great for the rock garden or for the front of any border.

Divide when clumps get too large. When cutting back for fall cleanup, cut only the foliage and stems. Avoid cutting into the eyes of the crown.

Spring planting is best for these plants because they have shallow roots. Mulch lightly in the North to prevent the plant from heaving. Water in drought periods.

Coralbells
(Heuchera).

GENUS/COMMON NAME: *Hosta*/Plantain Lily
FLOWER: white or blue in July–September
HEIGHT: 1–3'
ZONE: 3–9
SUN: partial/shade
SOIL: average/wet
SPACING: 2'

Hostas will brighten up any shady nook. Although they have pretty flowers, hostas are really grown for their wonderful foliage. You'll find hostas in unusual colors like blue-gray or bright green, as well as in variegated forms with yellow or white streaks. The interesting textures of hostas are also of note. You can use a smooth-leafed plant to create a soft look, or a very coarse, large leaf to make a bold statement.

Some hosta varieties have wonderful scents. One of these is *H.* 'Royal Standard,' whose flowers have a lily-of-the valley-like scent. It also makes a nice cut flower.

Hostas are great because they are extremely hardy and their big leaves keep weeds from popping through the soil.

They can be planted in the spring or fall, and dug and divided in either season, as well.

Cut back the foliage and flower stems to ground level for fall cleanup.

GENUS/COMMON NAME: *Iberis*/Candytuft
FLOWER: white in May–June
HEIGHT: $^1/_2$–1'
ZONE: 3–9
SUN: full/partial
SOIL: average
SPACING: 1'

Iberis, a semi-evergreen plant in the North and evergreen elsewhere, is a low-growing perennial. Iberis belongs in the front of the border or the rock garden—it will sprawl over anything, including stone walls. Its white color makes it easy to work into any garden design. It's especially beautiful in the Moon or Winter garden.

Deadhead iberis after the first show of flowers in the spring. This will help grow more blooms and strengthen and neaten up the plant for summer's growth.

Don't cut back in the fall. In the spring, trim it up.

> GENUS/COMMON NAME: *Iris*/Iris
> FLOWER: white, blue, lavender, pinks, yellow, reds in May–June
> HEIGHT: 6"–3'
> ZONE: 3–9
> SUN: full/partial
> SOIL: average/wet
> SPACING: 8"–2'

There are many types of irises to choose from, with a very wide variety of flower colors as well. All irises have swordlike foliage, although it will vary in height and stiffness. The flowers also vary in size and width, but all irises have the elegant flower with its unique shape.

The following are four iris species:

➤ Crested iris *(Iris cristata)* only reaches 6 inches. The flowers bloom in May in colors of blue or white. Throughout the season, the foliage makes a nice ground cover of short, swordlike foliage. *I. cristata* loves partial shade and a moist soil.

➤ Japanese iris *(I. ensata, I. kaempferi)* has a color range in blues, purples, pinks, and whites. The 3- to 6-inch flower heads sit flat and put on quite a show in June and July. The upright swordlike foliage is erect with a slight bend at the tip. Give *I. ensata* full sun and water during drought periods. Deadhead to keep plant looking neat.

➤ Yellow flag *(I. pseudacorus)* and blue flag *(I. versicolor)* are grouped here together because they both love the sun and wet or damp areas. Yellow flag can reach 3 feet and has yellow or white 2- to 5-inch flowers that bloom in June. Blue flag's color range is blues and purples with flowers 2 to 4 inches across. Blue flag's grasslike foliage is narrower than the yellow flag's and a bit shorter, 2 inches in height.

➤ Siberian iris *(I. siberica)* have smaller 2- to 4-inch flowers that come in a range of colors—white, blue, purple, red, and pale yellow. This very delicate flower blooms in July. The foliage is tall, grasslike, and turns a beautiful golden yellow for fall display. Keep the seed pods on the plants for added fall attraction.

All irises can be planted and divided in spring or fall. Fall cleanup for all but *I. cristata*: Trim foliage down to 2 inches above ground. *I. cristata* can be trimmed just a couple of inches.

GENUS/COMMON NAME: *Lavandula*/Lavender
FLOWER: white, blue, pink, or purple in June–August
HEIGHT: 2–3'
ZONE: 3–9
SUN: full
SOIL: average/dry
SPACING: 1–2'

Lavender's well-known scent and pretty flowers make it a must in the informal English cottage. Use it as a hedge in the formal garden, to line a walkway, or as a specimen plant in a sunny garden. The foliage is attractive when the plant isn't in bloom. Lavender comes in colors from blue-green to gray-green.

Grow lavender to use in potpourris and dried flower arrangements. It's best to cut the flowers just before they peak. They make a wonderful cut flower as well.

Don't cut lavender back in the fall. In the spring, cut back only if there was any winter kill. At this time you may want to trim the plant for a neater look.

GENUS/COMMON NAME: *Liatris*/Gayfeather
FLOWER: white, pink, purple in July–September
HEIGHT: 2–3'
ZONE: 3–9
SUN: full
SOIL: average/dry
SPACING: 1'

Flower Power!
Try liatris (purple flowers) with echinacea (pink flowers) and *Salvia x superba*.

Liatris has an unusual shape—it's a tall, straight spike with whiskery flowers up and down and the spike. Butterflies love liatris.

These plants can be dug and divided in the spring, but you may not want to touch the charming clumps of liatris. They will self-sow, so be careful during spring weeding not to weed out the seedlings. Leave the seedlings alone the first year to let them grow and transplant them where you wish the second year.

Plant liatris in the spring twice as deep as their width and cut back in the fall to ground level.

GENUS/COMMON NAME: *Linum*/Flax
FLOWER: white, blue, and yellow in June–September
HEIGHT: 1–2'
ZONE: 4–9
SUN: full
SOIL: average/dry
SPACING: 1'

Linum is graceful, light, and airy; a soft touch to every sunny garden. While their flowers only last a day, the plants produce so many buds you'd know never it. They will self-sow, which is great because linum are difficult to divide. Linum is also a very drought-tolerant plant and likes a sandy soil.

Cut back to 3 inches from the ground for fall cleanup.

GENUS/COMMON NAME: *Lysimachia*/Loosestrife
FLOWER: white or yellow in June–September
HEIGHT: 2–3'
ZONE: 4–8
SUN: full/partial
SOIL: average/wet
SPACING: 2'

Two loosestrifes that are fairly common are *L. clethroides* and *L. punctata*. The first, *L. clethroides*, has graceful, arching white flowers and grows about 3 feet tall. The other loosestrife, *L. punctata*, has large, yellow, star-shaped flowers.

Lysimachia love moist soils and make nice pond plants. They spread quickly by underground runners, and you may have to pull up runners in the spring to keep them from taking over neighboring plants. They grow so fast, they'll make their own garden if you let them. They'll grow in full sun or partial shade.

Cut back to the ground for fall cleanup. Lysimachia are easy to divide, so you could also replant shoots you pull up in the spring.

GENUS/COMMON NAME: *Malva*/Mallow
FLOWER: white or pink in June–September
HEIGHT: $2^{1}/_{2}$– $3^{1}/_{2}$'
ZONE: 4–9
SUN: full
SOIL: average/dry
SPACING: 2'

Flower Power!
Try malva (pink flowers) with perovskia (blue flowers) and lysimachia (white flowers).

The soft pink or white flowers on these bushy 3-foot plants are simple and pretty, making malva just right for the cottage garden.

Malva prefer a dry and sandy soil so they can grow their deep root system. If soil conditions are right, you'll have your plant forever. It will grow into a good-size plant and will self-sow readily.

Cut back the old flowering stems to the ground for fall cleanup.

GENUS/COMMON NAME: *Monarda*/Bergamot, Bee Balm
FLOWER: red, pink, white, purples in July–August
HEIGHT: $2^1/_2$–4'
ZONE: 3–8
SUN: full/partial
SOIL: average
SPACING: 2'

Butterflies and hummingbirds love monarda. So do gardeners because of its brilliant, globe-shaped flowers and pleasant, mint-scented foliage. Even when the flowers fall off,

Bet You Didn't Know...
You can recognize plants in the mint family by their square stems.

the round head of the flower is still attractive. Use monarda in a sunny border or light shade. Monarda is easier to grow in cooler regions; it may die out in hotter climates.

Dig and divide the plants in the spring. For fall cleanup, cut back to the ground. Two weeks later you'll see a mat of tiny rosettes forming—these are the same rosettes you'll see in the spring.

GENUS/COMMON NAME: *Nepeta*/Catmint
FLOWER: blue, lavender in June–September
HEIGHT: 1–3'
ZONE: 4–8
SUN: full/partial
SOIL: average/dry
SPACING: 2'

Nepeta's gray-green foliage is quite handsome by itself and, when the plant is in bloom, it's a real beauty. There are many different forms, from a floppy, sprawling ground cover to uprights that can reach 3 feet high.

Green Meany
Caution: Cats love nepeta. Although it can't hurt them, you may lose your plant!

The shorter species are wonderful for the fronts of borders, especially *N. x faassenii*. If you deadhead nepeta after the first show of blooms, you may get a second bloom in the late summer. Taller varieties may need staking.

Cut back to ground level for fall cleanup.

> GENUS/COMMON NAME: *Perovskia*/Russian Sage
> FLOWER: blue in July–September
> HEIGHT: 3–5'
> ZONE: 4–9
> SUN: full
> SOIL: dry
> SPACING: 3'

Perovskia's aromatic scent (and square stems) tells you it's in the mint family. The soft blue flowers and silvery, gray-green foliage give perovskia a wonderfully open and airy feeling. It's a great accent plant for the back of any garden or border.

Flower Power!
Plants with silver foliage tend to do well in seaside conditions.

Dig a big hole for perovskia when planting because these plants have stiff and woody root systems. For fall cleanup, cut back, leaving 5 inches of stem and buds for the following year.

> GENUS/COMMON NAME: *Phlox*/Phlox
> FLOWER: white, pink, red, orange, blue, or violet in May–September
> HEIGHT: 6"–4'
> ZONE: 4–8
> SUN: full/partial
> SOIL: average
> SPACING: 1–2'

Flower Power!
Phlox subulata will grow where no other plants will: in hot and dry conditions. It's perfect for the tops of banks.

Phlox is another genus with many species each with different habits, shapes of foliage, and bloom times. All of them are wonderful.

A woodland or shade garden isn't a garden without *P. divarica*. Another old favorite is *P. div. lamhamii*.

Its periwinkle-blue flowers on 8- to 12-inch stems put on a real show. Another partial shade lover and ground cover is *P. stolonifera*, which comes in blue, lavender, and pink.

A ground-covering phlox that loves the sun is *P. subulata*. It's also semi-evergreen and can manage with drier conditions. It's almost needlelike foliage is very different from the other phlox ground covers, whose leaves are round or oval-shaped.

The taller garden phlox, known as *P. paniculata*, have large terminal clusters of flowers. These phlox bloom during the summer months, while the lower-growing species flower in the spring. *P. carolinas*, also a taller phlox, blooms earlier in the summer and is less prone to powdery mildew than *P. paniculata*. Their flowers are white and rosy-pink.

Garden Talk
"Terminal" is the growing point on a plant— the tip of a stem or branch.

Both types of taller phlox should be thinned out early in the spring when the stems reach a foot high. Cut back all but five to eight of the strongest shoots. This will improve the air circulation for the plant and help control powdery mildew. It will also give the plant more energy to produce larger and stronger flowers and stems. The flowers will also last longer.

To keep the tall phlox vigorous, it should be dug and divided in three- to four-year cycles. You'll want to deadhead phlox just after blooming to keep it from self-sowing. The seedlings don't come up true, so they won't be the color of your plant. In time, the seedlings will take over your phlox. All phlox, except *P. subulata*, like a fertile, moist, well-drained soil.

Flower Power!
Try *Phlox paniculata* (pink flowers) with Achillea (yellow flowers) and Perovskia (blue flowers).

For fall cleanup on tall phlox, cut back to old flowering stems, about 1 inch from ground level. The ground-covering types should be left alone except for *P. divaricata*, which can be trimmed to neaten it up.

GENUS/COMMON NAME: *Platycodon*/Balloon Flower
FLOWER: pink, blue, or white in June–September
HEIGHT: 1$\frac{1}{2}$–3'

ZONE: 3–8
SUN: full/partial
SOIL: average
SPACING: 1'

*Balloon flower
(Platycodon).*

Platycodon is a very hardy and reliable gem with numerous balloon-shaped buds that open to a five-petaled star. The tall blue platycodon and yellow hemerocallis make a great combination. There are dwarf forms that are great for the front of any sunny border. Even though some platycodon will tolerate partial shade, the pink varieties seem to keep their color better.

Platycodon make a wonderful cut flower and will self-sow if conditions are right. Dig and divide in the spring for more plants, being careful to dig deep enough to get all of the fleshy, tubular root system. If you don't want more plants, don't divide them, and they'll live a long life without being touched. They prefer a slightly acid, light, and well-drained soil.

Cut back the plants and mark the area where your plant is for fall cleanup. Platycodon are slow to start in the spring, and you don't want to plant something else on top of them in the spring.

GENUS/COMMON NAME: *Primula*/Primrose
FLOWER: purple, white, red, pink, yellow, or blue in April–June
HEIGHT: 6"–2'
ZONE: 5–8
SUN: partial/shade
SOIL: wet/average
SPACING: 1'

Primulas are colorful flowers that look great when massed together. With a color range so wide, you're bound to find the colors you want.

The most common and easiest to grow are *P. denticulata*, whose 6-inch flowers are either blue or white. The single flowers are born on a rounded head. Sometimes the flowers will appear before the foliage does. The flower and stem are 10 inches tall.

Other primulas are *P. japonica*, whose 1-inch flowers are irregularly toothed and borne in a more open whorl. *P. x polyantha* is shorter—only a foot tall. These are also easy primulas to grow. Their color range has everything: Solids, bicolors, primary colors, and pastels. *P. sieboldii* is able to withstand more sun than the other primulas, but it will go dormant in the summer. The flowers are $1^1/_2$ inches wide and come in white, rose, and purple. *P. vulgaris* has somewhat crinkled and more individual flowers. Their foliage is either round or oblong and looks like a single-lettuce leaf.

Primulas need a moist soil; ponds and bogs suit them fine. If you don't have these conditions, you'll need to add peat moss and organic matter to the soil to keep the area moist. Cold and wet winters benefit primula more than hot and dry summers. If the summers are too hot, or your area goes through a drought, the primula will go into an early dormancy to protect itself.

Primulas should be divided every fourth year to renew their vigor. Some will self-sow. Remove spent leaves as they appear in the season. There is no fall cleanup.

GENUS/COMMON NAME: *Rudbeckia*/Black-eyed Susan
FLOWER: yellow or orange in July–September
HEIGHT: 2–3'
ZONE: 3–9
SUN: full/partial
SOIL: average
SPACING: 2'

Rudbeckia is a daisylike plant that can be found along the roadsides and meadows of North America. But there are cultivated species that do very well in the garden. They are fuller plants with more flowers. Rudbeckia blooms into the fall and is a great accent to any fall coloration.

Flower Power!
Try rudbeckia (yellow/orange flowers) with Asclepias (orange/red flowers) and coreopsis (yellow flowers) together.

R. fulgida is the name of the species found in the wild. *R. fulgida* 'Goldstrum' is the variety commonly grown in gardens. It's more compact than the wild, but still has the yellow-orange petals with the dark brown cone in the center. There are double forms called *R. nitida* 'Goldguelle.' This is a wonderful plant that needs no staking.

Cut back to ground for fall cleanup. Rudbeckia also makes a wonderful cut flower.

GENUS/COMMON NAME: *Salvia*/Sage
FLOWER: blue, lavender in June–August
HEIGHT: 1–3'
ZONE: 4–8
SUN: full
SOIL: average
SPACING: 1'

Salvia thrive in hot, dry, sunny locations and are perfect for seashore gardens. Most have silvery gray-green foliage that is aromatic.

Whether you use the large, gray-leafed varieties whose flower stems reach 3 feet tall or the shorter, compact salvias, you won't find a more beautiful plant with the same gorgeous blue shades. Be careful in choosing salvias because there are many annuals and biennials on the market. Usually the reds belong in the warmer climates and are annuals for the North. Their spike-shaped flowers last a long time on the plant, which is a great asset. *S. x superba* grows numerous flower stems and even when the flowers fall off, the reddish bracts the plant is still very attractive. They are good for use as dried flowers.

Fall cleanup for the large-leafed salvia is to leave it alone unless the leaf looks spent; Small-leafed varieties: Cut back to 1 inch from the ground.

GENUS/COMMON NAME: *Scabiosa*/Scabious, Pincushion Flower
FLOWER: white, blue, pink in June–August
HEIGHT: 1–2'
ZONE: 3–7

SUN: full
SOIL: average
SPACING: 1'

These lacy 3-inch flowers whose centers look like pin cushions are one of the best cut flowers you can grow. They bloom all summer and will bloom into the fall if you dead-head.

The dwarf varieties are great for the front of the border and will also bloom into the fall. Some people use the seed pods for dried flowers.

Scabiosa like average soil that's slightly alkaline, so add a little lime in the spring and your plant will reward you with plenty of flowers. In very hot climates you may need to keep the soil a little moister than usual. You could also try planting scabiosa where they can get some afternoon shade.

Cut back to ground level for fall cleanup.

GENUS/COMMON NAME: *Sedum*/Stonecrop
FLOWER: red, pink, white, or yellow in July–October
HEIGHT: 4"–2'
ZONE: 3–9
SUN: full
SOIL: average/dry
SPACING: 1–2'

Sedum have tiny flowers in clusters and their thick, supple leaves tell you they're succulents, like cactus plants. They are perfect for rock gardens or as ground covers. And like other succulents, they prefer very well-drained soil and can withstand the heat. Some sedum are even evergreen. Most of them are low growing, and the shorter ones work well in stone walls or between stepping stones. All sedum work well in containers, provided you don't overwater.

The taller species are great for the perennial border. *S. spectabile* can reach 18 inches. *S. sieboldii* grows to 6 to 9 inches tall. Another sedum, *S. telephium* 'Autumn Joy,' is one of the tallest sedums, reaching 2 feet. This species is a great plant with rust-colored flowerheads that deepen as the weather gets colder. The sturdy stems will hold the flowers up all winter, so use this plant for winter color.

Sedum is easily increased by stem cutting. You can root the stem in water or by sticking the cutting directly into the garden just after a rain. If you aren't using the plant for a winter garden, cut back to the ground in the fall. Try using *S. telephium* 'Autumn Joy' as a cut flower or for drying.

> GENUS/COMMON NAME: *Stokesia*/Stoke's Aster
> FLOWER: white, blue in July–September
> HEIGHT: $1^1/_2$'
> ZONE: 5–9
> SUN: full
> SOIL: dry
> SPACING: 1'

Stokesia's flowers are like asters. The 3- to 4-inch blooms are beautiful and seem to bloom all summer. They belong in every perennial border and make a great cut flower.

Stokesia can tolerate some shade but prefer full sun. They will live a long life if they can have a light or sandy soil. Damp conditions or wet winters could do this little charmer in.

Flower Power!
Try stokesia (blue flowers) with alchemilla (yellow flowers) and hemerocallis (yellow flowers).

Cut back to basal foliage for fall cleanup.

> GENUS/COMMON NAME: *Tradescantia*/Spiderwort
> FLOWER: shades of white, red, pink, blue, or purple in June–August
> HEIGHT: 1–2'
> ZONE: 4–9
> SUN: partial/shade
> SOIL: average
> SPACING: 2'

Tradescantias grow by underground runners and, if conditions are right, this plant will grow everywhere—even between cracks in walls! So be forewarned. But tradescantia is a useful plant because it works so well in shade. The flowers have three petals and are about one inch wide. They open in the morning and close in the heat of the day.

Cut the plant back half way after the blooming period is finished to get a second bloom. Cutting back will also rejuvenate the plant if it gets too leggy. Tradescantias need some organic matter in the soil.

Cut back to ground level for fall cleanup. You can dig and divide in the spring to make more.

GENUS/COMMON NAME: *Veronica*/Speedwell
FLOWER: blues, red, white, or pinks in May–August
HEIGHT: 6"–2'
ZONE: 4–7
SUN: full
SOIL: average
SPACING: 1'

Speedwell (Veronica).

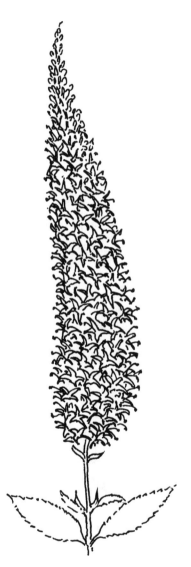

Veronica's blue flowers are beautiful, and although you can find white and red varieties, the blues really stand out. Their habits vary from low ground covers to upright forms that can reach 2 feet. Veronicas are perfect for the middle of the perennial border. Use the taller veronica for cut flowers or deadhead them to get more flowers. The shorter forms work well in rock gardens or for edging plants.

Veronica would prefer dry conditions to wet ones. Spring planting is best.

For fall cleanup, cut back taller varieties to ground level, leave ground covers alone.

> GENUS/COMMON NAME: *Vinca*/Periwinkle
> FLOWER: blue or white in April–May
> HEIGHT: 6"
> ZONE: 4–9
> SUN: partial/shade
> SOIL: average
> SPACING: 1'

The flowers are either blue or white and make a lovely show in the spring. Use vinca around shady trees where the grass won't grow or on a shady bank where you can't mow. It's quite charming to plant daffodils in a carpet of vinca.

Vinca is actually a vine that runs along the ground, making it a great ground cover plant. They root in several places along the stem so it is easy to take cuttings and replant the cuttings the same day.

No fall cleanup. Spring trim to keep under control.

> GENUS/COMMON NAME: *Viola*/Violet, Sweet Viola
> FLOWER: white, red, yellow, blue in May–August
> HEIGHT: 6"
> ZONE: 5–9
> SUN: full/partial/shade
> SOIL: average
> SPACING: 1'

Violas are small in stature, colorful, and well-loved. They are wonderful anywhere: in containers, in woodland gardens, in the rock garden, in the front of the border, as edging along pathways.

There are hundreds of different species of violas. The small 1-inch blue or white flowers on *V. odorata* are well known for their sweet fragrance. *V. odorata* will take sun or shade. *V. cornuta*, on the other hand, should be grown in the sun only where summers are cool. *V. cornuta's* flowers are about 1 to 2 inches wide, and come in a wide range of colors, solids, and two-tones.

V. odorata will flower throughout the season and self-sow readily. They are also easy to dig and divide. They naturalize easily, making a nice ground cover. If *V. cornuta* plants become leggy, cut them back hard and they'll rejuvenate. In the fall, trim back to neaten up the plant. Violas are best planted in the spring.

Perennials Are More Than Just Flowers

Perennials are not just ornamental flowers, but also include foliage plants like ferns, and ornamental grasses, that belong in any garden for the texture, shape, and definition that they contribute.

Ferns

As you discovered in Chapter 3, green foliage can enhance the colors of any garden by providing a backdrop for the garden.

The following are five great ferns, listed by genus and species and common names.

GENUS/COMMON NAME: *Adiantum pedatum*/Maidenhair
HEIGHT: 12–26"
ZONE: 3–10
SUN: sun/shade
SOIL: moist
SPACING: 1'

This fern's dainty, bright green fronds grow on a shiny purple-black stem in an almost horizontal direction. It needs a moist location and is slow to spread.

GENUS/COMMON NAME: *Athyrium goeringianum* 'Pictum'/Japanese Painted Fern
HEIGHT: 2'
ZONE: 3–10
SUN: partial/shade
SOIL: average/moist
SPACING: 1'

The Japanese painted fern is one of the most popular ferns because of its colorful design of deep red on the silver-gray foliage. It stands out in any garden.

> GENUS/COMMON NAME: *Dennstaedtia punctilobula*/Hay-Scented Fern
> HEIGHT: 20–30"
> ZONE: 3–10
> SUN: full/shade
> SOIL: average
> SPACING: 1'

Hay-scented fern grows very fast and is wonderful for naturalizing. The fronds have a fine texture, and if you pick them, you'll catch the scent of hay.

> GENUS/COMMON NAME: *Matteuccia pennsylvanica*/Ostrich Fern
> HEIGHT: 5'
> ZONE: 3–10
> SUN: full/partial
> SOIL: moist
> SPACING: 2'

This fern grows quickly—5 feet in one season. Ostrich fern gives nice height and definition to a garden. It needs wet conditions.

> GENUS/COMMON NAME: *Osmunda cinnamomea*/Cinnamon Fern
> HEIGHT: 2–5'
> ZONE: 3
> SUN: full/partial
> SOIL: moist
> SPACING: 2'

Cinnamon fern looks great in all seasons: In spring the fronds are a light green; in summer they turn a golden color; and in the fall, the fronds turn bronze. This is another great fern to use in the back of the border or for adding definition to the garden. It will grow in the sun if it has moisture, which it needs throughout the growing season.

Ornamental Grasses

Ornamental grasses come in a wide variety of different heights, colors, and textures. Grasses give wonderful definition to any garden, whether formal or informal, and make striking specimen plants. They are a must for the winter garden and are beautiful and useful screens and wind breaks in summer and winter gardens.

The following are five grasses, listed by genus and species and common name.

GENUS/COMMON NAME: *Festuca*/Fescue
HEIGHT: 8–12"
ZONE: 4–8
SUN: full
SOIL: average
SPACING: 2'

The beautiful gray-blue leaves of this small, tufted grass make it a striking plant for edging or a low ground cover. Prefers dry conditions once established, but should be watered regularly during prolonged summer drought as roots like moisture. Plant in spring. Cut foliage to ground before spring growth starts. Divide in spring every 3 to 4 years.

GENUS/COMMON NAME: *Miscanthus sinensis* 'Zebrinus'/Zebra grass
HEIGHT: 5–7'
ZONE: 5–10
SUN: full/partial
SOIL: average
SPACING: 3–5'

An excellent background grass for perennial or seaside gardens, with broad, yellow, irregularly spaced marks across its blades, and white flower sprays. Also works well in container plantings. There are many *M. sinensis* grasses to choose from: *M. sinensis* 'Gracillimus' grows up to 7 feet in a graceful arching clump, with airy green blades and silvery plumes during the summer that turn tan in the winter. M. *sinensis* 'Variegatus' has green blades with distinct white stripes up the center. Plant in the spring or fall. Cut back foliage before spring growth starts. Blooms persist through winter to add an interesting touch.

GENUS/COMMON NAME: *Pennisetum setacceum*/Fountain grass
HEIGHT: 3–4'
ZONE: 7–10
SUN: full
SOIL: average-dry
SPACING: 4'

This grass is treated as an annual in the north, for it can not withstand freezing temperatures. The leaves are narrow and its habit is very graceful as it arches and curves. Fountain grass comes in beautiful rose to copper shades that add wonderful color as well as form to the garden. The plumes are bristly and grow up to 1 foot long, and work well in containers as they are a nice accent in combination plantings. A cautionary note: this plant can be invasive in frost-free areas.

GENUS/COMMON NAME: *Phalaris arundinacea picta*/Ribbon grass
HEIGHT: 2–4'
ZONE: 2
SUN: full
SOIL: dry/poor
SPACING: 2'

This grass grows by underground stolons. Give it the poorest soil conditions in full sun and watch it grow like a weed. It can be mowed down to rejuvenate it. If planted in good soil it can become too leggy. The flowers are inconspicuous. It is grown just for its semi-evergreen foliage that is great for a ground cover where nothing else will grow.

GENUS/COMMON NAME: *Stripa pennata*/European Feather Grass
HEIGHT: 4–7'
ZONE: 6–9
SUN: full
SOIL: average
SPACING: 2–3'

Very graceful grass with tall, elegant, oat-like stems and silvery flowers that glisten through the summer. Divide clumps every 3 to 4 years. Cut back foliage before spring growth begins.

The Least You Need to Know

➤ Ten of the easiest perennials to grow and maintain are: achillea, alchemilla, astilbe, chrysanthemum, hemerocallis, hosta, iris, lysimachia, phlox, and sedum.

➤ Ten of the best blue perennials are: baptisia, campanula, nepeta, perovskia, platycodon, salvia, scabiosa, stokesia, veronica, and vinca.

➤ Remove spent flowers to neaten up the plant's appearance and to get, if possible, another show of flowers.

➤ Properly space perennials when planting to make weeding easier and allow the plant to receive the right amounts of light, rain, and nutrients.

Chapter 9

The Idiot's Guide to the Easiest Shrubs

In This Chapter

➤ The top 40 shrubs for beginner gardeners

➤ Descriptions of shrubs, including flowers, foliage, and shapes

➤ Use of plants in landscape

➤ Where to plant shrubs

First-time gardeners often shy away from planting shrubs—they seem unglamorous, unwieldy, and perhaps, too much work. Nothing could be further from the truth!

Although shrubs don't provide the instant gratification that annuals do, you'll see that they're the most attractive and useful plants for any garden. Well-placed shrubs in a garden give it backbone. Whether the shrub is evergreen or deciduous, its shape will define the structure of your garden. They are the long-term providers of color and beauty—the real workhorses in the plant world.

> **Garden Talk**
> "Deciduous" shrubs and trees shed their foliage in the autumn. The opposite is true of evergreens, which keep their leaves all year round.

What Is a Shrub?

Shrubs are woody plants, either deciduous or evergreen, branching from the ground, usually under 15 feet. Shrubs include everything from a low-grower like creeping juniper (*Juniperus horizontalis*) to a tall camelia bush (*Camelia japonica*), which will grow as tall as 25 feet and seems to have nothing in common with the evergreen Juniper. Even so, they are both evergreen shrubs, and both make valuable contributions to the landscape.

The Many Shapes of Shrubs

Shrubs vary so much in shape that it should be your first consideration in determining what you like. Color, particularly flower color, should be your second consideration.

Shrubs can be tall or short, thin or wide, evergreen or deciduous. They can form naturally round shapes or have branches that arch, weep, spray, curve upward, or spread outward. When considering a shrub's shape, keep in mind how wide the plant will get. You can always keep a plant from getting too tall by pruning it, but you'll have little control over its width.

Growing Shrubs for Year-Round Color

Shrubs can give your garden or landscape four seasons of color because they offer much more than just flowering periods. In addition to their flowers, many shrubs also have colorful berries and fruits. Many of the deciduous shrubs develop brilliant leaf coloration in the fall and their stems make nice winter displays against the snow. Evergreen shrubs, of course, stay green all winter.

Shrubs and Their Flowers

We mostly think of spring as the season for shrubs, especially when we see the blossoms on rhododendron, azaleas, forsythia, and lilacs. But shrubs also flower in the summer and fall. Some popular summer-flowering shrubs are buddliea and cytisus; fall bloomers include caryopteris and hydrangeas. If you combine the right shrubs in your garden, you will have flowering shrubs in spring, summer, and fall!

Red Is the Color of Foliage, Berries, and Even Bare Stems

Because many shrubs have brightly colored berries and foliage, they are great contributions to any garden or landscape. For instance, the fall foliage on burning bush (*Euonymus alata*) is a magnificent red. Another shrub, Siberian dogwood (*Cornus alba*), has brilliant red stems that stand out dramatically in the winter. And the red berries on common winterberry (*Ilex verticillata*) appear in the fall and stay on the shrubs all winter.

The Green of Evergreen Shrubs

Gardeners in Northern climates who get the thrills and chills of winter each year will be glad for the glorious green that evergreen shrubs provide. Broad-leaved evergreens, like rhododendrons, and narrow-leafed, like yews and junipers, give the winter landscape color. And Southern gardeners can grow these as well as camellias and gardenias.

Where to Use Shrubs

Shrubs are not only varied, but also versatile—the real question then becomes not finding the right location for a shrub, but finding the right shrub for the location.

Beauty Close to Home: Foundation Shrubs

When choosing a shrub for a foundation plant, think about whether you want an evergreen or deciduous shrub (the choice is yours; some people prefer evergreens for winter color).

Green Meany
Don't plant a thorny shrub, like those in the *Ilex* genus, next to a door. Ouch!

The amount of sun your shrub is likely to get is important to note. For sunny exposures, try chamaecyparis, deutzia, or potentilla. On shady sides of the house, plant kalmias, pieris, or rhododendron.

Good Hedges Make Good Neighbors

Shrubs are invaluable as screens. A row of shrubs placed between you and the street will give you privacy, as well as muffle any street noise. Hedges as screens are also handy along property lines, nicely separating your yard from your neighbor's. Some good candidates for shrubs to use for hedges include privet, yews, and forsythia.

A Focal Point in the Landscape

A single shrub in the landscape, called a specimen shrub, gives the landscape a focal point. A good rule of thumb when choosing a specimen shrub is to pick one that's large enough to dominate the area. Some of the larger shrubs in the Cornus genus, for instance, are perfect as specimen shrubs.

Backdrops for a Garden

Finally, there are plenty of shrubs that make perfect backdrops to gardens. You learned earlier in this book how the background color to a garden greatly influences the colors in the garden. A garden with a green backdrop will enhance the flowers' colors, so consider planting a row of Hinoki false cypress (*Chamaecyparis obtusa*) as a border behind your garden. This cypress hedge would also be a good wind barrier, minimizing the wind and offering protection to the plants in the garden.

Inheriting Shrubs on Your Property

Before you do away with any unwieldy and overgrown shrubs you have on your property, think about whether the neglected shrubs can be resuscitated by feeding and pruning. A "hard pruning," which means cutting back the plant by as much as one-third, will revive the poor plant. It will then bloom in its season like never before.

Getting Shrubs off to a Healthy Start

Shrubs are relatively easy to maintain, requiring only annual prunings and feedings. However, getting them off to a good start is essential. It's important to plant them properly, and look after them for the first few years. Water deeply if there's a drought in your area, and watch the shrub for signs of any trouble. In subsequent years, most shrubs will require only annual prunings, while other shrubs, like rhododendron, will benefit from deadheading after they flower.

Plan Right: Give Your Shrubs Room to Grow

Remember to give your shrubs enough room to grow. The rule of thumb for providing adequate room is to allow for a distance of one half the shrub's width from other plants or objects. This would mean a shrub with a width of 5 feet should be planted at least $2^1/_2$ feet from other shrubs. If your shrub will be planted near a foundation, tack on an extra 1 foot. Thus the shrub with a width of 5 feet would be properly planted $3^1/_2$ feet from the foundation.

Plant Right: Give Your Shrub's Roots Room to Grow

Your shrub's roots also need room to spread out. Get the roots off to a healthy start by digging a hole twice the size of the root ball. Proper planting is essential.

What Information Is Included on the Shrubs List?

You'll find the following information listed with each shrub, and what you can expect from the categories.

Genus Species

Species names are included on this list because many of the shrub genera are huge, and you need to know the species name. For instance, mugo pine (*Pinus mugo*), a shrub, is in the same genus as white pine (*Pinus strobus*), which is a tree that grows 60 feet tall!

Common Name

The common names can be acquired any number of ways. They can be descriptive, like showy crabapple, or just pretty, like beauty bush.

Flower

This category tells you about the shrub's flowers: their shapes, choices of colors, and whether it flowers in the spring, summer, or fall.

Foliage

This category tells you whether the shrub is evergreen or deciduous.

Height

This category tells you the average height for the shrub.

Zone

The hardiness zones indicate the coolest to warmest climates a plant will withstand. Be sure to keep your own zone in mind when reading and choosing shrubs.

Sun

This category tells you how much sun the shrub requires. The answers are either "full," "partial," "shade," or some combination of these.

Soil

This category tells you the kind of soil the plant requires. Some shrubs prefer drier conditions; some prefer moist; some need an acidic soil. Average soils are well-drained and moderately rich.

The Idiot's Guide to the Easiest Shrubs

GENUS SPECIES: *Berberis thunbergii*
COMMON NAME: Japanese Barberry
FLOWER: yellow in spring
FOLIAGE: deciduous
HEIGHT: 3–6'
ZONE: 4
SUN: full/partial
SOIL: average; tolerates dry soil

Berberis thunbergii is a thorny shrub and a vigorous grower, with great year-round color. In the spring, the small yellow flowers are sometimes hidden by the leaves. In the fall, the leaves turn a deep red. In the winter, showy scarlet berries remain on the plant all season.

B. thunbergii will grow where nothing else will. Plant it where you can't get anything else to grow. It makes a wonderful hedge and looks nice in groupings because of its deep red leaf color. Beware of the spiny protrusions on the stems!

GENUS SPECIES: *Buddleia davidii*
COMMON NAME: Buddleia, Butterfly Bush
FLOWER: whites, pinks, blues, purple, red from summer through fall
FOLIAGE: deciduous
HEIGHT: 6–8'
ZONE: 5–9
SUN: full
SOIL: rich, loamy

Buddleia flowers are sweetly scented and a favorite of butterflies and hummingbirds. The more you deadhead buddleia, the more flowers for you and the butterflies. The long terminal spikes of flowers come in a wide range of colors, including whites, pinks, blues, purples, and reds, depending on the variety of the plant. It makes a great plant for the back of the perennial border.

Buddleia, Butterfly bush (Buddleia davidii).

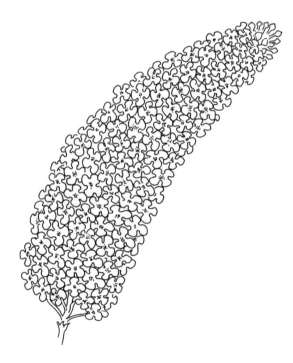

B. davidii's tops aren't hardy, and it flowers on new wood, so each spring cut the plant back to about 1 foot from the ground.

GENUS SPECIES: *Callicarpa dichotoma*
COMMON NAME: Purple Beautyberry
FLOWER: pink in the summer
FOLIAGE: deciduous
HEIGHT: 2–4'
ZONE: 5–8
SUN: full/partial
SOIL: rich, loamy

This small shrub with tiny pink flowers blooms at the end of summer. It can grow quickly,—up to 2 to 4 feet in one season. In the fall, pretty purple berries form along the stems. They are easy to spot since the foliage turns yellow and falls off early in the fall. It's a wonderful shrub for the shrub border or perennial garden.

C. dichotoma bears fruit on new wood, so cut it back to 5 inches from the ground in late winter.

GENUS SPECIES: *Camellia japonica*
COMMON NAME: Camellia
FLOWER: white, pink or red, October through April
FOLIAGE: evergreen
HEIGHT: 6–15'
ZONE: 7
SUN: partial
SOIL: well-drained, neutral–acid

This is a large shrub that will grow to 25 feet under the right conditions. It has thick, glossy, dark-green leaves and waxy petaled flowers that come in colors from white and pink to red. The flowers are either single or double: The single varieties have clusters of showy yellow stamens in the center and the double are so full of petals you can't see the stamens. Some varieties have flowers that are 5 inches wide and some are as small as 2 inches wide.

Camellias can get large, so if your garden is restricted in size choose a variety that's compact and upright. Or plant a camellia in a large container for use in a sheltered area, like against a wall. It also looks nice as a specimen plant—even when not in bloom, the glossy foliage is attractive. Prune to shape after flowering.

Bet You Didn't Know...
To make cut camellias last longer, stand them in slightly salty water for an hour before transferring them to fresh water in a vase.

GENUS SPECIES: *Caryopteris x clandonensis*
COMMON NAME: Hybrid Bluebeard
FLOWER: lavender blue in August
FOLIAGE: deciduous
HEIGHT: 4'
ZONE: 5–8
SUN: full
SOIL: moderately rich, well-drained

Caryopteris' long shoots of small blue flowers, along with their blue-gray foliage, appear just as the fall colors of yellows and oranges are arriving. Use caryopteris anywhere, in the perennial garden, or in the shrub garden, as a small hedge.

While caryopteris will tolerate dry soil, it would prefer moderately rich and well-drained soil. In colder climates, the tops may die back. Hard prune in the spring to promote better flowers and keep the plant from getting too big.

GENUS SPECIES: *Chaenomeles speciosa*
COMMON NAME: Flowering Quince
FLOWER: white, pink, or red in early spring
FOLIAGE: deciduous in north; semi-evergreen to evergreen in South
HEIGHT: 6–8'
ZONE: 5–8
SUN: full
SOIL: well-drained

Green Meany
These plants have thorns! Be careful when pruning.

Flowering quince has a dense, spreading habit with glossy, deep-green foliage. Flowers ranging in colors from whites and pinks to reds, form single, semi-double, to doubles. The flowers appear before the leaves in the spring, and the green, applelike fall fruits can be used to make delicious jelly. Prune after flowering.

Flowering quince can be used as a specimen plant.

GENUS SPECIES: *Chamaecyparis obtusa*
COMMON NAME: Hinoki False Cypress
FLOWER: inconspicuous
FOLIAGE: evergreen
HEIGHT: dwarfs are 3–6'
ZONE: 4
SUN: full
SOIL: average soil

There are many different shapes and sizes of *C. obtusa*, including trees 120 feet tall! We'll be talking here about the dwarf varieties. False cypress have flat sprays of evergreen foliage, drooping slightly at the tips. Depending on the variety, foliage can be bright or dark green to shades of yellow and red.

The dwarf varieties are very slow-growing and make ideal specimen plants when properly grown. Choose a selection of different varieties with varying colors and textures to create a beautiful hedge. Use mulch to keep the soil moist in the summer. Prune in the spring.

> **Flower Power!**
> If you've in-herited overgrown cypress on your property and want to bring it back to size and shape, remove from the shrub every third branch.

GENUS SPECIES: *Choisya ternata*
COMMON NAME: Mexican Orange
FLOWER: white in the spring
FOLIAGE: evergreen
HEIGHT: to 8'
ZONE: 8–10
SUN: full
SOIL: rich, loamy soil, well-drained

This is an aromatic evergreen with clusters of pure white, fragrant, starlike flowers in the spring. It makes a great plant for an entryway. *C. ternata* may need some pruning to keep it compact, but it's usually pretty neat and well-behaved.

GENUS SPECIES: *Clethra alnifolia*
COMMON NAME: Summersweet
FLOWER: pink or white in summer
FOLIAGE: deciduous
HEIGHT: to 8'
ZONE: 4–9
SUN: full/partial

This fragrant shrub with spikes of pink or white flowers is perfect for moist areas. It does well in seashore conditions and will adapt to poorer soil conditions with an organic mulch. The medium-green foliage turns to lovely shades of yellow and orange in the fall.

Plant clethra where you can best enjoy the plant's clovelike fragrance. Try it by your kitchen window or in a container for your terrace.

GENUS SPECIES: *Cornus* (see species below)
COMMON NAME: Dogwood
FLOWER: see below
FOLIAGE: deciduous
HEIGHT: see below
ZONE: see below
SUN: full sun/light shade
SOIL: acid-rich loam

There are more than 45 species in the *Cornus* genus to choose from, and a dogwood for every part of the United States except the hottest and driest areas.

Siberian dogwood *(Cornus alba)* is a shrub that grows to 9 feet and is hardy in zones 2 to 8. This shrub is a vigorous grower and, if pruned in the spring, will create more young shoot growth. In May, it has small, 2-inch, yellowish-white flat flowers in a cluster. The fall berries are white to pale blue. Both the green and variegated foliage are attractive, and the variegated forms are useful for brightening up a shady nook. *C. alba*'s most significant trait is its red stems, which are beautiful in the winter garden. Whether *C. alba* is in the garden or alone as a specimen plant, you can't miss the scarlet red bark in winter.

C. alba likes a moderately rich to moist soil.

Flowering Dogwood *(Cornus florida)* is actually a small tree that grows to 25 feet in zones 5 to 8. It flowers in the spring, and the shrub produces four notched, white or pink bracts, or leaves, which most people assume to be flowers. The flowers are, in fact, small yellow clusters in the center of the large bracts. Bright red berries follow the flowers in the fall, along with beautiful scarlet leaves. Plant *C. florida* as the centerpiece of a shade garden.

Japanese Dogwood *(Cornus kousa)* is becoming very popular because it's less prone to disease than *C. florida*. It, too, is hardy in zones 5 to 8. But the habit of *C. kousa* is different: The branches hide the trunk, giving the plant a very round habit. *C. kousa* blooms in the summer when it's covered with white bracts. The berries in the fall are round red fruits, somewhat like large raspberries, making a beautiful scarlet autumn coloration. *C. kousa* is best used as a specimen tree.

GENUS SPECIES: *Cotinus coggygria*
COMMON NAME: Smoketree
FLOWER: pink in the summer
FOLIAGE: deciduous
HEIGHT: 10 to 15'
ZONE: 5–9
SUN: full
SOIL: average soil

Cotinus coggygria is a spreading shrub that grows to 15 feet and gets its common name from the smoky effect its flowers make. These pinkish to grayish panicles hang from the tree for weeks in the summer. The foliage is spectacular, changing from a chartreuse to a purple color in the summer, then turning to a bright orange in the fall.

Give *C. coggygria* plenty of water for the first two years, while it is getting established. After that, it will take care of itself.

> GENUS SPECIES: *Cotoneaster horizontalis*
> COMMON NAME: Rock Cotoneaster
> FLOWER: white or pink in the spring
> FOLIAGE: evergreen in the South; semi-evergreen in the North
> HEIGHT: 3'
> ZONE: 5–9
> SUN: full
> SOIL: average/dry soil

This shrub spreads horizontally 5 to 6 feet wide and grows 3 feet tall. The arching branches resemble the spine of a fish. *Horizontalis'* white or pink flowers in the spring are small but very showy. A show of bright red berries follow. There are many different forms of *C. horizontalis*, including a variegated form you might prefer to the green varieties.

C. horizontalis makes an excellent ground cover for steep banks, and its unique form also lends itself to the rock garden.

> GENUS SPECIES: *Cytisus scoparius*
> COMMON NAME: Scottish Broom
> FLOWER: yellow in spring
> FOLIAGE: deciduous
> HEIGHT: 6'
> ZONE: 5–9
> SUN: full
> SOIL: well-drained, not overly rich

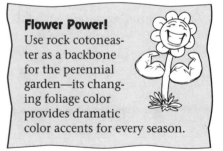

Flower Power!
Use rock cotoneaster as a backbone for the perennial garden—its changing foliage color provides dramatic color accents for every season.

Scottish broom
(Cytisus scoparius).

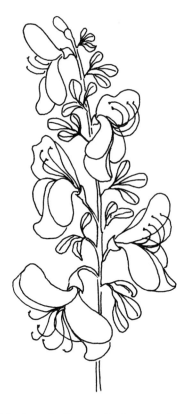

Cytisus scoparius has a real Old World plant feeling to it: Its upright stems and tiny pealike yellow flowers cover it in spring from top to bottom. The stems reach 6 feet tall and almost as wide. *C. scoparius* will brighten any spot in your garden, and while it's deciduous, the twiggy stems stay green all winter, giving Northerners a plant for the winter garden.

While these shrubs prefer full sun, they can tolerate partial shade. They also prefer an acid soil. It's best to plant young plants, as there will be less of a transplant shock and the plant will take more quickly and easily.

GENUS SPECIES: *Daphne x burkwoodii*
COMMON NAME: Burkwood Daphne
FLOWER: white or pink in early spring
FOLIAGE: evergreen in the South and deciduous in the North
HEIGHT: 5'
ZONE: 5–9
SUN: full
SOIL: well-drained, fertile soil

Daphne x burkwoodii is a vigorous grower with an appealing powdery scent. The conspicuous heads of white or pink flowers come early in the spring, and foliage is either dark green or variegated. Their fruits are red berries, about 3 inches wide. Daphne may rebloom late in the summer. While all daphne prefer full sun, they can also be grown in light shade.

Another species, February daphne *(D. mezereum)*, grows only to 3 feet and has fragrant, rosy pink flowers in February in the South and in April in Northern climates. In the late summer, scarlet berries appear, which attract the birds. This is a wonderful plant for underplanting in a tall shrub border, or as a ground cover. Plant *D. mezereum* near the house so you can enjoy the sweet scent, or cut some flowers to enjoy indoors.

Start with young plants, as *D. mezereum* don't transplant easily.

> GENUS SPECIES: *Deutzia gracilis*
> COMMON NAME: Slender Deutzia
> FLOWER: white in the spring
> FOLIAGE: deciduous
> HEIGHT: 1–4'
> ZONE: 5–9
> SUN: full sun/light shade
> SOIL: average to well-drained

This low-growing shrub is very graceful and produces white flowers in racemes in the spring. *D. gracilis* is one of the most dependable of all Deutzias—good for low hedges and foundation plantings. *D. gracilis* may require pruning in the spring. Remove the dead wood and thin out old shoots after bloom.

> GENUS SPECIES: *Eleagnus angustifolia*
> COMMON NAME: Russian Olive
> FLOWER: yellow in the summer
> FOLIAGE: deciduous
> HEIGHT: 12 to 20'
> ZONE: 2–9
> SUN: full
> SOIL: average to dry

Eleagnus angustifolia, not a true olive tree, has attractive narrow, silver-gray foliage and fragrant (though inconspicuous) yellowish flowers in the summer. The small, yellow-coated berries are also attractive. Its crooked trunk with shredding bark gives it a picturesque shape and can be pruned in late summer to keep it bushy.

Russian olive does well anywhere: as a specimen plant, in the shrub border, as a hedge. It loves seashore conditions and can withstand sandy, dry soils and open, exposed areas.

GENUS SPECIES: *Euonymus alata*
COMMON NAME: Redwinged Euonymus, Burning Bush
FLOWER: inconspicuous in early summer
FOLIAGE: deciduous
HEIGHT: 15'
ZONE: 4–9
SUN: full/partial
SOIL: average

E. alata grows 15 feet tall and is just as wide. The yellow-green flowers are ornamentally unimportant, blooming in early summer, and the red fruits are borne under the foliage. The orange-red seeds are the ornamental part of the fruit. The stems on *E. alata* are unusual and interesting; you'll notice corklike wings protruding from the sides, which identify this shrub. The leaves are flat and medium to dark green all summer. But in the fall, the leaves turn a bright pink then a brilliant red. The colors are never disappointing.

There are unlimited uses for *E. alata* as a landscape plant. It makes an excellent hedge, screen, or mass planting. It can also be used as a specimen plant or foundation plant. Prune *E. alata* to your heart's content or leave alone for the wild look. Try pruning the underbranches to get a fountain look, and plant a shade garden underneath.

Wintercreeper euonymus (*E. fortunei*) is an evergreen ground cover or high climber (when planted against a wall), hardy in zones 5 to 9. It grows quickly and has handsome, dark-green leaves and insignificant white flowers. The scarlet pink color capsule is the showy part, which opens to expose orange-red seeds in the late fall. The seeds will hold on until early winter. *E. fortunei* can be used as a ground cover, or let it climb walls or a low hedge. Try it in a mass or group plantings for a screen.

GENUS SPECIES: *Forsythia x intermedia*
COMMON NAME: Border Forsythia
FLOWER: yellow in early spring
FOLIAGE: deciduous
HEIGHT: 10'
ZONE: 5–9
SUN: full
SOIL: any condition but damp

Forsythia grows 10 feet tall and 12 feet wide. There are upright forms with arching canes, as well as pendulous varieties and weeping forms. Forsythia are grown chiefly for the bright yellow flowers that appear in early spring. In the fall, the green leaves turn a yellow-green color.

Forsythia are great for the shrub border, or as screens, massed, or group plantings. Plant forsythia on a bank or slope. In the landscape, forsythia is best left natural and not pruned. For a hedge look, trim right after the bloom period.

GENUS SPECIES: *Fothergilla gardenii*
COMMON NAME: Dwarf Fothergilla
FLOWER: white in early spring
FOLIAGE: deciduous
HEIGHT: 2–3'
ZONE: 6 to 9
SUN: full/partial
SOIL: sandy loam and good drainage

This slow-growing shrub is small but often spreads widely with slender, crooked-spreading branches. The small, white, bottlebrush flowers are very fragrant and appear early in spring before the foliage. The dark-green foliage is also an attractive feature. But the fall color is the reason to grow Fothergilla: It turns a brilliant yellow to orange to scarlet and is simply gorgeous.

Plant fothergilla as a foundation plant or use in the border. Moist loam with plenty of peat moss is best, and fothergilla likes acid soils. If you have these soil conditions, you must have this plant.

GENUS SPECIES: *Gardenia jasminoides*
COMMON NAME: Gardenia
FLOWER: white all season
FOLIAGE: evergreen
HEIGHT: 6'
ZONE: 8–10
SUN: full sun to light shade
SOIL: acid, rich loam

G. jasminoides has white, waxy flowers with a familiar fragrance that everyone loves. The flowers come in single or double forms and bloom continuously. The thick glossy leaves are very handsome. Plant *G. jasminoides* near the house for the fragrance. Gardenia is grown in the outdoors in the South and as a houseplant in the North.

Flower Power!
If you have gardenia in a container, be sure to water well and use an acid-tone fertilizer in the spring.

GENUS SPECIES: *Hydrangea* (see below)
COMMON NAME: Hydrangea (see below)
FLOWER: late summer

FOLIAGE: deciduous
HEIGHT: 3–5'
ZONE: see below
SUN: full sun/partial shade
SOIL: well-drained, rich loamy soil

The following are three species of hydrangea shrubs:

Smooth hydrangea *(H. arborescens)* is a low-growing shrub that is sometimes wider than it is tall. Hardy in zones 4 to 9, it's a fast grower. The long-lasting white flowers are born in flat clusters called "corymbs," and the leaf color is a bright dark green all summer with no fall coloration. *H. arborescens* flowers on new wood in late summer, so be sure to prune back hard in the early spring. *H. arborescens* belongs in the shrub border or perennial garden.

Panicle hydrangea *(H. paniculata)* is an upright, semi-arching small tree or large shrub that grows to 20 feet and varies in width. It's hardy in zones 4 to 8. Whether grown in a tree form or a shrub form, this is another fast grower. The long, pyramidal, panicle-shaped flowers change colors, starting out white in the summer, then changing to pink in the early fall. The plant has dark-green leaves all summer with a hint of yellow in the green foliage in the fall. Use as a specimen plant or in the shrub border.

Oakleaf hydrangea *(H. quercifolia)* is a slow-growing, upright, irregular shrub that grows 4 to 6 feet high and 3 to 5 feet wide. It's hardy in zones 5 to 9. The panicle-shaped flowers are white, changing to purplish pink in the fall. The foliage is the reason to grow *H. quercifolia*, which turns from green to red, orange, brown, and purple in the fall. Plant *H. quercifolia* in a shrub border or mass or place in a shady nook. The culture for *H. quercifolia* is the same as for *H. arborescens*, but note that this shrub flowers on the previous year's wood, and sometimes in the North the tops may suffer winter damage. But it is still worth considering because of its beautiful foliage.

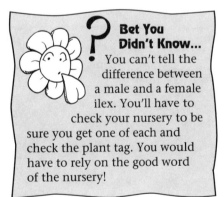

Bet You Didn't Know...
You can't tell the difference between a male and a female ilex. You'll have to check your nursery to be sure you get one of each and check the plant tag. You would have to rely on the good word of the nursery!

GENUS SPECIES: *Ilex* (see below)
COMMON NAME: Chinese Holly, Common Winterberry
FLOWER: white in the spring
FOLIAGE: evergreen
HEIGHT: 10'
ZONE: 6–9
SUN: full/partial
SOIL: slightly acidic

Chinese holly *(I. cornuta)* has a dense, round form and can reach 10 feet both high and wide. The shiny, dark foliage remains on the plant summer and winter. Be sure to get one male and one female plant of the same species and plant them in same yard in order for the male plants to pollinate the females. The females produce the bright red berries.

I. cornuta can be used for foundation plantings, a hedge or screen, or even as a specimen shrub or container plant. Its foliage has prickly spines, so avoid planting near entry ways or walkways.

Prune back as hard as you like in late spring for desired height.

Common winterberry, black alder *(I. verticillata)* is hardy in zones 4 to 9. This hardy, deciduous, twiggy shrub grows 6 to 9 feet tall and almost as wide. The summer flowers aren't showy, but the pretty red berries that appear in the fall stay on the female shrubs until December. The leaves are a deep, rich green with no fall coloration. These make handsome plants for the woodland gardens.

I. verticillata is a slow grower, but growth can be quickened with fertilizer and water. They prefer moist, acid soils with high organic matter.

> GENUS SPECIES: *Juniperus* (see below)
> COMMON NAME: Juniper
> FLOWER: inconspicuous
> FOLIAGE: evergreen
> HEIGHT: 5–10'
> ZONE: see below
> SUN: full
> SOIL: any soil condition

Junipers are grown in many different shapes and sizes, from very low-growing forms, just inches from the ground, to trees that reach 36 feet. Their color ranges from blue-greens to gray-greens, light greens to dark ones; some even take on yellow and purple tones in the winter months.

The use of junipers in the landscape is unlimited, from foundation plantings to open fields. Use it as a ground cover or as a screen. Their culture is easy—all they need is sun. Any soil condition will do—from sandy to clay, even moderately moist to dry situations. Juniper will tolerate city pollution as well as any conifer.

Common Juniper *(J. communis)* is hardy in zones 3 to 7. It is a slow-growing, extremely hardy evergreen that can reach 5 to 10 feet tall and 8 to 10 feet wide. This sprawling shrub with needlelike gray-green to blue-green foliage sometimes turns a yellow or brownish green in the winter. *J. communis* is grown for its evergreen foliage, not the flower. The fruits are bluish-black, ripening the second year. *J. communis* is used as a ground cover for sandy areas, and can also be used for underplanting in a shrub border or for naturalizing.

Creeping juniper (*J. horizontalis*) is hardy in zones 3 to 9 and grows only 1 to 2 feet in height, spreading 8 feet wide. The plumelike foliage is a bluish-green or steel-blue in the summer, turning to a plum purple in the winter. It withstands hot, dry, sandy locations. Use as a ground cover, on slopes and mass plantings. It's great for foundations and in containers.

GENUS SPECIES: *Kalmia latifolia*
COMMON NAME: Mountain Laurel
FLOWER: white, pink, or red in early summer
FOLIAGE: evergreen
HEIGHT: 7–15'
ZONE: 5–9
SUN: full/partial
SOIL: acidic, cool, moist

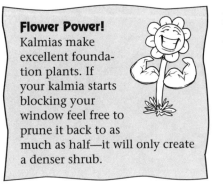

Flower Power!
Kalmias make excellent foundation plants. If your kalmia starts blocking your window feel free to prune it back to as much as half—it will only create a denser shrub.

Kalmia latifolia are slow to grow and, if not crowded, will become a dense shrub. They grow as wide as they grow tall. The flower colors range from pure white and pink to rose and red. Some flowers are solid colors, some have bands of another color, some have red or even purple markings. The light-green leaf color in the spring turns darker in the summer, then the rich, dark-green foliage stays glossy all through the winter.

Kalmia will grow in full sun or deep shade but will flower more in full sun. It requires an acidic, cool, moist soil. This broad-leaved evergreen is great for naturalizing or for the shady border. To keep your plant compact and producing lots of flowers, you should remove the sticky flowers a few weeks after the plant flowers. To do this, twist the old flower cluster with your index finger and thumb. Kalmias can become open and leggy in old age but will always be picturesque with their irregular trunk shapes.

GENUS SPECIES: *Kolkwitzia amabilis*
COMMON NAME: Beauty Bush
FLOWER: pink in early summer
FOLIAGE: deciduous
HEIGHT: 6–10'
ZONE: 5–9
SUN: full
SOIL: average

K. amabilis is an upright, arching shrub with a fountain-shaped habit that grows up to 10 feet with a smaller spread. It's a fast-growing shrub with pink, bell-shaped flowers and foliage that turns yellow to reddish in the fall.

Prune out any old wood and weak shoots of *K. amabilis* after the flowering period has finished.

> GENUS SPECIES: *Ligustrum vulgare*
> COMMON NAME: Common Privet
> FLOWER: inconspicuous white flowers in spring
> FOLIAGE: semi-evergreen in the South; deciduous in the North
> HEIGHT: 10–15'
> ZONE: 5–9
> SUN: full/partial
> SOIL: average to poor

Privet is grown mostly as a hedge and has white flowers in the summer followed by small black fruit. This plant thrives at the seashore. The best way to care for privet is to prune it to a foot or two in the first year, and in subsequent years just trim to shape up any time during the growing season.

> GENUS SPECIES: *Magnolia* (see below)
> COMMON NAME: Magnolia (see below)
> FLOWER: big or small, depending on species, in spring
> FOLIAGE: deciduous
> HEIGHT: 20–25'
> ZONE: 5–9
> SUN: full
> SOIL: moist, rich loam

The following are two species of magnolias:

Saucer magnolia *(M. x soulangeana)* has low branches that spread almost as widely as the higher branches. The spring flowers are white-pink to purple, as big as 5 to 10 inches in diameter, and the flowers have a sweet fragrance. The leaves are 6 inches. Plant in full sun, but don't plant too deeply. The soil conditions should be moist, rich loam. Adding a leaf mulch and peat moss will help keep the soil moist.

Star magnolia *(M. stellata)* is a smaller version of the saucer magnolia. It grows to 15 or 20 feet tall and its habit is a dense, wide shrub or small tree. Flowers are the same but smaller, about 3 inches in diameter. This magnolia flowers earlier than the saucer

Flower Power!
Star magnolias are great in the inner city for their ability to withstand high concentrations of air pollution.

137

magnolia, and the foliage is a dark green, often turning a yellow-bronze color in the fall. Use these shrubs as specimen plants or, if your house is very large, use them as foundation plantings. Culture for star magnolia is the same as for saucer magnolia. To protect these shrubs from losing flowers in a cold snap, plant in any exposure but directly southern. The buds risk opening faster in southern exposures.

GENUS SPECIES: *Malus floribunda*
COMMON NAME: Showy Crabapple
FLOWER: white flowers in spring
FOLIAGE: deciduous
HEIGHT: 15–25'
ZONE: 5–8
SUN: full
SOIL: average

These small trees have dense branches that curve upward, giving the trees a round habit. The fragrant flowers begin as red buds, turn pink, then fade to white. Crabapple's showy fruits are yellow or red and almost an inch in diameter. You can use crabapples to make preserves.

Very little pruning is necessary. Just eliminate dead wood or shape trees as you wish in late winter.

GENUS SPECIES: *Philadelphus coronaris*
COMMON NAME: Sweet Mockorange
FLOWER: white in late spring, early summer
FOLIAGE: deciduous
HEIGHT: 10–12'
ZONE: 5–9
SUN: full sun to light shade
SOIL: rich, loamy soil

Mockoranges are fast-growing, rounded shrubs with stiff, straight branches that begin to arch with age. The fragrant white flowers come in single or double varieties, and are about 1 to 2 inches across. Mockoranges mix well with other flowering shrubs and are great for the shrub border or used as part of a screen planting. They can become leggy with age, so prune dead wood after flowering.

GENUS SPECIES: *Pieris japonica*
COMMON NAME: Japanese Pieris, Andromeda
FLOWER: creamy white in spring
FOLIAGE: evergreen

HEIGHT: 5–8'
ZONE: 5–8
SUN: partial shade
SOIL: rich, acid loam

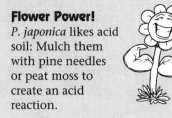

Flower Power!
P. japonica likes acid soil: Mulch them with pine needles or peat moss to create an acid reaction.

P. japonica is an upright, evergreen shrub. Its pink buds form on pendulous clusters for the next year's flowers and open to creamy white, forming slightly fragrant tassels for weeks. The new buds that form in the fall make pieris attractive throughout the winter. When the plant is young, the foliage is a rich bronze, changing to a dark green at maturity.

This plant works well in shade around the foundation of a house, or when used in a shrub border or with other broad-leaved evergreens. It's also hardy in containers in terraces and can withstand tough city conditions. To maintain its nice, round form, deadhead after flowering for the first couple of years.

GENUS SPECIES: *Pinus mugo*
COMMON NAME: Mugo Pine, Dwarf Pine, Swiss Mountain Pine
FLOWER: inconspicuous
FOLIAGE: evergreen
HEIGHT: 10–15'
ZONE: 3–7
SUN: full/partial
SOIL: moist loam

This pine grows very slowly and keeps a nice round shape. It grows almost three times as wide as it does tall, so keep this in mind when choosing a site for it. The needles, typical of pines, are bright to dark green and about 2 inches long. *P. mugo* works well in large containers or as a foundation planting. It's very winter-hardy and can withstand the harsh conditions on city terraces. Very little pruning is necessary—just shape it to keep its shape compact.

GENUS SPECIES: *Potentilla fruiticosa*
COMMON NAME: Bush Cinquefoil
FLOWER: yellow, white, apricot, orange from summer until frost
FOLIAGE: deciduous
HEIGHT: 1–4'
ZONE: 3 to 8
SUN: full
SOIL: fertile, well-drained soil

P. fruiticosa is a slow-growing, delicate-looking shrub with small $^1/_4$- to 1-inch leaves on three to seven leaflets. The flowers look like tiny buttercups and come in bright yellow, pale yellow, white, apricot, and orange. They will flower for a long time, from summer to fall. The leaves have a fine texture when opening, then turn a bright green all summer. In the fall, they turn a yellow-green.

This is a great shrub for foundation plantings because of its neat appearance and long flowering season. Use it also in the shrub or perennial border, or as a low hedge or massing. Plant in full sun for the best colors, although *P. fruiticosa* will tolerate partial shade. It will also tolerate poor, dry soils and extreme cold, but grows best in a fertile, well-drained soil.

> GENUS SPECIES: *Prunus* (see below)
> COMMON NAME: Common Chokeberry, Yoshino Cherry
> FLOWER: white or pink in spring
> FOLIAGE: deciduous
> HEIGHT: 20–30'
> ZONE: see below
> SUN: full
> SOIL: average soil

Chokeberry *(P. virginia)* is hardy in zones 3 to 8. This small tree with arching branches has small, white flowers in spring that grow on 3- to 6-inch racemes. The fruits are a lustrous dark purple, almost black and open in the early summer. The foliage starts green and then changes to a reddish color. Use chokeberry as a specimen tree.

Another species, yoshino cherry *(P. yedoensis)*, hardy in zones 6 to 8, grows up to 40 feet with fragrant white to pink flowers. These are the well-known cherry trees in Washington D.C. that bring visitors to see their spectacular blooms every spring.

> GENUS SPECIES: *Rhododendron* (see below)
> COMMON NAME: Rhododendron (see below)
> FLOWER: see below
> FOLIAGE: (see each species, below)
> HEIGHT: see below
> ZONE: see below
> SUN: full/partial
> SOIL: acid rich loam

The following are four species of rhododendron:

Carolina rhododendron (*R. carolinianum*) is a slow-growing, broad-leaved evergreen that grows 3 to 6 feet tall with a similar spread. It is hardy in zones 6 to 8. In spring, clusters of flowers are born on the terminal bud, and flower colors range from whites to pale rose and pinks to rosy purples. Use Carolina rhododendron in the shrub border, in groupings, or in foundation plantings. It thrives in woodlands or along streams. Water in drought periods and mulch with decomposed leaves.

Flower Power!
For Northerners, plant rhododendrons in full sun to get the most flowers.

Catawba rhododendron (*R. catawbiense*) is a heavier evergreen shrub, with larger leaves, hardy in zones 5 to 8. It grows to 6 to 10 feet tall and 5 to 8 feet wide. This, too, is a slow grower. Flowers bloom in late spring and early summer. There is a wide variety of colors and shades to choose from in whites, pinks, reds, and purples. The leaves are dark green. In extreme cold, you may see some yellowing. Use Catawba rhododendron for mass plantings and in shrub borders.

Japanese azalea (*R. japonicum*) is hardy in zones 6 to 8 and is a deciduous shrub. It grows to 6 feet tall, flowering in the spring in colors of bright red, yellow, and orange. Azaleas like light shade and an acid-rich loam. Japanese azalea is wonderful naturalized in woodland gardens.

Korean azalea (*R. mucronulatum*) is hardy in zones 5 to 8 and is also a deciduous shrub. It grows 4 to 6 feet tall with about the same spread. It's a slow grower with bright, rosy purple flowers in the spring. There are cultivars with pink flowers that are also very attractive. Korean azaleas are very neat in appearance, with soft green foliage that changes to yellow, then bronze/crimson in the fall. Korean azalea likes light shade and, while adaptable to an acid to neutral soil, always needs a rich, loamy soil.

Rhododendrons should be deadheaded a few weeks after the flowering period ends. To accomplish this, take the old flowerhead between your forefinger and thumb and twist it until it falls off. You'll get more flowers from your shrub the following year when you deadhead, and your rhododendron will keep a nice round shape.

> GENUS SPECIES: Rosa (see below)
> COMMON NAME: Rose (see below)
> FLOWER: see below
> FOLIAGE: deciduous
> HEIGHT: see below
> ZONE: see below
> SUN: full
> SOIL: rich soil with good drainage

Roses fall into different classes and subclasses. There are climbers or ramblers, floribundas, grandifloras, hybrid teas, miniatures, old garden roses, and shrub roses.

Climbing roses and ramblers are not true climbers in that they do not climb by tendrils or other means, but they have a flexible cane that you can train to climb up a trellis, arbor, or building. R. 'Blaze' is a climber with large scarlet flowers that is hardy in zones 4 to 9. It grows 7 to 9 feet. R. 'New Dawn,' also hardy in zones 4 to 9, grows 12 to 15 feet and has beautiful, soft pink flowers.

Flower Power!
The best mulch to use on any rose is a mixture of leaf and manure compost. The best fertilizer is a seaweed or fish emulsion.

Floribundas is a modern group of roses, the result of crossing hybrid teas with polyanthas. They make great hedges and work well in a shrub border. Try R. 'Europeana,' which grows $2\frac{1}{2}$ to 3 feet and is a dark red, or R. 'Iceburg,' which grows 4 feet and is very white. These floribundas are hardy in zones 4 to 9.

The grandiflora class is a cross between hybrid teas and floribundas. These are hardier than hybrid teas and have long stems. R. 'Queen Elizabeth' grows 5 to 7 feet and is a soft pink. It's hardy in zones 4 to 9.

Hybrid teas is the most popular class of roses of all. These are the familiar long-stemmed varieties in a wide range of colors. Hybrid teas are less hardy than the other classes, and hardy in zones 5 to 9. While they can grow from $2\frac{1}{2}$ to 7 feet, most will grow about 3 feet tall. Hybrids must be pruned each year and deadheaded. A popular hybrid tea is R. 'Peace,' a colorful yellow and apricot blend.

Miniature roses grow about 6 to 20 inches tall, with $\frac{1}{2}$-to-$1\frac{1}{2}$ inch wide flowers. They are useful in the garden as ground cover or as a low hedge. They are also great in containers and window boxes. Two of the easiest to grow are R. 'Baby Darling,' an orange pink, and R. 'Pixie Rose,' a deep pink. Miniatures are hardy to zone 4.

Old garden roses include alba, Bourbon, China, damask, gallica, moss, and tea roses. Most old garden roses are extremely hardy.

Shrub roses include hybrid musk, hybrid rugosa, and polyantha roses. Polyanthas are usually about 2 feet tall, but some can reach 4 feet. They have many small flowers in clusters from spring to fall. They are hardy to zone 4.

Roses need five to six hours of full sun, preferably morning sun. They need water (morning is the best time), a mulch to keep in the moisture, and good air circulation—don't plant them too close together. Roses also need a rich, well-drained soil.

GENUS SPECIES: *Spiraea x bumalda*
COMMON NAME: Burmalda Spirea
FLOWER: pinks, whites, and reds in summer
FOLIAGE: deciduous
HEIGHT: 4–5'

ZONE: 5–8
SUN: full
SOIL: average

The following are three species of spirea:

Burmalda spirea (*Spiraea x bumalda*) is a low-growing shrub that grows 3 to 5 feet tall and just as wide. It's densely twiggy, with upright branches and flowers that are white to deep pink in the summer. The flowers are on corymbs, about 4 to 6 inches wide. The pinkish red leaves turn blue-green in the summer. Plant Burmalda spirea where it can spread out, but don't plant it where the soil is wet. This is a great plant for massing, or for those empty spaces in the garden. It also makes a nice cut flower.

Japanese spirea (*S. japonica*) is a shorter shrub, growing 2 to 4 feet and just as wide. It has stiff, upright branches and is a little more coarse in texture. Flowers on flat-topped corymbs are white, pale pink, or deep pink. Use Japanese spirea in the foreground of shrub borders, in foundation plantings, in mass plantings, or in containers on a terrace.

Thunberg spirea (*S. thunbergii*) grows 3 to 5 feet tall and just as wide. It's also a bushy shrub but is very graceful, with slender, arching branches. The leaves are yellow-green in the summer and turn yellow-bronze in the fall. The flowers are tiny and white. It's a nice plant for the foundation and one that thrives on neglect.

GENUS SPECIES: *Symphoricarpos albus*
COMMON NAME: Common Snowberry
FLOWER: insignificant flowers in summer
FOLIAGE: deciduous
HEIGHT: 3–6'
ZONE: 4–7
SUN: full/partial
SOIL: average

This shrub's main attraction are the large white berries that appear for several weeks in the fall. The small pink flowers are inconspicuous and appear in the summer on the current season's growth. The foliage is a bluish-green. This is a very twiggy bush that grows quickly. Snowberry is a wonderful shrub for shady nooks. Because it grows suckers freely, it's a great shrub for holding back banks.

Snowberry will grow in sun or shade with average soil, but it loves clay. Feed it lime in spring. Pruning is also done in early spring to produce new growth for more berries.

GENUS SPECIES: *Syringa meyeri*
COMMON NAME: Meyer Lilac
FLOWER: spring

143

FOLIAGE: deciduous
HEIGHT: see below
ZONE: see below
SUN: full
SOIL: average

The following are two species of lilac:

Meyer lilac (*S. meyeri*) is hardy in zones 4 to 7 and grows 4 to 8 feet tall and just as wide. This dense, neat, rounded shrub with dark-green leaves grows at a slow rate. Meyer lilac produces many flowers and will cover the entire shrub with its lavender-scented flowers. Meyer lilac is never bothered by powdery mildew, a disease that plagues many of the lilacs. Full sun is best for flower development in average, well-drained soil. Deadhead lilacs after they bloom to prevent the plant from using all its energy to make seeds. You'll have more flowers the following year as well as a nice shape to your shrub.

Common lilac (*S. vulgaris*) is hardy in zones 4 to 8 and can grow 8 to 15 feet with a spread of 6 to 12 feet. It's an upright shrub that can sometimes get leggy, and its extremely fragrant flowers in the spring come in shades of whites, pinks, and purples. The heart-shaped leaves are gray-green to blue-green in the summer.

Plant common lilac in the shrub border or in groupings. Be sure you don't crowd the plant—it needs adequate air circulation. It has the same culture as Meyer lilac.

GENUS SPECIES: *Taxus cuspidata*
COMMON NAME: Japanese Yew
FLOWER: inconspicuous flowers
FOLIAGE: evergreen
HEIGHT: 10–40'
ZONE: 5–7
SUN: full/partial
SOIL: moist, sandy loam

Green Meany
Don't add fertilizer to the hole when planting shrubs, let your shrub acclimate to the native soil first.

This slow-growing, multistemmed, evergreen shrub grows 10 to 40 feet tall with an equal spread. There are many dwarf (slow-growing) varieties from which to choose. The dark- green, needlelike leaves have a leathery texture. The flowers are inconspicuous and the fruits are red. Landscape uses for Japanese yew include many possibilities, from foundation plantings to hedges, screens, groupings, or bank covers. They also make nice topiaries for the more ambitious gardeners. Yews will tolerate any soil but prefer a moist, sandy loam. They also tolerate city conditions with dust and smoke and can withstand any amount of pruning.

Viburnum (Viburnum x burkwoodii).

GENUS SPECIES: *Viburnum* (see below)
COMMON NAME: Viburnum (see below)
FLOWER: spring
FOLIAGE: deciduous
HEIGHT: see below
ZONE: 5–8
SUN: full sun to light shade
SOIL: moist, well-drained soil

The following are two Viburnum:

Burkwood viburnum (*V. x burkwoodii*) is a multistemmed, upright deciduous shrub that grows 8 to 10 feet with a similar spread. This is a slow to medium grower. The sweetly scented flowers start as pink buds, opening to white flowers in the spring. Leaf color is a dark green all through the summer, changing to a wine red in the fall.

Burkwood viburnum is one of the best choices for the shrub border and looks nice in combination with broad-leaved evergreens such as rhododendron. Plant it near the house to enjoy the fragrance.

V. carlesii is hardy in zones 5 to 9 and smaller than Burkwood viburnum, growing 4 to 5 feet, with a greater spread. This is a round, dense shrub with stiff, spreading branches. The flower buds are an attractive pink to red, then opening with fragrant white flowers on a rounded cluster in the spring. The leaves turn a wine red in the fall.

Use these two viburnums the same way—in the shrub border or near the house.

GENUS SPECIES: *Weigela florida*
COMMON NAME: Old-Fashioned Weigela
FLOWER: pink flowers in late spring
FOLIAGE: deciduous
HEIGHT: 6–9'
ZONE: 5–9
SUN: full
SOIL: average soil

This is a dense, spreading deciduous shrub with an arching habit. It grows to 9 feet with as wide a spread. The rosy pink, tubular shaped flowers are borne in late spring or early summer, and the dark-green foliage is charming in the summer, turning to a bronze-purple in the fall. Weigela is great for the shrub border or group plantings. Some cultivars have white flowers.

The Least You Need to Know

➤ Most flowering shrubs should be pruned immediately after their flowering period to maintain the plant's shape and produce more flowers for the following year.

➤ When deciding on a shrub, your first consideration is the size of the shrub. You can prune a shrub to keep it shorter, but have little control over how widely it will spread. The second consideration is color.

➤ Shrubs with nice round shapes are berberis, caryopteris, choisya, deutzia, daphne, ilex, potentilla, pinus mugo, spiraea, and japonica.

➤ Shrubs with wonderful fragrance are clethra, choisya, daphne, fothergilla, gardenia, malus, philadelphus, syringea, and viburnum.

➤ Shrubs with arching or weeping stems are buddleia, forsythia (unpruned), *Hydrangea paniculata*, kolkwitzia, *Spiraea thunbergii*, and weigela.

➤ Shrubs that tolerate seashore conditions are berberis, buddleia, caryopteris, chamaecyparis, clethra, cornus, cytisus, forsythia, hydrangea, juniperus, kolkwitzia, potentilla, prunus, spiraea, syringea, taxus, viburnum, and weigela.

➤ Always check the hardiness tolerance for shrubs you buy, and only buy shrubs that are hardy in your zone.

Chapter 10

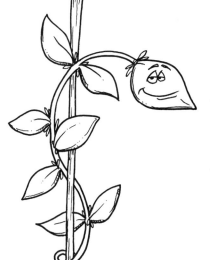

The Idiot's Guide to the Easiest Vines

In This Chapter

➤ The 20 easiest vines to grow

➤ Descriptions of annual and perennial vines (how they grow, their colors and sizes)

➤ The best places to grow vines

➤ Tips on growing vines

You were introduced to vines in Chapter 2, and now you'll get a foolproof list of twenty easy and reliable vines that you'll feel comfortable growing.

What Is a Vine?

Some vines are annuals, some are biennials, and some are perennials. It's not the length of their life-cycles that defines them, but rather their habit of growth.

Some vines are grown for their colorful flowers, such as honeysuckle (*Lonicera*), while others are grown for their foliage, such as Boston ivy (*Parthenocissus*). While the ivy vine also flowers, the flowers are inconspicuous and insignificant—the foliage itself is the attraction.

Annual and Perennial Vines

Annual vines are quick-growing plants that will clothe fences, banks, and walls, continuing to flower until the first frost. Morning glory (*Ipomoea purpurea*), with its pretty, star-shaped flowers, is an extremely vigorous annual vine.

Perennial vines may be slower to establish themselves, but once established, they will return every year with the same wonderful color and foliage. The perennial vine wisteria, for instance, known for its long panicles of fragrant flowers, will come back every year with a vengeance, growing stronger every year.

How Do Vines Grow?

All vines grow in one of the three following ways:

1. *Some vines twine.* Some vines, like honeysuckle (Lonicera), grow by twining. These slender-stemmed plants will grow upward, reaching for support. When they get hold of that support, from a trellis, fence, or branch of a tree, the plants then wrap their terminal shoot around the trellis or branch and continue the move upward.

Green Meany
Don't allow vines that grow by suction cups to climb up wood structures because they can damage the wood by rotting it. Either grow them on other materials (brick, cement, stone) or install a trellis.

2. *Some vines have tendrils or leaf stalks.* Other vines have tendrils or leaf stalks to help them climb. While these vines also grow upward and are slender-stemmed, they have little side shoots which wrap themselves around the trellis, fence, for tree for support. Sweet pea (*Lathrus odoratus*) is an example of a plant that grows with tendrils. Clematis is an example of a vine that grows by leaf stalks.

3. *Some vines cling.* The third kind of vine grows by clinging: Small disks or suction cups attach themselves to walls or buildings. Plants in this category include *Hydrangea anomala*, subsp. *petiolaris*, and English ivy (*Hedera helix*). These plants are usually grown on strong supports: the sides of buildings (everything except wood sidings) and sturdy walls of brick or stone.

Flower Power!
Use quick-growing annual vines like morning glories (*Ipomoea purpurea*) to clothe a chain-link fence or chicken wire around your vegetable patch.

Where Vines Belong

Vines can be used anywhere there is support for them. If they climb by twining or with tendrils, use them on fences, trellises, arbors, or even in containers with wire support. Cardinal climber (*Ipomoea x multifida*) is a wonderful, tropical-looking vine perfect for a pot with a trellis in it. This annual climber has a lavish supply of crimson flowers that look good all summer.

Vines as Ground Cover

Another great place for a vine is on a slope, as a ground cover. *Clematis paniculata* is something of a workaholic and is perfect for the job. It's a rampant grower that can reach up to 30 feet and has small, fragrant, pure white flowers that literally cover the entire plant. Place this clematis at the bottom of the slope; it will grow up the slope, covering it with beautiful flowers.

Vines to Soften Walls or Foundations

Use vines that grow by clinging with disks wherever there is enough support for them. They can soften the look of building wall or stone foundation, or provide beautiful color to stone or brick chimneys.

Lush English ivy (*Hedera helix*) can make even ordinary brick buildings look stately and distinguished. (It's worked for the Ivy League schools!)

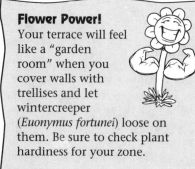

Flower Power!
Your terrace will feel like a "garden room" when you cover walls with trellises and let wintercreeper (*Euonymus fortunei*) loose on them. Be sure to check plant hardiness for your zone.

What Information Is Included on the Vines List?

You'll find the following information listed with each vine, and what you can expect from the categories.

Genus Species/Common Name

Plants are listed with both the genus species and the common names. For more information about plant names, refer to Chapter 2.

Flower

This tells you the color or colors of the flowers and, if the vine is a perennial, when it flowers. In the cases of vines grown for their foliage, the description of the flower will indicate that the flowers are inconspicuous. In other words, the flowers may be very small and difficult to see.

Foliage

Foliage is listed as a category because it is the beautiful foliage that makes many vines unique. Ivies, for instance, have beautiful colors in their leaves in different seasons. This category will also tell you whether the vine is evergreen or deciduous.

Height

When you read about the heights of vines, keep in mind that the heights given are the *approximate* height the vines will grow. Remember that perennials and annuals grow very differently; morning glory, for example, a popular annual, may grow more than 15 feet in one year. Trumpet creeper, a perennial, may grow only 2–3 feet the first year, and after several years you may have the 30-foot-tall plant you want.

Zone

Zones are listed for the perennial vines. If the vine is an annual, then the zone category is marked "annual."

Sun

This category tells you how much sun the vine requires, either "full," "partial," or "shade," or some combination of these.

Soil

This category tells you the kind of soil the vine requires. Some vines may prefer drier conditions, some prefer moist, and some need a rich soil. Average soils are well-drained and moderately rich.

Spacing

This tells how far apart to space the plants.

Climbs By

This information is useful because you don't want to place a vine that climbs by clinging to a structure it could potentially damage. For more information about how vines climb, refer to Chapter 2.

The Idiot's Guide to the Easiest Vines

The following list of vines is tailored for the beginning gardener. There's nothing tricky about these plants.

GENUS SPECIES: *Aristolochia durior*
COMMON NAME: Dutchman's Pipe
FLOWER: insignificant brownish-purple
FOLIAGE: deciduous
HEIGHT: 30'
ZONE: 4

SUN: full
SOIL: average
SPACING: 8–10'
CLIMBS BY: twining

This ivy grows small flowers shaped like a meerschaum pipe. Twelve-inch leaves sometimes hide the small flowers. Dutchman's pipe is a vigorous grower and can get out of hand. If it does, cut it back 3 feet from the ground.

GENUS: *Bougainvillea*
COMMON NAME: Common Bougainvillea
FLOWER: the 1" long bracts are reds, pinks, purples, yellow, and orange
FOLIAGE: evergreen in the South, deciduous in the North
HEIGHT: 15–20'
ZONE: 10
SUN: full
SOIL: average
SPACING: 6–10'
CLIMBS BY: twining

Bougainvillea is a vigorous grower that will cover fences, trellises, or porches quickly. Its colorful bracts, which are generally leaves and not flowers, are the show stoppers on this vine.

Bougainvillea can be used in southern climates as a low-growing hedge to cover a bank, provided it is pruned back. In northern climates it is used outside in summer months and brought in for the winter months. Prune it when the leaves fall off, and keep the soil dry in the dormant winter stage. Double-flowering bougainvillea plants hold on to their dead flowers for a long time, which can make the plant look messy. Look for single-flowering varieties.

Garden Talk
Bracts are modified leaves—they are often large and brightly colored. Poinsettia, for example, have colorful bracts that are bright red, pink, or white.

GENUS SPECIES: *Campsis radicans*
COMMON NAME: Trumpet creeper
FLOWER: orange
FOLIAGE: deciduous
HEIGHT: 30'
ZONE: 4–7
SUN: full
SOIL: average
SPACING: 6–10'
CLIMBS BY: clinging

Trumpet creeper may require extra support because the 9- to 11-inch leaves can get extremely heavy. The trumpetlike flowers are 2 inches wide, and although orange is the most common color, trumpet creeper also comes in scarlet and yellow varieties. The fruits are long dry pods.

GENUS SPECIES: *Cardiospermum halicacabum*
COMMON NAME: Balloon-Vine
FLOWER: white
FOLIAGE: deciduous
HEIGHT: 10'
ZONE: annual
SUN: full
SOIL: average
SPACING: 1–2'
CLIMBS BY: tendrils

Balloon-vine is grown for its fruit, which are shaped like balloons and are about an inch in diameter. The black seeds have a white, heart-shaped spot on them about the size of a pea.

Plant directly where you want them to grow when the soil warms up.

GENUS SPECIES: *Clematis sp.*
COMMON NAME: Clematis
FLOWER: white, pink, purple, blue, red; early bloomers flower in June, summer bloomers in July
FOLIAGE: deciduous
HEIGHT: 12' or more
ZONE: 4–7
SUN: full/partial
SOIL: cool
SPACING: 12'
CLIMBS BY: leaf-stalks

Green Meany
Mulching clematis will cause more harm than good, as it will trap moisture and not allow enough air to circulate around the stem and soil.

The Clematis genus includes many varieties from which to choose. Some bloom early in the summer; other varieties bloom later. *C. montana*'s pink or white 1- to 2-inch flowers bloom in June. *C. x jackmanii* blooms in July with 4- to 5-inch flowers, in colors that range from whites and pinks to blues, purples, and reds. *C. paniculata* can grow to 30 feet and has tiny fragrant white flowers that cover it in late August.

Clematis prefer a moderately rich and cool soil condition. The soil should never be too dry or too wet. The best way to keep the soil cool is to plant an annual or perennial in front of your clematis to shade the roots.

Prune clematis when the plants are young to promote branching; then prune only to shape or rejuvenate growth. The time to prune your vine will depend on the variety—whether it's early- or late-blooming. Early flowering varieties should be pruned just after they flower. Clematis that bloom later in the summer or early fall should be pruned the following year, early in the spring.

GENUS SPECIES: *Cobaea scandens*
COMMON NAME: Cup and Saucer Vine, Cathedral Bells
FLOWER: lavender or violet
FOLIAGE: deciduous
HEIGHT: 15' or more
ZONE: annual
SUN: full
SOIL: average
SPACING: 3'
CLIMBS BY: tendrils

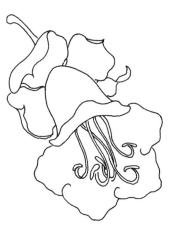

Cup and saucer vine or cathedral bells (Cobaea scandens).

These graceful stems produce pendulous, lavender- to violet-colored flowers that bloom mid-summer to frost. The decorative bell-shaped flowers have ruffles around the edges.

This is a great plant for the container plant with a trellis.

GENUS SPECIES: *Dolichos lablab*
COMMON NAME: Hyacinth Bean
FLOWER: purple, white
FOLIAGE: deciduous

HEIGHT: 15' or more
ZONE: annual
SUN: full
SOIL: average
SPACING: 2'
CLIMBS BY: twining

This tropical-looking vine is a great summer screen for a fence or trellis. The pealike flowers are about an inch long and cover the vine in mid-summer. The seed pods are flat, 2 to 3 inches long and are still a deep, showy purple, but are not a true bean. Hyacinth bean loves the heat.

Direct sow when all dangers of frost are gone.

GENUS SPECIES: *Euonymus fortunei*
COMMON NAME: Wintercreeper
FLOWER: inconspicuous white flowers
FOLIAGE: evergreen
HEIGHT: 30'
ZONE: 5
SUN: full/partial
SOIL: average/dry
SPACING: 5'
CLIMBS BY: clinging

The inconspicuous flowers of this vine produce showy orange berries. This is one of the best vines to use as a screen because of its dark, shiny, evergreen leaves. Use it on your stone, brick, or cement foundation.

Don't let this vine cling to wooden structures or the clinging vines will damage the wood.

GENUS: *Hedera helix*
COMMON NAME: English Ivy
FLOWER: inconspicuous yellowish-green flowers
FOLIAGE: evergreen
HEIGHT: 30'
ZONE: 6
SUN: shade
SOIL: average
SPACING: 4'
CLIMBS BY: clinging

This is a very popular vine that roots easily. Use as a climbing vine or as a ground cover in the shade. Be careful not to allow this vine to grow on wooden structures because the roots can cause damage to wood. The inconspicuous flowers produce black berries and the leathery foliage is dark green and almost 4 inches in length. Ivy climbing on brick or stone buildings is an elegant sight.

GENUS SPECIES: *Hydrangea anomala* subsp.
petiolaris
COMMON NAME: Climbing Hydrangea
FLOWER: creamy white
FOLIAGE: deciduous
HEIGHT: 30'
ZONE: 4
SUN: full/partial
SOIL: average
SPACING: 4'
CLIMBS BY: clinging

Flower Power!
When your climbing hydrangea gets out of control, use sharp pruners to cut it back as hard as you wish.

This woody vine produces lacy flowers in mid-June and covers a large area in a few years. It will climb up everything—old oak trees, stone walls, brick chimneys—and is one of the most gratifying of ornamental climbers.

GENUS SPECIES: *Ipomoea purpurea*
COMMON NAME: Morning Glory
FLOWER: white, blue pink, red
FOLIAGE: deciduous
HEIGHT: 15' or more
ZONE: annual
SUN: full
SOIL: average
SPACING: 12"
CLIMBS BY: twining

Morning glories bloom all night and into the cool summer mornings.

Let these plants grow on their own—they need little fertilizer and water. Do give them plenty of sun and room to grow. Morning glories are easy to start from seed, but soak the seeds for about an hour before planting for easier germination.

GENUS: *Ipomoea x multifida*
COMMON NAME: Cardinal Climber
FLOWER: red
FOLIAGE: tropical
HEIGHT: 10'
ZONE: annual

SUN: full
SOIL: average
SPACING: 1'
CLIMBS BY: twining

The 2-inch long crimson flower on this vine attracts hummingbirds from July to September. The foliage has a tropical look with palmlike leaves. It's another vine that loves the heat of the summer.

GENUS SPECIES: *Jasminum officinale*
COMMON NAME: Common Jasmine
FLOWER: white
FOLIAGE: semi-evergreen
HEIGHT: 25'
ZONE: 7
SUN: full/partial
SOIL: average
SPACING: 5'
CLIMBS BY: clinging

This is a wonderfully fragrant, semi-evergreen vine for the South. It quickly climbs fences and covers arbors. In the North, jasmine is grown mainly as a houseplant for the fragrant flowers that appear on it in winter.

GENUS SPECIES: *Lathyrus odoratus*
COMMON NAME: Sweet Pea
FLOWER: pink, white, shades of purple, rosy reds
FOLIAGE: deciduous
HEIGHT: 6' or more
ZONE: annual
SUN: full/partial
SOIL: rich
SPACING: 12"
CLIMBS BY: tendrils

Flower Power!
Soak sweet pea seeds for two hours before planting to soften the shells.

Sweet peas sound edible but they are strictly ornamental flowers! This wonderful, sweet-smelling flower comes in many different colors: pinks, white, shades of purples, and rosy reds. Sweet peas prefer cool climates, so southerners must plant in winter months in order to grow; northerners should plant in early spring.

Sweet peas are easy to sow directly into the ground.

GENUS SPECIES: *Lonicera sp.*
COMMON NAME: Honeysuckle
FLOWER: orange, red, yellow, pink in spring or summer
FOLIAGE: deciduous
HEIGHT: 10' or more
ZONE: 3–9
SUN: full/partial
SOIL: lime/average
SPACING: 5'
CLIMBS BY: twining

Most honeysuckles have a sweet fragrance and trumpet-shaped flowers. Fruit colors range from bright red and yellows to blues and black. Look for a honeysuckle that grows as a native in your own area because some plants can be invasive. Invasive plants will run rampant in your garden, taking over surrounding plants and edging them out. Keep pruning honeysuckle to keep it under control. Varieties that bear their fruit in the fall seem to last for weeks, providing lots of autumn color.

GENUS SPECIES: *Parthenocissus sp.*
COMMON NAME: Creeper (Boston Ivy)
FLOWER: inconspicuous greenish flowers
FOLIAGE: deciduous
HEIGHT: 30' or more
ZONE: 3–8
SUN: full/partial
SOIL: average
SPACING: 5'
CLIMBS BY: clinging

This is an attractive vine whose foliage turns brilliant scarlet in the fall. It has blue fruits that birds love. Most are quick growers and come in many different varieties available with different sizes of foliage and shades of green.

Green Meany
Don't plant Boston ivy in damp, shady areas because it is prone to powdery mildew.

GENUS SPECIES: *Passiflora sp.*
COMMON NAME: Passion Flower
FLOWER: blue, pink, white, purple
FOLIAGE: tropical
HEIGHT: 8' or more
ZONE: 7–10
SUN: full/partial

SOIL: moist/average
SPACING: 3'
CLIMBS BY: tendrils

These unusual and interesting flowers look like flat circles with pointed tips, which are solid or multicolored. They last a long time. In the North they are grown as houseplants, and in the South they can tolerate the heat if given plenty of water.

GENUS SPECIES: *Phaseolus coccineus*
COMMON NAME: Scarlet-Runner Bean
FLOWER: scarlet
FOLIAGE: deciduous
HEIGHT: 6–8'
ZONE: annual
SUN: full
SOIL: average
SPACING: 1–2'
CLIMBS BY: twining

This vine grows quickly for summer coverage. It's great for the fence around the pool. Late in the summer, the pods are about a foot long.

GENUS SPECIES: *Thunbergia alata*
COMMON NAME: Clockvine, Black-eyed Susan Vine
FLOWER: white to orange-yellow
FOLIAGE: deciduous
HEIGHT: 6'
ZONE: annual
SUN: full/partial
SOIL: moist/average
SPACING: 2–3'
CLIMBS BY: twining

The dark purple center of this flower gives it a resemblance to a black-eyed Susan. In the summer the vine is covered with numerous flowers. Clockvine is very popular in the South, where it grows on pillars, porches, and trellises. In the North, it is best used in hanging baskets and window boxes. It should always be kept watered during dry periods.

GENUS SPECIES: *Wisteria sp.*
COMMON NAME: Wisteria
FLOWER: white, blue, pink in May
FOLIAGE: deciduous

HEIGHT: 30'
ZONE: 5–10
SUN: full/partial
SOIL: rich/average
SPACING: 10'
CLIMBS BY: twining

Wisteria is one of the most beautiful of the ornamental vines and an incredibly vigorous grower. The pendulous flowers are usually very fragrant in May.

Wisteria grows on a thick woody trunk and needs strong support from an arbor, trellis, or tree. Wisterias prefer well-drained but moist soil.

Never give wisteria nitrogen or the plant will produce all leaves. Feed it superphosphate in the spring to help it develop its root system, flowers, and seeds. Prune wisteria back hard in late winter, to the third lateral bud (see illustration). Prune again after the wisteria flowers, and continue pruning throughout the season. Continual pruning of the slender stems that grow in all directions, called *whips*, is very important.

It's important to continue pruning the wisteria whips.

cut here
lateral buds
new growth
(this year's stem)
old growth
(last year's stem)

159

The Least You Need to Know

➤ Vines grow by twining, growing tendrils or leaf stalks, or attaching disks.

➤ A quick-growing annual vine like morning glory (*Ipomoae purpurea*) will decorate a mailbox or cover an unsightly fence with flowers in no time.

➤ Use climbing hydrangea (*H. anomala* subsp. *petiolaris*), a perennial vine, to cover walls and chimneys.

➤ Make a note of the vines that appeal to you and think about incorporating them into your garden scheme.

Chapter 11

The Idiot's Guide to the Easiest Herbs

In This Chapter

➤ A list of the ten easiest herbs to grow

➤ Descriptions (color, height, shape) of herbs

➤ Best places to grow herbs

➤ Harvesting herbs

Herbs are some of the easiest plants you'll ever grow. In the list that follows, you'll get a good sampling of the easiest of the easiest. No doubt you'll recognize some of the plants in this chapter by their common names (and the song): parsley, sage, rosemary, and thyme.

What Are Herbs?

Botanically speaking, herbs are sort of hard to define. The word *herb* is short for "herbaceous," meaning nonwoody. But this would eliminate herbs that are evergreen shrubs, such as rosemary. In a broader sense, herbs are plants whose stems, leaves, flowers, or seeds contain some medicinal, savory, or aromatic value.

At any rate, herbs are wonderfully versatile plants that have been put to a wide variety of uses. Among them, herbs have been grown for their culinary uses, cultivated for their medicinal or "folk remedy" values, steeped for teas and other beverages, harvested for dyes, and dried for scented potpourris.

The list in this chapter highlights some herbs for you to enjoy as ornamental plants, and when the mood strikes, to put to work in the kitchen.

Herbs Are Annuals and Perennials

Remember that annuals flower, set seed, and die in the same year. Both basil (*Ocimum basilicum*) and dill (*Anethum graveolens*) are annuals, so you'll want to keep in mind that these plants will reach their full heights in the same year you plant them. These annuals are planted in early spring, either by sowing seeds directly into the ground or by planting seedlings.

Garden Talk
Gardeners use the term *invasive* to describe plants that spread aggressively.

Perennials live from year to year. Perennial herbs will return every year to your garden. Some perennial herbs, like spearmint (*Mentha spicata*), are invasive and will grow so vigorously that you will want to keep them from getting out of control.

Ornamental Herbs for the Garden

All the herbs selected for our list are great as ornamental plants in flower beds, borders, and containers. Ornamentation is one of the best reasons to grow herbs, especially for gardeners who want their flower beds to have interesting and varied aromas in addition to colorful flowers.

Herbs in Flower Beds and Borders

Ornamental herbs like chives (*Allium schoenoprasum*), with their purplish-pink flower heads on stalks a few feet tall, and rosemary (*Rosmarinus officinalis*), with its pretty, needlelike foliage, are perfect in perennial beds. Don't think of them as herbs—think of them as you would any ornamental plant and place them in the flower bed for best visual effect.

Herbs in Containers

One of the nicest things about herbs is that all of them work well in containers in direct sunlight, whether it's a clay pot, window box, or hanging basket. If you are planning a container garden on your deck or terrace, nothing could be easier to use than herbs in your pots and baskets.

Chives (Allium schoenoprasum).

Flower Power!

If you want your herbs to do double-duty in the kitchen, be sure to place the containers with herbs close to the kitchen door to save yourself a trip across the lawn.

Harvesting Herbs for Use in the Kitchen

The list that follows includes many herbs whose leaves we use in cooking, like basil and French tarragon. If you want to use fresh herbs for culinary purposes, keep pinching the plants throughout the growing season to keep them from flowering. Basil, for instance, has pretty, spiked flowers above the foliage, but in order to keep the plant from putting

Flower Power!
When cooking with fresh herbs, always use twice as many fresh herbs as dried herbs, and always add the fresh herbs at the end.

energy into producing flowers, pinch the flowers off the plant. Pinching will also give your plant a nice, bushy shape.

You should also keep in mind when harvesting herbs that you need to leave at least one-third to one-half of the plant's foliage on the plant. Never take off more than half the plant's foliage.

Pinch the flowers off your basil plant to maintain its shape and keep it growing strong.

Drying Herbs

Herbs can be dried in any warm location that is not in direct sunlight. If the area is well-circulated, so much the better, as good air circulation speeds up the drying process. The quicker the herbs dry, the fewer essential oils they lose. To dry, tie herbs in small bunches and hang the bunches upside down or spread them on a screen to dry. Turn the herbs over a few times until they are completely dried; store the herbs in an airtight container when finished and label the container with the name of the herb.

Never Use Chemicals on Herb Plants You Harvest!

As you become used to gardening and acquainted with the unpleasant diseases and bugs that like your plants as much as you do, you may be tempted to get rid of your problems with herbicides, insecticides, pesticides, and other toxic quick-fix remedies. But don't use these dangerous chemicals; instead learn how to eliminate pests in nontoxic ways. It's especially important to never, never, never use chemicals on herb plants you intend to harvest.

Herbs Need Sun and Average Soil

All herbs need full sun, at least six hours a day, and prefer a soil that is average and not too fertile. If you have these conditions, you should have herbs. There are a few herb plants, like basil (*Ocimum basilicum*), that need a more fertile soil (which is noted in their plant descriptions).

What Information Is Included on the Herbs List?

You'll find the following information listed with each herb, and what you can expect from the categories.

Genus Species

The list is alphabetized by genus, which is always capitalized, followed by each plant's species name, which is in lowercase. The species names are included on this list so that you know exactly which plant to get. For instance, if you want a particular salvia, common sage, called *Salvia officinalis*, you don't want to make the mistake of just asking for a "salvia." You may get *Salvia leucantha*, a pretty Mexican bush sage you definitely do not want to eat!

Garden Talk
To find an herb on the list by its common name, refer to the index at the back of the book.

Common Name

The common names for herbs on the following list are the names you know the plants by, like basil and thyme.

Flower

This category tells you the color of the herb's flowers, or if the flowers are insignificant. Most herbs, annuals, and perennials flower in the summer.

Height

This category tells you the average height for the herb. The heights of the herbs will vary since you will probably be cutting the plants back (when you want fresh herbs). Annuals will reach full maturity the same year you plant them. Perennial herbs, since they grow for many years, will take longer.

Zone

The hardiness zones indicate the coolest to warmest climates a perennial herb can with-stand. Herbs that are annuals are designated "annual" in this category. Be sure to keep your own zone in mind when reading and choosing perennial herbs.

The Idiot's Guide to the Easiest Herbs

Here's the list:

> GENUS SPECIES: *Allium schoenoprasum*
> COMMON NAME: Chives
> FLOWER: pink in the spring
> HEIGHT: 12"
> ZONE: 3–10

Chives' small, round purplish-pink flower heads appear above the grasslike foliage. This is a charming plant for the perennial border or the herb garden. The flowers will dry well for arrangements or as a cut-flower. Chives are great for container plants, especially since they will overwinter in plastic or wooden containers.

Cut the plant to 2 inches from the ground just after the flowers are at their peak and use the flowers either as cut flowers or for drying. You'll get a second flush of growth in foliage and flowers in two to three weeks. Chives will readily self-sow everywhere. Divide in the fall or the spring. If you want fresh chives in winter, cut the foliage just after the second flush of growth, chop it, and freeze it in zip-lock bags. Or use the flowers and foliage fresh from the garden any time during the growing season.

> GENUS SPECIES: *Anethum graveolens*
> COMMON NAME: Dill
> FLOWER: greenish-yellow in summer
> HEIGHT: 2–3'
> ZONE: annual

Dill's feathery foliage and tall flower heads make it a great plant for the garden.

It is best to grow dill by seed since it resists transplanting. If you do buy dill as seedlings, make sure the plants are in individual pots so you don't risk disturbing the root systems when you plant. Dill self-sows readily.

Use fresh dill foliage during the season or harvest the seeds to dry and use to flavor dressings.

GENUS SPECIES: *Artemisia dracunculus*
COMMON NAME: French Tarragon
FLOWER: insignificant
HEIGHT: 2'
ZONE: 5–9

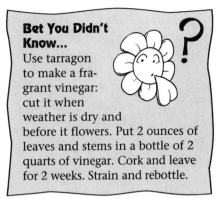

Bet You Didn't Know...
Use tarragon to make a fragrant vinegar: cut it when weather is dry and before it flowers. Put 2 ounces of leaves and stems in a bottle of 2 quarts of vinegar. Cork and leave for 2 weeks. Strain and rebottle.

This perennial has a distinctive and pungent flavor—sort of like anise—and its narrow leaves are a pretty blue-green color. Keep French tarragon's flavor strong by dividing the plant every 2–3 years.

French tarragon is drought- and heat-tolerant. Well-drained soil is important—it won't survive in a poorly drained site.

Use the leaves of French tarragon fresh during the growing season or dry them to use later.

GENUS SPECIES: *Mentha spicata*
COMMON NAME: Spearmint
FLOWER: white in summer
HEIGHT: 2'
ZONE: 5–9

Mints are some of the most notoriously invasive plants around, and gardeners are always trying to come up with ways to contain these plants. But no one wants to stop growing them—the strong aroma of these plants is irresistible. Spearmint leaves are serrated and pointed at the tips. All mints have square stems. Mints grow by underground runners, which you can try to contain by burying the plant in a pot.

Use fresh mint leaves in teas and as garnishes on desserts.

GENUS SPECIES: *Ocimum basilicum*
COMMON NAME: Sweet Basil
FLOWER: pink spikes in summer
HEIGHT: 2$\frac{1}{2}$'
ZONE: annual

Sweet basil is an annual with attractive pink flowers. However, if you want to grow it for harvesting, you'll be pinching the flowers to keep the plant from putting energy toward producing flowers. Start with seeds, directly sown into the ground. If you want a longer growing period, start with seedlings. Either way, the only caution for growing basil is to beware of severe temperature drops below 65 degrees F; basil doesn't like the cold, either in the day or the night.

Give basil a rich, well-drained soil; pinch back plants often when young to produce bushy plants and you'll be rewarded all summer with fresh basil leaves for harvesting. Use the leaves in sauces, soups, and salads. Basil also dries easily.

Flower Power!

Want a plant with dark purple foliage and pretty lavender-colored flowers in your garden? Try *O. basilicum*, "Purple Opal," (purple basil). It blooms all summer and is very ornamental in the garden. The leaves are a beautiful garnish on all dishes!

GENUS SPECIES: *Origanum vulgare*
COMMON NAME: Italian Oregano
FLOWER: pink in summer
HEIGHT: 2–3'
ZONE: 7–10

Italian oregano is a hardy perennial with small leaves and flowers that last throughout the summer. There are other varieties of origanum that are more ornamental, but *O. vulgare* is the best of them for harvesting. Start with small plants. Cut oregano back during the growing season to keep it looking neat and to use fresh in the kitchen. You can also start to dry oregano for use throughout the winter. This perennial herb grows quickly, so divide it every few years to keep it under control. It needs full sun and no fertilizers. Italian oregano is great for container plants and in combination with other perennials.

GENUS SPECIES: *Petroselinum crispum*
COMMON NAME: Parsley
FLOWER: feathery green foliage
HEIGHT: 2–3'
ZONE: 3–8

Parsley is an herb you're probably familiar with, since it is used so often as a garnish for all kinds of dishes. Its flavorful leaves, which are either flat Italian parsley (*P. crispum* var. *neapolitanum*) or curled French parsley (*P. crispum* var. *crispum*) have an attractive yellow-green tint to them. This is a great plant for an herb garden, in a container, or as an edging plant for a flower garden. Parsley is a biennial, so seeds sown the first year will flower the second year and then die. Plant seeds directly into the ground when temperature is above 50 degrees. You can also purchase seedlings and plant them after danger of frost. This biennial does self-sow.

You can freeze chopped parsley or whole sprigs in plastic bags for fresh parsley all year round.

> ## Flower Power!
>
> Speed up the process! Parsley seeds sown directly into the ground can be very slow to germinate, taking up to six weeks, which can be too long a wait for gardeners in cool climates. But if you soak the seeds overnight in warm water, your parsley will germinate much sooner.

GENUS SPECIES: *Rosmarinus officinalis*
COMMON NAME: Rosemary
FLOWER: pale blue or white in early summer
HEIGHT: 2–4'
ZONE: 8–10

Rosemary's attractive, needlelike foliage is a pretty gray-green, and in early summer the plant is covered with tiny blue or white flowers. Where winters are mild, use rosemary as a small hedge to border gardens or as an edge to a pathway. Where the plant isn't hardy, gardeners can use rosemary as a specimen plant in decorative containers. You'll want to keep the shape of your rosemary shrub looking neat by trimming any protruding branches that make it look untidy. For ambitious gardeners, rosemary can be trained into topiary shapes.

> ## Garden Talk
>
> A good way for Northern gardeners to get rosemary in and out of the garden easily is to plant the rosemary in pots, then bury the pots in the soil. This way, when it's time to bring the rosemary indoors for the winter, it's already set in its pot.

Use sprigs of fresh rosemary to flavor poultry and other meat dishes, or add it to fresh vegetables as well as tomato sauce.

If you do bring your potted rosemary indoors, bring it inside before the autumn leaves turn. In other words, bring it in early in the fall so that the plant has time to acclimate to its new indoor environment. You don't want to wait until the difference in temperature between indoors, with the heat on, and the outdoors is extreme. Also, be sure to keep the plant properly watered throughout the winter, taking care not to let the soil dry out.

169

GENUS SPECIES: *Salvia officinalis*
COMMON NAME: Common Sage
FLOWER: blue in early summer
HEIGHT: $2^1/_2'$
ZONE: 3–10

Sage has pretty grayish-green foliage and violet-blue, tubular-shaped flowers. There are many different types of sage, all with different types of foliage, from yellow to tricolored with purple, green, and cream, to one colored with purple, green, and cream to a purple-red. All of the foliage on sages is very showy, as are the flowers, making these plants nice additions to the garden. Start with potted plants. Cut sage back to keep it in shape. It tolerates dry conditions.

Sage, fresh or dried, is a popular seasoning for stuffings and stews.

GENUS SPECIES: *Thymus vulgaris*
COMMON NAME: Common Thyme
FLOWER: lilac, pink, or white in summer
HEIGHT: 1'
ZONE: 4–9

There are many types of thymes, but the most commonly used variety for cooking is *T. vulgaris*. It has a neat, attractive appearance and looks great in rock gardens or borders. It is also a good container plant with mixed herbs. This perennial loves sandy soil, making it perfect as a filler for cracks between paving or rock gardens. Creeping varieties of thyme make wonderful ground covers.

Add a few sprigs of thyme to all your dishes. You can never have too much thyme in a garden.

The Least You Need to Know

➤ All herbs like sun, so if you have a sunny spot and plant herbs you won't go wrong.

➤ Ornamental herbs are perfect in perennial beds. All the herbs on the list work well in flower beds.

➤ Plant herbs in containers and set them by your kitchen door for handy harvesting.

➤ Always harvest herbs just before they flower. This is when the flavor in the leaves is the strongest. Remember, the more herbs you use, the more you get. When you pick leaves for harvesting, you get a neater appearance to the plant plus all the herbs you need for your kitchen.

➤ Never use any chemicals on herb plants you intend to harvest, no matter how pesky your pests.

Chapter 12

The Idiot's Guide to the Easiest Bulbs

> ### In This Chapter
>
> ➤ The easiest bulbs for beginner gardeners
>
> ➤ Descriptions of bulbs, corms, tubers, and rhizomes
>
> ➤ Use of bulbs in the garden
>
> ➤ Naturalizing bulbs in the landscape

Bulbs and bulblike plants are some of the most rewarding flowering plants you'll ever grow. Tulips, daffodils, dahlias, tuberous begonias, lilies—these are just a few of the most popular bulbs and bulblike plants you'll want to include in your garden and landscape.

Here you'll get a basic understanding of what these plants need, as well as where to best plant them. The list that follows includes all the easiest bulbs a beginner gardener can grow.

What Are Bulbs?

Bulbs are storage organs. They consist of a modified bud, surrounded by fleshy scales and/ or swollen, modified leaf-bases on a much reduced stem. These storage organs are usually underground.

What Are Corms, Tubers, and Rhizomes?

Corms, tubers, and rhizomes are shaped differently from bulbs. We put bulbs and bulb-like plants in the same category since they all share the underground storage organ as a major characteristic.

Bulbs and bulblike plants are also alike in that they are herbaceous: They have no permanent woody stems above ground, and all are perennial or tender perennial in that they continue to live from year to year.

Bulbs in Bloom

Bloomers like daffodils and crocus come early in spring with their bright and glorious colors. But you can also grow bulbs that bloom in summer, like most of the plants in the lily *(Lilium)* genus, as well as in the fall, like autumn crocus *(Colchicum)*.

The Bulbs of Summer

Some of the most wonderful plants are in the summer-blooming bulb group, including most of the plants in the dahlia *(Dahlia)* genus. Montbretia *(Crocosmia)* is very colorful and also a summer-bloomer.

Bulbs in the Fall

Fall-blooming bulbs are a real treat in any garden, especially since you're not likely to find many plants blooming at this time. Treat yourself to a mass of fall crocus *(Colchicum)* in a rock garden for a gorgeous display of color in autumn. There are other fall-blooming bulbs on the list that follows.

The Life Span of a Bulb

Some bulbs live quite a long time, but much depends on where the bulbs are being grown. Tuberous begonias, for instance, will live about seven years, whereas tulips and hyacinths in the Northeast may last only a few years. But tulips and hyacinths, which love the Oregon weather, will multiply rapidly there, living, it seems, forever. Daffodils multiply quickly in the Northeast and will multiply in this area the way tulips and hyacinths do in Oregon.

Some Bulbs Are Hardy, Some Are Tender

Bulbs that can take freezing temperatures are "hardy." Bulbs that can't take freezing temperatures are "tender."

Hardy Bulbs

Lots of plants, like the hyacinths named earlier, can withstand the cold temperatures during winter months, making them hardy. They'll need very little care. Other hardy bulbs include glory-of-the-snow *(Chionodoxa)* and snowdrops *(Galanthus).* These bulbs can stay in the ground year after year.

Tender Bulbs Need Winter Protection

Tender bulbs are bulbs that can't tolerate freezing conditions, so you'll have to dig these up in the fall if you live above the frost line. Even gardeners in southern climates should dig and divide tender bulbs to keep them healthy and strong.

The plants themselves will tell you when to bring them in—the foliage will start to turn yellow and the plant may fall over. Don't worry if the plant gets hit with a slight frost, but bring it in before the first killing frost. Winter storing instructions are included with the plants listed later in this chapter.

Flower Power!

Treat tender bulbs like annuals: If you want to grow some of the tender bulbs but worry about winter care, use the less expensive tender bulbs, such as small dahlias. Discard at the end of the season and replace the following year with new dahlia tubers.

Where the Bulbs Are: Everywhere!

There are some traditional places to plant bulbs, like tulips in beds and borders and daffodils in lawns and fields. Tulips are rather formal-looking, with their stiff, upright stems and neatly cupped flowers. But don't let convention be your only guide. Plant your bulbs where you want, provided you give them what they need in terms of sun and soil, and they will be fine anywhere—in lawns, on slopes, in garden beds, in containers.

Naturalizing Daffodils and Blue Squill

Some plants, like daffodils *(Narcissus)* and blue squill *(Scilla siberica)* naturalize very well. They look natural growing where nature might have intended them to grow—but where they were, in fact, planted intentionally.

173

GardenTalk
To *naturalize* means to grow plants as if they were in the wild.

Daffodils look perfectly natural planted in drifts in fields, or under and around deciduous trees. Blue squill's carpet of flowers in April and May will get bigger every year. They work well planted right in the lawn—after they bloom all that's left is the short foliage, which is hardly noticeable.

In the Garden

Bulbs for garden beds tend to have a slightly more formal shape to them, like the tulips mentioned earlier. Lilies are great additions to any garden and come in lots of colors. Hyacinths are also great in the garden since their shape is also pretty from all angles.

Flower Power!

Enter bulb planting information in your garden notebook. This way you'll know that you planted scilla in front of the forsythia and not under the azalea. You'll know where not to dig and save yourself the extra work of planting new bulbs on top of existing ones.

Plant Bulbs Where You'll Most Enjoy Them

Since spring flowers are such a wonderful sight, plant your spring-flowering bulbs where you can't miss them the minute they come up. Try them just outside the door to your house or in full view from a window.

Bulbs in Containers

You can always plant bulbs in containers and place the containers wherever you want them—on the porch, on the terrace, in the middle of a lawn. Lilies tend to do well in containers—try planting some in a whiskey barrel or add lilies to a mixed-flower container.

What Bulbs Need

Green Meany

Standing water is a bulb's worst enemy! Never let bulbs sit in water—plant well away from wet areas.

All bulbs need a well-drained, loamy soil. Most of the spring flowering bulbs will also need full sun, but given that most deciduous trees won't have their leaves when these plants bloom, adequate sun is usually not a problem.

Some larger bulbs will need to be planted several inches deep, 6 to 8 inches, while smaller bulbs can be planted more shallowly.

Plant "Right Side Up"

You'll also want to plant the bulb "right side up." This can be difficult since you may not be able to recognize the top of the bulb, nor the small roots on the bottom. Generally, the smaller end of the bulb is the top, so try to place the bulb in the hole with the smaller end facing up.

Flower Power!
If you don't know which end of a bulb is up, plant the bulb on its side.

Plant Bulbs with Fertilizer

When you dig a hole for your bulbs, add a handful of bulb fertilizer to the hole before setting bulbs in it. Bulb fertilizers are typically "9–9–6," which means the fertilizer is 9 percent nitrogen, 9 percent phosphorus, and 6 percent potassium. In future years, to keep the bulbs going, you'll "top dress" the soil, which means you'll add bulb fertilizer to the top of your soil where the bulbs are.

Deadheading

You'll want to deadhead the larger flowering plants, such as tulips and lilies, so that the plant doesn't expend energy making a seed pod. With the exception of scilla, most bulbs do not self-sow, so they won't need the seeds. Don't forget to cut some flowers for the kitchen table or the office. This actually helps the deadheading process!

Storing Tender Bulbs

Some corms and tubers, like gladiolus and dahlia, respectively, are not cold-hardy and will need to be stored in the winter months.

You'll need to store bulbs in a cool, dry location, where the temperature remains around 50 degrees. First, dig the bulbs up after you see signs of dormancy. Next, cut back the tops of the plants about 2 inches from the bulb and shake off any soil. You should then put dry peat on the bottom of a grocery bag; add your bulbs and more peat to cover the bulbs; close up the bag; and label what bulbs are in there.

Tender Bulbs in Containers

If you've planted tender bulbs in containers, you can let these bulbs stay there over the winter. Just make sure the soil is dry before putting the pot away for the winter in a location that is cool and dry. Otherwise the bulbs may rot. In the spring, take out the bulbs and repot.

What Information Is Included on the Bulbs List?

You'll find the following information listed with each bulb or bulblike plant, and what you can expect from each of the categories.

Genus/Common Name

Bulbs are listed with their genus name and common name, and alphabetized according to the genus name. To find a plant by its common name, refer to the index. In some cases, a species name follows a genus name, and the species name is included for reasons of specificity.

Flower

This category tells you the color or color range, and when the flower will bloom. For instance, a spring-blooming bulb that blooms as early as March in the South may bloom as late as May in the North. It will be listed as "spring." These are the average times this plant will bloom.

Height

Most bulbs and bulblike plants reach full height in the first year following the year they were planted. Some fall-blooming bulbs are exceptions. Remember: The bulbs must be planted at the right time, either spring or fall.

Flower Power!
Check the zone map for your zone before continuing this chapter! The zone map can be found in Chapter 4.

Zone

This category tells you the plant's hardiness zone.

Sun

This category tells you how much sun the bulb requires. While most spring-flowering bulbs require full sun, other bulbs can make do with less sun. Tuberous begonias, for instance, are lovely plants for the partial-shade garden.

Spacing

This category indicates how far apart to space the bulbs when planting. For instance, *1'* would tell you that you should plant it 1 foot apart from other plants in all directions.

The Idiot's Guide to the Easiest Bulbs

GENUS/COMMON NAME: *Allium*/Onion
FLOWER: see species below
HEIGHT: see species below
ZONE: 4–9
SUN: full/partial
SPACING: 3"

The following are two species in the Allium genus. Don't let the idea of growing flowers that smell like onions put you off. It's only the foliage that reminds you these plants are in the onion family; the flowers themselves are very pretty.

In early summer, golden garlic *(A. moly)* has small, starlike flowers that grow in clusters about 3 inches wide with a flattened flower head. The bright yellow color will complement any blue flower near it. The stiff, gray-green foliage is about an inch wide.

Another Allium, giant onion (*A. giganteum*) has huge 5-inch purple flowers in perfect ball-shapes in summer that grow atop 4-foot stems. Because the stems have no foliage, it's a good idea to place a low growing perennial in front of it. *A. giganteum* is popular in the garden and makes a great cut flower as well. The flowers will last in water for weeks. They also work well in dried-flower arrangements.

Plant Allium in the fall.

GENUS/COMMON NAME*: Anemone*/Wind Flower
FLOWER: blue/pink, lavender, white in spring
HEIGHT: 4–6"
ZONE: 6–8
SUN: partial shade
SPACING: 3"

Flower Power!
Soak the tubers for *A. blanda* for 8 to 10 hours before planting.

Wind flowers are daisylike flowers that appear in the spring. You can have a carpet of flowers by planting them close together.

A. blanda are grown from small, tuberous roots. They can be grown as far north as zone 5 if they have a protective mulch or if they are planted in a protected area, like the side of a house.

Plant in early spring or fall.

GENUS/COMMON NAME: *Begonia*/Begonia
FLOWER: every color but blue, blooming summer till frost
HEIGHT: 2'
ZONE: 10
SUN: partial shade
SPACING: 2'

Flower Power!
The pendulous begonias are great for hanging baskets.

The begonias in this chapter are tuberous begonias (*Begonia x tuberosa*), as opposed to the wax begonias you read about in Chapter 7. Tuberous begonias, like all begonias, are beautiful, romantic plants and perfect for the shade garden. The ruffled or smooth flower forms with either single or double flowers and comes in a wide range of colors. There are reds, yellows, and oranges, as well as shades of pink, rose, cream, and salmon—everything but blue. There are also two-toned begonias with edges lined in complementing colors.

The fleshy tubers of begonias are planted shallowly so the plant may require staking. Also, these plants need good air circulation, so keep them outside no matter how tempted you are to bring the plants indoors. Tuberous begonias may need a little extra care, but they're worth the time and effort.

Flower Power!
To enjoy lovely begonias indoors, cut a flower or two and float them in water.

While begonias like bright light and can take up to three hours of morning sun, don't let them have more than this or the foliage may burn.

To get the biggest flower from your begonia, try disbudding the smaller flowers: On either side of a flower bud you will notice two smaller buds. Pinch off these two small buds . This process of disbudding will allow the middle flower to grow into a longer-lasting and larger flower.

Begonias need to go dormant for about four months of the year and do so naturally when the days get shorter and the nights get colder. In warmer climates, you can force begonia tubers to go dormant by withholding water from them. Don't make the mistake of fertilizing begonias in August, as they are getting ready to go dormant, or you will hurt their natural rhythm. They won't have time to store food for the following year.

Plant begonias in the spring. Fertilize tuberous begonias with a balanced mix every two or three weeks, stopping in the middle of July.

> GENUS/COMMON NAME: *Chionodoxa*/Glory-of-the-Snow
> FLOWER: blue, pink, or white in the spring
> HEIGHT: 5–10"
> ZONE: 3–9
> SUN: full/partial
> SPACING: 3"

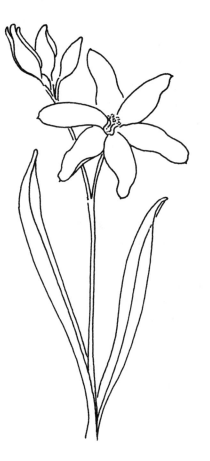

Chionodoxa's common name is glory-of-the-snow.

These little gems with starlike flowers are some of the first bulbs to come up in the spring. They have grasslike foliage and are great for the rock garden or the woodlands.

Plant in the fall. Glory-of-the-snow will multiply by creating new bulbs or seeding themselves. Don't disturb them.

GENUS/COMMON NAME: *Colchicum*/Autumn Crocus
FLOWER: lavender/pink in the fall
HEIGHT: 4–10"
ZONE: 4–9
SUN: partial shade
SPACING: 12"

While crocuses are most commonly known as spring bloomers, these plants with single or double forms flower in autumn and are wonderful in the fall garden. The foliage, which appears in spring, is rough and unattractive, so it's best to hide it by either letting spring leaves collect around it or by letting the grass around it grow a little longer.

These bulbs will bloom the same season you plant. Plant in late summer (September) for early fall bloom. They love to multiply by themselves.

GENUS/COMMON NAME: *Crocosmia*/Montbretia
FLOWER: orange, red, or yellow in late summer
HEIGHT: 3–4'
ZONE: 5–8
SUN: full
SPACING: 12"

Flower Power!
For a nice combo in the garden, try crocosmia with either *Achillea* 'Coronation Gold' or echinacea (a white coneflower).

Crocosmia's brightly colored flowers grow on tall stems. This tall and graceful plant will reach its full height in one season.

Plant in the spring. Crocosmia aren't very hardy, so even in zone 5 they should be mulched, unless planted in a protected area.

GENUS/COMMON NAME: *Crocus*/Spring and Fall Crocus
FLOWER: blue, white purple, or yellow in early spring
HEIGHT: 3–6"
ZONE: 3–8
SUN: full/partial
SPACING: 4"

Spring crocuses, with their bright and cheery flowers, are some of the first signs of spring, popping up when few other flowers have. Their only drawback is that they don't make good cut flowers. So enjoy them outside and make sure you plant them where you can admire them from a window.

Spring crocuses grow from corms and should be planted early enough in the fall to allow the plants enough time to settle in for the winter.

Green Meany

If you have spring crocuses in the lawn, don't mow the foliage until it has completely died down. Crocuses need their foliage to create food and multiply.

Another wonderful bulb in the crocus family is the fall crocus. These are a pretty lavender color and look much like the spring crocuses. There are two very common species of fall crocus, known as *C. sativus* and *C. specious*. When you see these crocuses coming up in the fall, you'll know it's time to start planting your spring flowering bulbs.

Plant crocuses early in the fall. All crocuses naturalize well and are great for the rock garden or the edge of any border, under trees, even in the lawn.

> GENUS/COMMON NAME: *Dahlia*/Dahlia
> FLOWER: every color but blue, flowering in late summer
> HEIGHT: 1–4'
> ZONE: 8–10
> SUN: full/partial
> SPACING: 12–24"

Dahlias are a "must have" in the late summer to fall garden. They are wonderful for cut flowers and come in all different shapes and sizes.

Plant dahlias in the perennial border to fill in where other plants have already died back. The mignon or anemone forms are great to use in the front of a border.

Dahlias need a rich, loamy soil on the moist side whether in the ground or in a container. You should add mulch around the tuber to keep the moisture in the ground if summers are particularly hot.

Dahlias should be dug up for the winter where they are not hardy. In areas that are frost-free, dahlias can remain in the garden.

To dig up, take them up after a light frost. Dig them carefully out of the ground and cut back the top, leaving a 2-inch stem from the tuber. Let the tuber dry in the sun for an hour or two after you have carefully shaken off all the soil. Store the tubers in a cool, dry location for the winter, packed in dry peat moss.

Flower Power!
To get a head start on dahlia blooms, pot up tubers early in the spring and keep the pots protected from spring frost. Plant outdoors after the last frost date.

If you want to divide dahlias, do so in the spring, before you place them in pots. Using a sharp knife, cut down the center of an old stem. The "eyes," which are close to the old stem, will become next year's stems, so be careful not to knock them off. Dividing is up to you—if you choose not to, give them twice the room they took up last year.

GENUS/COMMON NAME: *Galanthus*/Snowdrops
FLOWER: white in early spring
HEIGHT: 3–6"
ZONE: 3–8
SUN: full/partial
SPACING: 3"

Little snowdrops are one of the first flowers to come up in the spring. Even a late snowfall won't hurt these bulbs. Their sweet, droopy flowers give a great show when clumped together.

Plant in the fall. Snowdrops work well in woodland sites and under shrubs. They will self-sow.

GENUS/COMMON NAME: *Galtonia*/Summer Hyacinth
FLOWER: white in summer
HEIGHT: 3–4'
ZONE: 6–9
SUN: full/partial
SPACING: 12"

Summer hyacinth's numerous, nodding, bell-shaped flowers are extremely fragrant. The 4-inch flower stalks combine well with any late-blooming perennial, and the white of the flowers looks great in any garden. Try a summer hyacinth in a container, conveniently placed where you'll most enjoy the heavenly scent.

GENUS/COMMON NAME: *Gladiolus*/Gladiolus
FLOWER: range of colors and mixed, in late summer
HEIGHT: 3'
ZONE: 8–10
SUN: full
SPACING: 8"

Gladioli are popular flowers for floral arrangements, so you've probably seen their tall, stiff foliage and the flowers that grow along the tall stalks. If you want to grow for cut flowers, cut when about half of the flowers are open. The rest of the flowers will open in water.

G. callicanthus has a very sweet fragrance with white flowers whose purple center is shaped like a star. The foliage on these is thinner than the typical gladiolus. This is another sweet-smelling plant to put on the side of your favorite chair on the terrace. They work well in containers.

Plant in the spring. All gladiolus corms in the North must be dug out and stored in a cool, dry location for winter.

> GENUS/COMMON NAME: *Hyacinthus*/Hyacinth
> FLOWER: blue, pink, white, red in the spring
> HEIGHT: 8–12"
> ZONE: 4–8
> SUN: full
> SPACING: 6"

The scent of hyacinths is well known, and many gardeners grow these bulbs just to enjoy the cut flowers indoors. But there are many species to consider for the rock garden, where they look nice. Just a few hyacinths will create a lot of color. Group a few here and a few there (making sure not to plant in a straight row), and you'll have an eye-catching attraction for many years.

Plant early in the fall so they can settle in for the winter. To keep them growing strong, give them a rich, well-drained soil and full sun.

> GENUS/COMMON NAME: *Lilium*/Lily
> FLOWER: every color but blue in the summer or early fall
> HEIGHT: 2–7'
> ZONE: 3–8
> SUN: full/partial
> SPACING: 12"

Lily (Lilium)—
flowers, foliage,
and bulb.

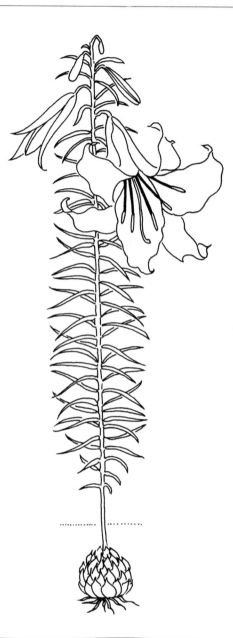

Flower Power

Side dress lilies with wood ashes to produce the best flower blooms you've ever seen.

There are many types of lilies from which to choose. They can vary quite a bit.

The Asiatic lilies have shorter stems and bloom earlier than the Oriental or trumpet lilies. Their short height allows them to work well in partial sun, where the taller Asiatic lilies might not do as well. Most Asiatic lilies have recurved petals.

Oriental lilies have huge flowers and are very fragrant. They bloom later in the summer, after the Asiatic types, and are much taller. These lilies are great for the back of the garden (don't worry, you'll still be able to catch the fragrance).

The trumpet lilies have long, trumpet-shaped flowers, and the most popular trumpet lily is the Easter lily. These lilies also have a strong fragrance, and most of them need to be staked. To do so, place a stake in the ground when you plant the bulbs (to lessen the chances of piercing the bulb later on). When the plant comes up, tie it loosely to the stake with twine.

All lilies like average, well-drained soil. Don't let them sit in water. After four or five years, dig and divide the bulbs.

If you decide to use lilies as cut flowers, leave a third of the stem as food for the bulb.

Plant lilies in the spring or fall, but divide only in the fall.

> GENUS/COMMON NAME: *Muscari*/Grape Hyacinth
> FLOWER: blue or white in spring
> HEIGHT: 6–12"
> ZONE: 3–9
> SUN: full/partial
> SPACING: 3"

No spring garden is complete without clumps of low-growing grape hyacinths. They come in wonderful shades of blue that will accent other early spring bloomers like tulips and daffodils.

Plant in the fall. Grape hyacinths multiply by creating more bulbs every year, providing you with bigger and bigger patches of flowers. Plant them wherever they can be seen.

> GENUS/COMMON NAME: *Narcissus*/Narcissus, Daffodils
> FLOWER: Yellow, orange, white, or pink in spring
> HEIGHT: 6–24"
> ZONE: 3–8
> SUN: full/partial
> SPACING: 8–12"

Everyone seems to love daffodils—they are one of the first signs of spring. Daffodils are some of the easiest bulbs to grow and to enjoy.

Bet You Didn't Know...
To make cut daffodil flowers last longer, stand them in an inch of cold water and store them in the refrigerator for a couple of hours. Then arrange.

There are many types of narcissus from which to choose. Shorter varieties, like the miniatures or poeticus, are perfect for the rock garden. Taller varieties work well naturalized in a large area. Try the large-cup, doubles, or split-cupped. One of the most common daffodils is the trumpet narcissus, which also multiplies freely. In southern climates, tazetta and jonquils will work best.

To naturalize daffodils in an area, plant patches of daffodils every year. Group three bulbs 12 inches apart, making as many groupings as you can. By the second and third years, you'll see each clump of daffodils getting bigger, filling in the 12-inch spaces you left.

Do not cut back the foliage until one-third of the leaves are yellow. When a third of the leaves are yellow, you can be certain that the bulbs have stored enough food.

Daffodils should be planted early enough in the fall to ensure they get a period of warmth that they need to set roots.

> GENUS/COMMON NAME: *Scilla*/ Spanish Bluebells, Blue Squill
> FLOWER: blue, pink, or white in spring
> HEIGHT: 6–15"
> ZONE: 3–8
> SUN: full/partial
> SPACING: 4"

Scilla are trouble-free and will multiply by themselves. The following are two well-known species.

Spanish bluebells (*S. hispanica*) are particularly showy flowers, available in beautiful shades of blue, pink, or white. They grow to 15 inches and are perfect for shade gardens. There is absolutely no work involved with these plants, except to stand back and admire.

Blue squill (*Scilla siberica*) is a much smaller plant, growing 4 to 6 inches with either blue or white small, nodding, star-shaped flowers in spring. One bulb will supply a few stems for each flower. Plant blue squill close together to get a nice clump. They naturalize well and self-sow to produce a carpet of blue or white.

Plant in the fall.

GENUS/COMMON NAME: *Tulipa*/Tulip
FLOWER: all but blue in spring
HEIGHT: 6–36"
ZONE: 3–8
SUN: full/partial
SPACING: 6"

Flower Power!
Keep tulips bloom-
ing longer by
giving them
plenty of water
while they are in
their bud stage,
continuing into their
blooming period. However,
don't let them sit in water.

Tulips are available in every color but blue, and in
every height from 6 inches to 3 feet. The choices are
vast, including solid colors, striped, single-petaled or
double-petaled, early flowering or late flowering. You
could plant a combination of early and late flowering for a succession of bloom.

The miniature types of tulips work well in the rock garden or on a slope combined with
ground cover perennials. Taller tulips are wonderful in any garden or container.

Most tulips, with the exception of the smaller ones, require full sun in northern climates.
Miniature tulips can take partial sun. All tulips in warm, southern climates should get
partial sun.

Flower Power!

The trick to tulips: Plant tulips outdoors in late fall when you are sure
the temperature will not go above 40 degrees. You may want to wait as
late as December (depending on which zone you are in). You don't want
the tulips to break their dormancy and thus become weak, which will
happen if the ground suddenly warms up.

Plant tulips in the late fall. After the tulips have flowered and the foliage is turning
yellow, gently pull the foliage out of the ground. If the stem comes out easily, fine, if not,
wait a week or two and try again.

GENUS/COMMON NAME: *Zantedeschia*/Calla Lily
FLOWER: pink, white, yellow, red, apricot, lavender in summer
HEIGHT: 1–2'
ZONE: 9–10
SUN: full/partial
SPACING: 1–2'

Calla lilies are tropical-looking with large, funnel-shaped flowers and pretty, arrow-shaped foliage. Some varieties have speckled leaves.

Calla lilies work well in containers and are ideal as cut flowers as they stand up well for a long time.

They are not hardy in the North, so gardeners will need to bring the bulbs in for the winter.

Plant in the spring.

The Least You Need to Know

> ➤ Plant spring-flowering bulbs in the fall. You'll be glad you did when you see all the flowers coming up the next year.

> ➤ Bulbs need a well-drained soil and should never sit in water during the growing or dormant season.

> ➤ Bulbs that stay in the ground year-round should be divided in the fall. Lilies are in this group.

> ➤ Don't apply heavy mulch on top of bulbs. You would only be making a home for rodents (and guess what they would eat: your bulbs!).

> ➤ Tender bulbs should be dried before storing for winter months.

> ➤ Note that the genera Allium, Anemone, and Begonias also have annual and perennial plants. Make sure when ordering bulbs for these plants that you know which species you want before making your purchase.

Part 4
Putting It on Paper

You have a list of the easiest plants to grow and you know what their basic needs are: sun, water, and food. Now you need a plan. In Part 4, you learn how to design your garden, from taking measurements in the yard to creating the design on paper.

If you want a ready-made plan at this stage, instead of creating your own, you can choose from one of the 14 specialized garden plans included in Chapter 14. One of them is bound to be right for you and your location.

Chapter 13

Measuring Up: Putting Plans on Paper

In This Chapter

➤ Taking measurements outside

➤ Transferring your findings to paper

➤ Designing the garden, spacing annuals, perennials, and shrubs

---

The whole idea of measuring a garden and putting plans on paper is probably what scares off most would-be gardeners. But it is truly not as hard as you would think—with a few colored pencils and a couple of sheets of graph paper, you will soon see that it only requires a little extra work, and it is really worth it.

First, you'll greatly impress your friends and family by getting the most perfectly designed garden bed, as opposed to plants thrown randomly into a sloppy garden. Second, you'll take the guesswork out of shopping for plants—you'll get exactly the number you need because you'll know how many your design requires. And third, you'll have your own perfect design for your garden on paper and can refer to it at any time. Makes good sense to take the time to measure up, right?

A Picture Is Worth a Thousand Words

Take a few photographs of the area where you intend to put your garden. Photographs will be extremely helpful for planning your garden. You'll be able to take them with you and refer to them when shopping around for plants and creating your garden design. Photographs also show you things you may have overlooked.

Get an Angle on It

Take pictures from different angles: standing away, close up, as well as from different angles that are different from how you'll be viewing the garden (for example, from the house, deck, or porch).

Taking Measurements

Garden Talk
Your first garden should be about 50 square feet.

This will take you about an hour (at most!) and can be done at any time of the day or year. If you do it in the winter, keep in mind that the available sunlight for your potential garden is different. Deciduous trees won't have their leaves, so you may have more shade than you think if trees are overhead. On the other hand, the sun will be higher in the summer, casting more light.

A List of What You'll Need

Here's a list of what you will need to measure your garden, most of which you should be able to find around your house.

➤ Tape measure   ➤ Pencil

➤ Yardstick   ➤ Hammer

➤ String   ➤ Stakes (or flour or ground limestone)

➤ Notebook   ➤ Rope or hose

For an Island Bed

Because an island bed is all curves with no straight sides, you'll want to make the curves by using stakes, each measuring the same distance from a center stake, or by a hose or rope laid out on the ground in the desired shape.

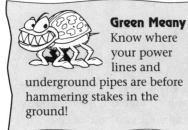

Green Meany
Know where your power lines and underground pipes are before hammering stakes in the ground!

First, place a stake in the middle of the plot. Starting with the long sides of the garden, measure one-half of a foot on either side of the center stake (in the direction of the narrow sides of the garden). Place a string around each of the side stakes and walk out 5 feet, the string in hand. Hammer in a stake at the 5-foot point. Do this in the opposite direction; this will give you the oval curve you desire.

Now for the shorter or narrower sides of the garden. Place the string on the center stake and walk out 3 feet from the center stake and mark again with a new stake. Repeat for the other side.

Now you have nine stakes in the ground: a center stake with two on either side, and six outside stakes. Take the rope or hose and butt it along the outside stakes to form an oblong shape. This garden will measure 6 × 10 feet.

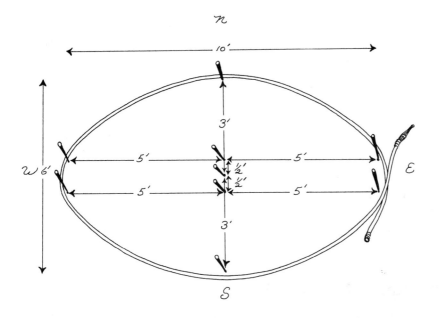

An island bed.

For a Border Garden

A border garden will border a wall, house, fence, or tree line. The back of this garden is straight, and the front can be straight or curved. One simple guideline to follow: The garden should be at least 2 feet wide and the length should be at least 2 feet longer than the width. A 6-foot long border should be 2 to 4 feet deep—any wider and the garden will look like a square plopped in the yard. For most borders, you'll work with what you have, like creating a garden in a nook where the house extends out on either side, or along a drive or walkway.

To measure out a border garden, start by measuring the straight line. Place stakes at both ends—the border for this illustration will be 10 feet long—and one in the middle (5 feet from either end). If your garden will have a straight line in the front, measure your desired width from each stake, placing a new stake for the front marker. If you want curves in front, measure the distance from the center, in this case, 5 feet, and place stakes

193

halfway between the ends (2½ feet from either end). To make the curves in the front, measure out 2 feet on the ends, 3 feet wide from the center/front of the bed stake, and 4 feet wide from the two stakes measuring 2½ feet from either end. Again, a hose or rope will help you see the outline of the bed.

A curved bed.

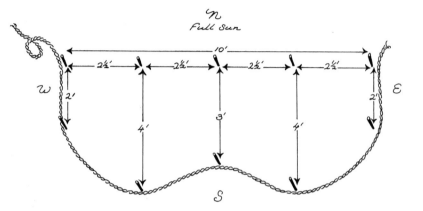

Now, with hammer and stakes in hand, or with flour or limestone, draw the outline of the garden. Using stakes is easier—you can move them if you change your mind, whereas with flour or lime you have to sweep it away before making new lines. You can also use a watering hose or rope to create curved lines.

For a Garden Against a House

If you're planning a garden against a house, take the same steps as you did in measuring for a border as indicated above, but consider outside features like windows and doors.

*A bed against
a house.*

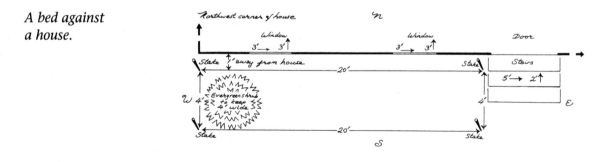

Measure at least a foot away from the house and hammer in a stake at each end of the garden. Always plan and plant at least one foot from a house in case you later need to work on the house, and to allow plants in foundation plantings the proper amount of air circulation, sun, and water.

Measure out the width of the garden plot, using the same method as the other plots. Measure any windows—height and width—and record the dimensions of the width with an arrow pointing horizontally. The height of the window is also important so you can plan for the correct height of a plant. Measure height from the ground to the base of the window and record measurements with an arrow pointing vertically. Any existing trees or shrubs that you will keep in the plan should also be measured and recorded.

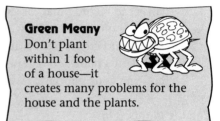

Green Meany
Don't plant within 1 foot of a house—it creates many problems for the house and the plants.

Putting Your Plans on Paper

Now that you have your measurements, you need to transfer them to your notebook in order to draw a plan for your garden. Your photographs will come in handy now.

You'll need the following things to make your plan:

➤ Your notebook with the list of plants you like

➤ Pencil (and colored pencils)

➤ Ruler

➤ Graph paper (or make the lines yourself)

➤ Plant lists

➤ Photographs of the area plot

Take your notebook into the garden and do the following:

➤ Draw a rough sketch of the shape of the garden as it is staked out.

➤ Label north, south, east, and west.

➤ Write down the dimensions of the garden—length and width and the positions of all the stakes.

➤ Note the date, time of day, and whether the garden is in sun or shade.

➤ Note any trees or shrubs in or next to the garden plot as well as any building structures.

Making a Map

Your first step to making a map is to make a legend. All maps have legends, and your map needs one, too. Use the lower-right corner of your plan for the scale you are using. You may, for example, want to use a simple scale such as this: $1/2" = 1'$. Use the upper-right corner to record polar directions (north, south, east, west). Use the lower-left corner to indicate symbols: circles with dots to symbolize trees, for example; an *x* can indicate the stakes; and circles with a number inside to symbolize plants. The legend should indicate the plant's name, color, and time of bloom. Refer to the diagram below for some tips on creating your symbols.

Placing plants: This chart was drawn for a perennial border shade garden.

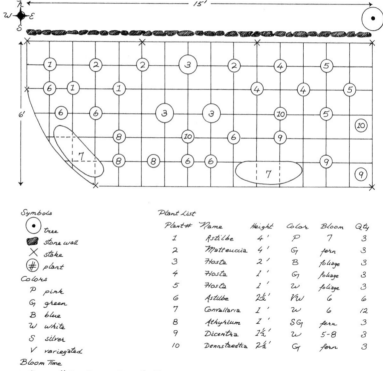

First, draw the line that is straight (if there is one), noting the dimensions on either end. Use your ruler to keep your lines straight. Take into account windows, doors, and existing trees and shrubs. Next, indicate on the paper all the stakes with an *X* and carefully draw the shape of the garden's outline.

Study your plan. Have you forgotten anything? A shrub, a window, or a huge rock in the middle of the garden? Look it over carefully, and add anything you might have forgotten.

Annuals

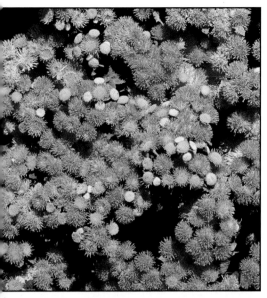

Ageratum/Ageratum

Antirrhinum/Snapdragon

Cleome spinosa/Spider Flower

Centaurea/Bachelor's Button

Annuals

Cosmos/Cosmos

Helianthus/Sunflower

Lobelia/Trailing Lobelia

Nicotania/Flowering Tobacco

Annuals

Nigella/Love-in-a-Mist

Portulaca/Portulaca

Petunia/Petunia

Papaver/Poppy

Annuals

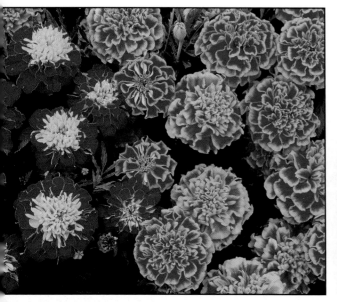

Tagetes/Marigold

Tropaeolum/Nasturtium

Verbena/Verbena

Zinnia/Zinnia

Perennials

Althaea/Hollyhock

Coreopsis/Tickseed

Campanula/Bellflower

Astilbe/Garden Spires

Perennials

Echinacea/Coneflower

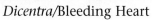

Dicentra/Bleeding Heart

Hemerocallis/Daylily

Hosta/Plantain Lily

Perennials

Iris/Iris

Nepeta/Catmint

Paeonia cultivars/Peony

Perovskia/Russian Sage

Perennials

Phlox/Phlox

Rudbeckia/Black-eyed Susan

Salvia/Sage

Sedum/Stonecrop

Shrubs

Berberis thurnbergii/Japanese Burberry

Buddleia davidii/Butterfly Bush

Caryopteris x clandonensis/Hybrid Bluebeard

Camellia japonica/Camellia

Shrubs

Clethra alnifolia/Summersweet

Cotoneaster horizontalis/
Rock Cotoneaster

Cornus/Dogwood

Cytisus scoparius/Scottish Broom

Shrubs

Rosa/Rose

Potentilla fruiticosa/Bush Cinquefoil

Viburnum/Viburnum

Syringa meyeri/Meyer Lilac

Vines

Clematis sp./Clematis

Hydrangea anomala subsp. *Petiolaris/*
Climbing Hydrangea

Ipomoea purpurea/Morning Glory

Wisteria sp./Wisteria

Herbs

Allium schoenoprasum/Chives

Anethum graveolens/Dill

Ocimum basilicum/Basil

Rosemarinus officinalis/Rosemary

Bulbs

Anemone/Wind Flower

Begonia/Begonia

Dahlia/Dahlia

Gladiolus/Gladiolus

Bulbs

Hyacinth/Hyacinth

Lilium/Lily

Narcissus/Narcissus, Daffodil

Tulipa/Tulip

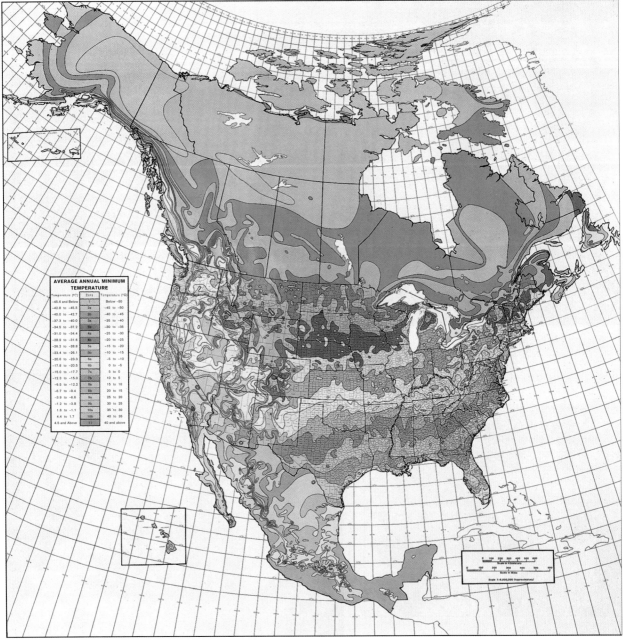

USDA Plant Hardiness Zone Map

Choosing Plants

Now it's time to think about the plants you want for your garden. If you've already made a list of all the ones that appeal to you, great.

You can also look through gardening catalogs, or just look back through the list of plants in this book. Pick out the plants you want for your garden, being careful about selecting perennials and shrubs hardy in your zone. Always check the plant's zone for hardiness in your area before you do anything else.

Consider Color and Time of Bloom

You'll be drawn to plants for many reasons, but probably the most for color. Remember to keep to one, two, or three colors in your design to create unity in your garden. Also, it's nice to use white as your neutral color—if you're unsure whether colors go with one another, put the white flowering plant in between them.

Time of bloom is also a consideration for all perennials and some shrubs. Choose plants that will bloom when you'll most appreciate them.

Consider Height, Unity, and Flow

In general, place tall plants in the back, shorter ones in the front for borders, and tall plants in the center in island beds. But there is no hard and fast rule to this. Some taller plants toward the front can give nice definition to a garden. If you don't like a perennial in a particular spot, you can always move it.

Unity is created when you repeat varieties—tying a garden together by creating patterns. Flow is created when a particular plant is woven throughout the garden, giving a sense of balance.

Consider 3's, 5's, and Accents

Plant in groupings of odd numbers, 3's and 5's, or use one plant as an accent. An accent could be a single plant used to make a statement in a garden. For example, buddleia is used as an accent plant in the Butterfly Garden described in Chapter 14.

Drawing the Plan

Use colored pencils. The more colored pencils you have, the more precise you can be. But remember that flowers bloom at different times, so don't let the colors on the plan fool you into thinking that everything will be in bloom at the same time!

Spacing the Plants

Every plant has an average growing diameter, and spacing is necessary to give each plant its proper space—not too close to other plants or objects (or they will be weak and spindly); nor too far apart (or the garden won't look full for years). They need enough space for light, water, and nutrients to grow into healthy plants.

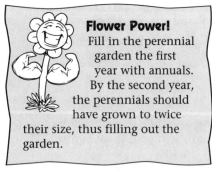

Flower Power!
Fill in the perennial garden the first year with annuals. By the second year, the perennials should have grown to twice their size, thus filling out the garden.

An average spacing distance in perennials is 1 to 2 feet. The general rule of thumb for spacing distance is half of the spread—a plant that spreads to 4 feet will need 2-foot spacing. Annuals, however, will not need as much space because they are only in the ground for one year, so they don't need the extra growing room.

Tips on Spacing Shrubs

Shrubs need to be carefully spaced. You'll be sorry if you have to replant five years down the road because you didn't leave enough space the first time. Nicely spaced shrubs look neater and are easier to get around to deadhead or prune. Give shrubs more room than less. Shrubs planted too close when young will tend to get tall and leggy.

Flower Power!
If you have extra perennials or annuals, pot them up for container gardens.

Knowing the Number of Plants to Buy

Planning your garden on paper saves time and money in the long run. It's much easier to work with a plan—you know the size of your garden and how many plants you will need. Marking it out foot by foot will give exact measurements so that your spacing will be correct.

The Least You Need to Know

➤ Take a few photographs of the area where you intend to put your garden.

➤ A simple guideline to a border garden: It should be at least 2 feet wide and the length should be at least 2 feet longer than the width.

➤ Every plant has an average growing diameter and needs proper spacing.

Chapter 14

Easy Garden Plans

In This Chapter

➤ Specialized gardens: what they are

➤ Descriptions and diagrams of 14 specialized gardens

➤ List of plants for each garden

➤ Alternative lists of plants for each specialized garden

In the last chapter, you learned how to measure your planned garden and transfer those measurements to paper. Now, you have all the tools and information to create a garden of your own.

And to make creating your own garden even easier, we have 14 different predesigned garden plans you can just follow! Or, if you'd like, you can make slight adjustments here and there depending on your preferences and site conditions. One of these garden plans is bound to be the right first garden for you.

Specialized Gardens: What They Are, What to Do with Them

The gardens we've designed for you in this chapter are referred to as "specialized" or "theme gardens." Each garden has a specific goal in mind—whether that is coloring up a wetlands area with a bog garden, creating a peaceful woodlands garden, or finding plants adaptable to sandy conditions. You may even want a garden to create a particular mood, such as the feeling that's created by a twilight garden.

What's Your Pleasure: Choosing Your Garden

Each specialized garden includes a description of that garden, the garden plan, and a list of the plants included in the plan.

While each of the plans have specific plants named for each design, feel free to substitute if you can't find exactly the same plant. The plant you use as a substitute should be in the same genus, but it may be a different height or color. At any rate, don't feel hemmed in. These plans are supposed to make gardening easier, not harder.

Here's a list of the types of gardens we'll discuss in this chapter:

Annuals for Sun Garden Plan	*Meadow Garden Plan*
Annuals for Dried Flowers Garden Plan	*Perennial Border (Sun) Garden Plan*
Annuals that Self-Sow Garden Plan	*Rock Garden Plan*
Bog or Wetlands Garden Plan	*Sandy Soil—Border Garden Plan*
Butterfly Garden Plan	*Shrubs for Screen in Sun Plan*
Cut-Flower Garden Plan	*Twilight or Moon Garden Plan*
Herb Garden Plan	*Woodland Garden Plan*

Annuals for Sun Garden

Gardens with annual flowers are somewhat easier to maintain than any other kind of garden. When you're working with annuals in a sunny location, you can choose among an enormous variety of annuals that love the sun, and they are trouble-free plants that are perfect for a beginner gardener.

The Advantages to Planting an Annual Bed

The biggest advantage is that annuals bloom all season long. Another nice thing about annuals is that you can try a new garden the following year using an entirely different color scheme.

Annuals for Sun Garden Plan (3 x 9)

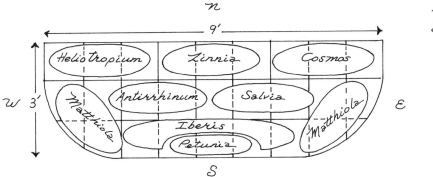

Annuals for sun garden.

Plant List

The annuals for this garden are usually available as small plants in "six-packs." These packs have six plant cuttings in them, and the individual cups protect the roots. If your garden center has six-packs, great, if not, you'll probably get "seedling flats," which will work just fine.

Quantity	Name	Height	Color
1 six-pack	Antirrhinum	20–36"	pink mix
1 six-pack	Cosmos	30–60"	white
1 six-pack	Heliotrope	24"	purple
1 six-pack	Iberis	18"	white
1 six-pack	Matthiola	12–30"	lavender
1 six-pack	Petunia	6–24"	purples
1 six-pack	Salvia	24–36"	blues
1 six-pack	Zinnia	24–36"	rose mix

Annuals for Dried-Flower Garden

When you have a dried-flower garden, you'll always have plenty of flowers for dried flower arrangements and wreaths.

201

Garden Design Plan for Annuals for Dried-Flowers (4 x 8)

Annuals for dried-flower garden.

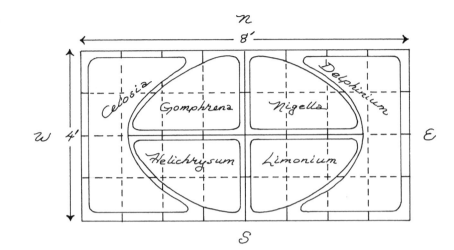

Plant List

Quantity	Name	Height	Color
2 six-packs	Celosia	12–42"	red
2 six-packs	Delphinium	12–36"	blues
2 six-packs	Gomphrena	18"	red
2 six-packs	Helichrysum	12–30"	mixed
2 six-packs	Limonium	24"	mixed
2 six-packs	Nigella	18–24"	mixed

Self-Sowing Annuals Garden

The first year, your self-sowing annuals garden will have plants where you planted them, but in later years your seedlings will be scattered about the garden, sowing themselves where the wind and birds take them.

Garden Design Plan for Self-Sowing Annuals (5 x 10)

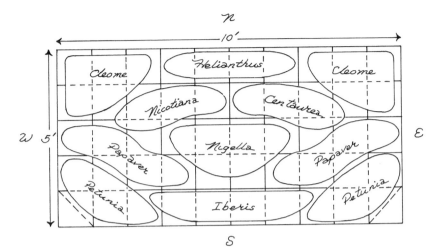

Self-sowing annuals garden.

Plant List

Quantity	Name	Height	Color
1 six-pack	Centaurea	1–3'	blue
2 six-packs	Cleome	3–5'	pink, purple
1 seed	Helianthus	5–6'	yellow
2 six-packs	Iberis	18"	white
1 six-pack	Nicotiana	18–24"	white
1 seed	Nigella	18–24"	pink
2 seeds	Papaver	12–24"	pinks
3 six-packs	Petunia	6–24"	purples

Bog or Wetlands Garden

Bogs and wetlands are low-lying parts of land surrounding ponds or streams. The soil in these areas generally stays damp for long periods of time. Gardens for these areas require plants that have adapted to living in wet and often partial shade conditions. Since bogs and wetlands usually don't carry much color, by creating a bog garden you can bring unexpected color and texture to these areas.

Luckily, many of the plants suitable to very wet areas are also very easy to grow. For instance, certain irises, like flag iris (*I. versicolor*), are wonderful by a pond. When you plant around ponds and streams, remember that the water table moves up and down, and that the level of water is usually highest in the spring. The design for this garden is one you can repeat.

Bog or Wetlands Garden Plan (6 x 10)

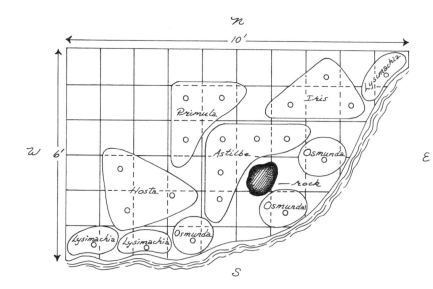

Bog or wetlands garden.

Plant List

Quantity	Name	Height	Color	Bloom Time
5 plants	Astilbe	18"–4'	white, pink	June/July
3 plants	Osmunda	2–5'	fern foliage	N/A
3 plants	Hosta	1–3'	white, blue	July/Aug
3 plants	Iris versicolor	3–4'	blue	June/July
3 plants	Lysimachia	2–3'	yellow, white	June/Sept
3 plants	Primula	6"–2'	many	April/Jun

Butterfly Garden

There are many plants that attract butterflies because of their colors or the nectar from the flowers. One of the best plants for attracting butterflies is buddleia, which is also called "butterfly bush." Often flowers that attract butterflies also attract hummingbirds, as well as little hummingbird moths. Butterfly gardens are great fun for children.

Garden Design Plan for Butterfly Garden (7 x 15)

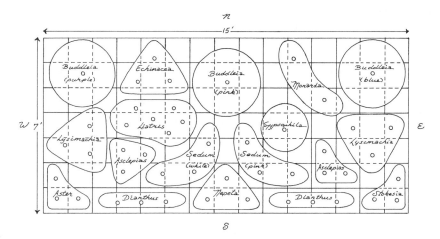

Butterfly garden.

Plant List

Quantity	Name	Height	Color	Bloom Time
6 plants	Asclepias	$2\frac{1}{2}'$	red	Jun/Sept
3 plants	Aster x frikartii	2'	blue	Jun/Aug
1 shrub	Buddleia	4'	purple	Jun/Sept
1 shrub	Buddleia	4'	pink	Jun/Sept
1 shrub	Buddleia	4'	blue	Jun/Sept
6 plants	Dianthus	1'	pink	Jun/Sept
3 plants	Echinacea	3'	pink	Jun/Sept
1 plant	Gypsophila	3'	white	Jun/Aug
6 plants	Liatris	3'	purple	Jul/Sept
6 plants	Lysimachia	2–3'	white	Jun/Aug
2 plants	Monarda	3–4'	scarlet	Jul/Aug
3 plants	Nepeta	2'	blue	Jun/Aug
3 plants	Sedum	2'	pink	Aug/Oct
3 plants	Sedum	$1\frac{1}{2}'$	white	Aug/Sept
3 plants	Stokesia	$1\frac{1}{2}'$	blue	Jul/Sept

Cut-Flower Garden

Since this garden is dedicated to providing fresh cut flowers, the cut-flower garden usually consists of plants that carry themselves on long stems and last a long time in water. Flowers with interesting shapes also make wonderful cut flowers.

Flower Power!
Bring a bucket of water out with you to the cutting garden and place flowers you cut into the water. They'll last longer.

When you choose your color scheme, keep in mind the color scheme in your house so your flower arrangements always complement it. Or, if you tend to throw a big party every Fourth of July, make your garden's color scheme red, white, and blue.

You should always cut flowers from the garden in the early morning or evenings, avoiding the heat of midday—this can cause the flowers to wilt. Set your flowers in fresh, clean water for an hour, then make a new cut before you arrange them in a vase. Be sure to check the water daily.

Garden Design Plan for Cut-Flower Garden (6 x 10 Oval)

Cut-flower garden.

Plant List

Quantity	Name	Height	Color	Bloom Time
3 plants	Achillea	2–3'	white	Jun/Sept
3 plants	Alchemilla	1–1$\frac{1}{2}$'	yellow	Jun/Aug
3 plants	Aster novi-belgii	2–3'	red	Aug/Sept
3 plants	Campanula carpatica	$\frac{1}{2}$'	blue	May/Aug
3 plants	Chrysanthemum x superbum	2–2$\frac{1}{2}$'	white	Jun/Aug
3 plants	Chrysanthemum (fall bloom)	2–3'	yellow	Jul/Aug
3 corms	Crocosmia	3–4'	red	Aug
3 plants	Gaillardia	1–1$\frac{1}{2}$'	yellow	Jun/Sept
1 plant	Gypsophila	3'	white	Jun/Aug
2 plants	Heliopsis	3$\frac{1}{2}$–4'	yellow	Jul/Sept
3 plants	Heuchera	1–2'	red	May/Aug
3 plants	Lysimachia	2–3'	white	Jun/Sept
1 plant	Monarda	2$\frac{1}{2}$–4'	red	Jul/Aug
3 plants	Platycodon	1$\frac{1}{2}$–3'	blue	Jun/Sept
3 plants	Salvia	2–3'	blue	June/Aug
3 plants	Veronica	$\frac{1}{2}$–2'	blue	May/Sept

Herb Garden

Herb gardens are one of the easiest gardens to grow. In fact, most herbs grow just like weeds, so if you're not careful, your carefully laid out garden may look like a messy jumble.

Most herbs are used for their foliage and, if allowed to flower, may become leggy or self-sow all over the garden. The best thing you can do is use the herbs—a lot! You might as well, since you must keep cutting back or pinching the plants to maintain them.

Herbs are perennials or annuals. Give them plenty of sun and bring them indoors in the fall for fresh herbs throughout the winter.

Garden Design Plan for an Herb Garden (6 x 8)

Herb garden.

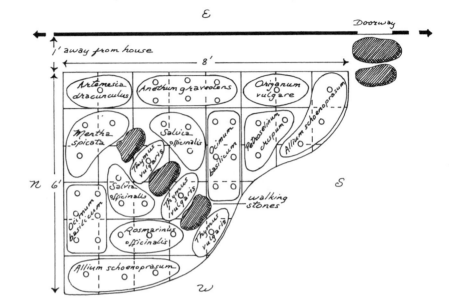

Plant List

The perennial herbs should be bought as plants and the annuals should be purchased as six-packs of seedlings.

Quantity	Name	Height	Color
1 six-pack	Anethum graveolens	2–3'	yellowish
6 plants	Allium schoenoprasum	1'	pink
1 plant	Artemesia dracunculus	2–3'	foliage
2 plants	Mentha spicata	$2^1/_2$'	white
2 six-packs	Ocimum basilicum	2'	foliage
1 plant	Origanum vulgare	2–3'	pinkish
1 six-pack	Petroselinum crispum	2–3'	foliage
3 plants	Rosmarinus officinalis	2–4'	blue
1 six-pack	Salvia officinalis	$2^1/_2$'	foliage
3 plants	Thymus vulgaris	1'	rose

Meadow Garden

Meadow gardens are made up of plants that naturalize by throwing their seeds into the soil or by having such strong root systems they can fight for a place in the meadow.

Meadows have flowers that bend and wave with the wind, and while a good deal of meadow plants have daisylike flowers, there are other nice flowers that have different shapes.

Garden Design Plan for a Meadow Garden (4 x 10)

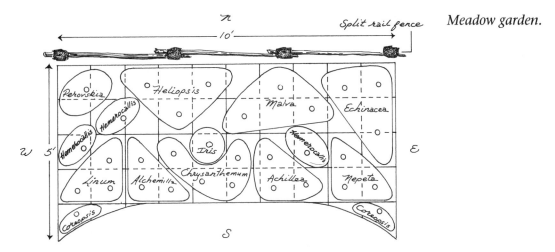

Meadow garden.

Plant List

Quantity	Name	Height	Color	Bloom Time
3 plants	Achillea	2 ¹/₂'	pink	Jun/Sept
3 plants	Alchemilla	1 ¹/₂'	yellow	Jun/Aug
4 plants	Chrysanthemum	2'	white	Jun/Aug
2 plants	Coreopsis	2'	yellow	Jun/Aug
3 plants	Echinacea	3–4'	white	Jun/Oct
3 plants	Heliopsis	4'	yellow	Jul/Sept
3 plants	Malva	3'	pink	Jul/Sept
3 plants	Nepeta	1–2'	blue	Jun/Sept
1 plant	Perovskia	4–5'	blue	Jul/Sept
3 plants	Hemerocallis	3'	yellow	Jun/Jul
1 plant	Iris siberica	3'	blue	Jun/Aug
3 plants	Linum	1–2'	blue	Jun/Sept

Perennial Border for Sun

Whether you have a perennial garden for sun or shade will depend on the available sunlight in your garden. A garden design for a perennial garden in shade was included in the last chapter, and below is a design for a garden in sun.

Border gardens typically have a backdrop, whether that backdrop is a concrete wall, a hedge of evergreens, shrubs, or a fence. Remember that whatever backdrop you choose, it will influence how you see the flowers. All colors look differently when placed against different backdrops.

Garden Design Plan for Perennial Border/Sunny (6 x 15)

Perennial border garden/sunny.

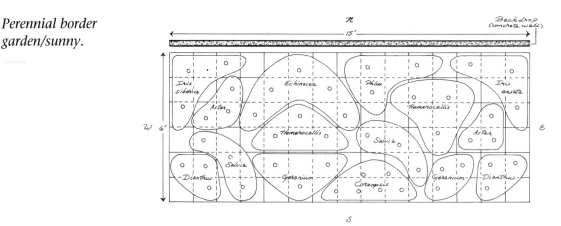

Plant List

Quantity	Name	Height	Color	Bloom Time
6 plants	Aster x frikartii	$2^1/_2'$	blue	Sept
6 plants	Coreopsis vert.	$1^1/_2'$	yellow	Jun/Sept
6 plants	Dianthus	1'	pink	Jun/Sept
5 plants	Echinacea	2–3'	white	Jun/Oct
6 plants	Geranium	1'	pink	May/Aug
6 plants	Hemerocallis	3–4'	yellow	Jul/Aug
3 plants	Iris siberica	3'	blue	May/Jun
3 plants	Iris ensata	3'	purple	Jun/Jul
3 plants	Phlox	3'	pink	Jul/Aug
6 plants	Salvia	2–3'	blue	Jun/Aug

Rock Garden

Rock gardens are usually filled with low-growing perennials that spread and creep along the ground. Some rock garden plants are rare and can be quite tricky, but the plants listed in this text are easy to grow.

There usually isn't enough soil in the ground where you plant rock gardens, so you'll want to add some soil before you plant. You may also want to play around with the rocks in the garden—raising and lowering them and maybe even adding more rocks—to get the design you want. A rock garden is fine in either sun or shade.

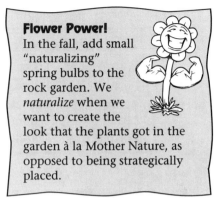

Flower Power!
In the fall, add small "naturalizing" spring bulbs to the rock garden. We *naturalize* when we want to create the look that the plants got in the garden à la Mother Nature, as opposed to being strategically placed.

Garden Design Plan for Rock Garden (4 x 10)

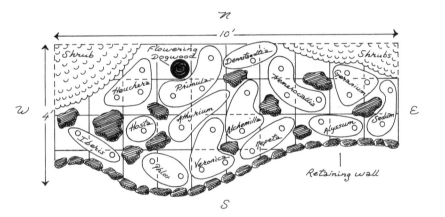

Rock garden.

Plant List

Quantity	Name	Height	Color	Bloom Time
2 plants	Alchemilla	$1^1/_2'$	yellow	June/Aug
2 plants	Alyssum	1'	yellow	May/June
2 plants	Athyrium	1–2'	foliage	N/A
1 plant	Dennstaedtia	$2^1/_2'$	foliage	N/A
3 plants	Geranium	1'	pink	May/Aug
3 plants	Hemerocallis	2'	yellow	May/Sept
3 plants	Heuchera	2'	red	May/Aug
1 plant	Hosta	1'	white	August
2 plants	Iberis	1'	white	May/June

continues

continued

Quantity	Name	Height	Color	Bloom Time
2 plants	Nepeta	2'	blue	June/Sept
2 plants	Phlox subulata	1'	white	April/May
3 plants	Primula	1'	blue	April/May
2 plants	Sedum	$1/4$'	pink	July/Aug
3 plants	Veronica	$1/2$'	blue	July/Aug

Seashore/Sandy Soil Garden

Creating a garden where the wind, sandy soil, and hot sun all seem to be working against you seems like a risky proposition. However, there are advantages to gardening in these conditions. First, the wind alleviates some of the diseases plants get. Second, the sandy soil can be a very good thing for plants, since roots have an easier time spreading in sandy soil. And third, there is a wide variety of sun-loving plants to choose from.

> **Flower Power!**
> Plants suitable for sandy soils often have clues in their foliage: They will have coarse or hairy, silver or blue, or succulent foliage.

Gardens in seashore or sandy soils need to have a peat moss/manure mix in the soil to help the soil retain moisture. Be sure to check the young plants every sunny day, and water them. You can begin to cut back on watering when the plants are about a foot high. This will help them to develop a deep root system so they can survive on their own. You'll find that annuals will need more water than perennials or shrubs. If you get hit with a drought, try to soak the plants during the cool parts of the day.

Garden Design for a Sandy Soil Garden (4 x 10)

Sandy soil garden.

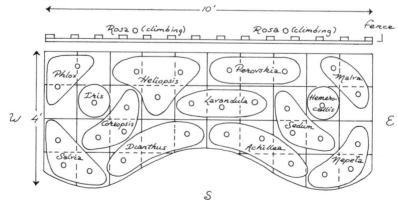

Plant List

Quantity	Name	Height	Color	Bloom Time
3 plants	Achillea	3'	white	Jun/Aug
3 plants	Coreopsis	2'	yellow	Jun/Sept
3 plants	Dianthus	$1/2$"–1'	pink	Jun/Sept
3 plants	Heliopsis	$3^1/_2$–4'	yellow	Jul/Sept
1 plant	Hemerocallis	3–4'	yellow	Jul/Sept
1 plant	Iris (German)	3'	blue	May/June
3 plants	Lavender	2–3'	blue	June/Aug
2 plants	Malva	$2^1/_2$–3'	pink	Jul/Sept
3 plants	Nepeta	1–3'	blue	Jun/Sept
2 plants	Perovskia	3–5'	blue	Jul/Sept
2 plants	Phlox	3–4'	pink	Aug/Sept
2 plants	Rosa (climbing)	10'	pink	Jun/Jul
3 plants	Salvia	2–3'	blue	Jun/Aug
3 plants	Sedum	2'	pink	Jul/Aug

Shrub Garden

Shrub gardens are great low-maintenance gardens. While the majority of shrubs flower in the spring, with careful planning you can have flowers throughout the growing season.

Shrubs' flowers are just one of their many attractions. Some have fruits, while others have interesting foliage and bark textures. In the fall, many shrubs have spectacular coloration. They also come in all kinds of shapes and habits, from round mounds to tall, graceful weeping forms.

Flower Power!
When planting shrubs around the house, keep in mind the height of the windows so you don't block your views from the inside.

Because shrub gardens require more space than other gardens, you'll want to be sure you have enough room for them. While you won't have tall trees in shrub gardens, often a small tree, no more than 15 feet tall, looks nice.

Shrubs for Screens

Many people think screens should be evergreen, assuming that only evergreens will cut down on noise and be fully effective. However, very twiggy shrubs can also slow down noise waves, so don't leave them out of your screen design.

Garden Design Plan for a Shrub Garden in Sun (15 x 18)

Shrub garden.

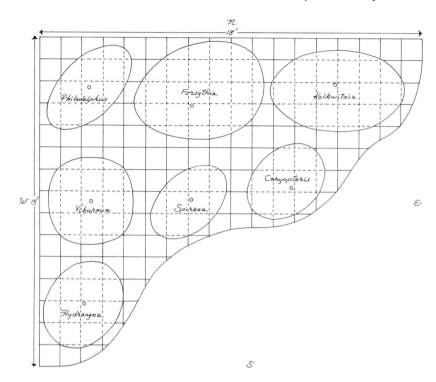

Plant List

Quantity	Name	Height	Color	Bloom Time
1 plant	Caryopteris	4'	blue	fall
1 plant	Forsythia	10'	yellow	spring
1 plant	Hydrangea arborescens	3–5'	white	fall
1 plant	Kolkwitzia	6–10'	pink	summer
1 plant	Philadelphus	10–12'	white	summer
1 plant	Spiraea x bumalda	3–5'	pink	summer
1 plant	Viburnum carlesii	5'	white	spring

Twilight or Moon Garden

A moon garden is made up of all white colors, coming alive during the night when the moon is out so the garden radiates with the pale colors. It's a very romantic garden—just right for placing where you can see it from an indoor window, like a bedroom window. Most white-flowering plants tend to open their flowers during the cool of the evenings and stay open through cool early mornings. The heat of the day can cause some flowers to close, but not all, so your garden can still be appealing in the day.

> **Flower Power!**
> Add annuals with white flowers for the first year when the garden is young and not yet filled in. Dapple them in for the full effect.

Garden Design Plan for Twilight Garden (6 x 15)

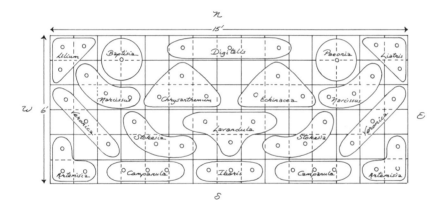

Twilight garden.

Plant List

Quantity	Name	Height	Bloom Time
6 plants	Artemisia 'Silver Mound'	1'	Jul/Sept
1 plant	Baptisia	3–4'	June
6 plants	Campanula carp. 'Alba'	1'	Jun/Jul
3 plants	Chrysanthemum (Shasta)	3'	Jun/July
3 plants	Digitalis purp. 'Alba'	3'	May/July
3 plants	Echinacea purp. 'Alba'	3–4'	Jun/Oct
3 plants	Iberis	1'	May/Jun
3 plants	Lavendula a. 'Alba'	2'	Jun/Aug
3 plants	Liatris	3'	Jul/Sept

continues

continued

Quantity	Name	Height	Bloom Time
3 bulbs	Lilium (any white)	3–4'	July
6 bulbs	Narcissus (any white)	18"	May
1 tuber	Paeonia (any white)	3'	June
6 plants	Stokesia	18"	Jul/Sept
6 plants	Veronica	18"	Jun/Aug

Woodland Garden

Woodland gardens are usually located either in the woods or along a side of the woods, incorporating the woods into the garden, but they certainly don't have to be. If you aren't close to a woods but want a woodlands garden, work with what you do have—a few existing trees, perhaps—to create this restful garden. Either way, creating a woodland garden is work. You may have to add soil and clear out certain trees or underbrush to allow more light, but it will be worth it. These gardens are some of the most peaceful places on earth.

Gardens in shade, like a woodland garden, have a different look to them and depend on other elements to make them work. The various shades of green foliage, for instance, are a big factor. The foliage can be *variegated*, which means the leaves have color in them—red, yellow, or white streaks or spots—or it can be anywhere from a bluish-green shade to a vibrant green. The shapes of the leaves can be quite interesting: big and bold or small and fernlike. The Hosta genus is huge and is known for the wonderful bold leaves the plants have. Hostas are perfect for shade. Where a sunny garden may be brilliant with colors, a shade garden uses the subtle interplay of textures and shadings to make the garden come alive.

Flower Power!
Plant lots of spring-blooming daffodil and blue squill bulbs during the fall in woodland gardens, where they naturalize so well.

Garden Design Plan for Woodland Garden (4 x 10)

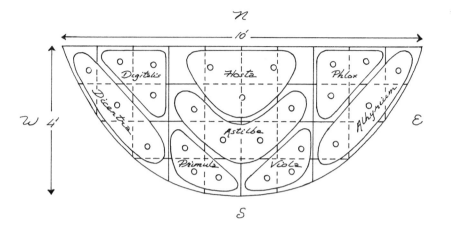

Woodland garden.

Plant List

Quantity	Name	Height	Color	Bloom Time
4 plants	Astilbe	2–2$^{1}/_{2}$'	pink	Jun/July
3 plants	Dicentra exima	1–2'	white	Jun/Sept
3 plants	Digitalis ambigua	1$^{1}/_{2}$–2'	yellow	May/July
3 plants	Athryium-Fern	1–2'	foliage	N/A
3 plants	Hosta	2–3'	blue	Aug/Sept
3 plants	Phlox divaricata	1$^{1}/_{2}$'	blue	May/June
3 plants	Primula denticulata	1'	white	May/June
3 plants	Viola odorata	$^{1}/_{2}$'	white	May/July

The Least You Need to Know

➤ Don't be afraid to substitute plants when you can't find the one listed in the plan. Look for another in the same genus with a different color, height, even bloom time.

➤ Annual gardens always benefit from cutting back and deadheading. The plants will produce more flowers.

➤ When you're creating rock and woodland gardens, you'll probably have to add more soil.

➤ Where a sunny garden may be brilliant with colors, a shade garden uses the subtle interplay of textures and shadings to make the garden come alive.

Part 5
Shopping Sprees!

If you like to shop, this part's for you! We'll give you a list of the "must haves"—a spade, spading fork, hoe, trowel, pruning shears, and hat—as well as a list of some purchases you may want to make later. Brightly colored plastic clogs may seem extravagant today, but you'll be grateful to have them in the early spring when the ground is pure mud!

We'll show you what to look for in tools in terms of quality, and which tools perform which tasks. There are tools for every task in the garden (such as watering, weeding, and pruning) and you'll want to be prepared.

Tool Time

You may have no real gardening tools to speak of. And you probably have struggled at one time or another with inadequate tools, like a square shovel, when what you really needed was a good-quality spade.

It's now important that you invest in some authentic gardening tools and avoid any unnecessary efforts that may make gardening uncomfortable. This should be enjoyable! This chapter will list some of the essential tools for gardening and show you what to look for in terms of quality.

Even if you only want the bare necessities, you still should know the difference between a tool that will only last a year and a tool built to last a lifetime. Knowing what to look for when you shop for tools, and investing in good quality items, will save you money in the long run.

If you like to shop, this chapter's the one you've been waiting for. Go wild and get all the wonderful new garden paraphernalia on the market—perhaps a few pairs of brightly colored gardening clogs. We'll list everything you need—from aprons to wheelbarrows.

What to Look for in Tools

Gardening tools, like everything else in life, run the gamut from well-constructed and good quality to poor and very, very poor quality. The Rolls Royce of wheelbarrows, one with a heavy-duty steel undercarriage, may seem pricey compared to the pretty plastic one that's lightweight—but consider how long you'll have the wheelbarrow and under what conditions (rain, sun, sleet, snow and filled with debris, mulches, rocks, tools, etc.). Now how attractive is the plastic one with the cheap price tag? And which one is likely to tip over?

Here you'll learn how to identify quality tools and to get an idea of what tools you need.

Quality Counts

A good-quality gardening spade can last you more than 25 years, and it's worth it. The tools you buy should be solidly constructed, noting the following:

Green Meany
Beware of tools with loose joints. Loose joints are a sign of inferior craftsmanship!

➤ Buy only steel-tempered tools or heat-treated. These tools will last the longest.

➤ Buy heavy-gauged stainless steel. Stainless steel won't rust if you accidentally leave it out in the rain.

➤ Buy tools with comfortable weights. Pick it up and hold it—make sure it's not too heavy for you.

➤ Check the wood on the tool's handle. Don't buy tools with knots or splinters in the wood.

Care for Your Tools

Buy good tools and you'll treat them well. Make it a point to always bring your tools in from outside when you aren't using them, and keep them in one location so they're always there when you need them. Periodically sharpen cutting and pruning tools.

The Essentials

These are the "must haves," organized by number— according to their use in the garden.

The "Must-Have" Tools for Preparing the Bed and Planting in the Bed

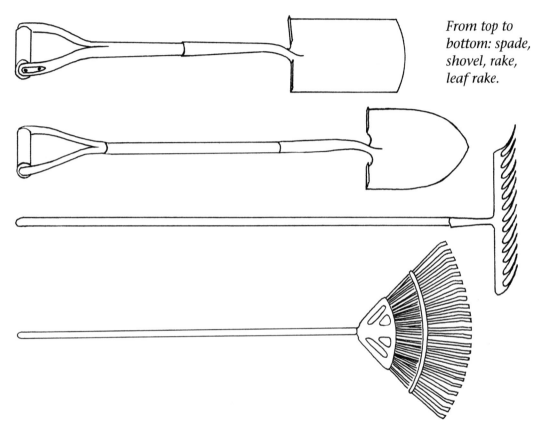

From top to bottom: spade, shovel, rake, leaf rake.

1. A flat-edged spade with a long or short handle

2. A hoe that's either long-handled or hand-held

3. A rake for the lawn or a level-headed rake for grading

4. A spading fork with a long or short handle (if you have problems bending, choose long-handled tools)

5. A shovel, round tipped or pointed, with a long or short handle for moving materials

6. A hand-held tool called a "trowel," which has a small, pointed blade for digging holes

223

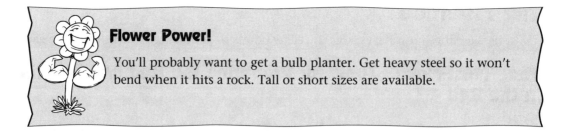

Flower Power!

You'll probably want to get a bulb planter. Get heavy steel so it won't bend when it hits a rock. Tall or short sizes are available.

The "Must-Have" Tools for Watering

1. A garden hose (get one that's durable and in a size that's right for you—25, 50, 75, or 100 feet)

Flower Power!

For gardeners above the frost line, be sure to drain water from hoses and store them indoors for the winter.

2. A nozzle for the hose (a good nozzle is essential for spraying unwanted bugs off plants)

3. A few plastic watering cans are necessities—just get the cheapest and save the money for quality tools

4. And for later: a soaker hose, which has holes in it, allowing the water to be distributed evenly and deeply; a sprinkler to attach to the end of a hose; and an in-ground sprinkler system—all "must haves" in certain parts of the country and not necessary in others (you'll know if you need it!)

Flower Power!

A soaker hose could well be your best investment in the garden. Bury it 2 inches under the soil, and place soil and mulch on top. It's very useful.

The "Must-Have" Tools for Weeding

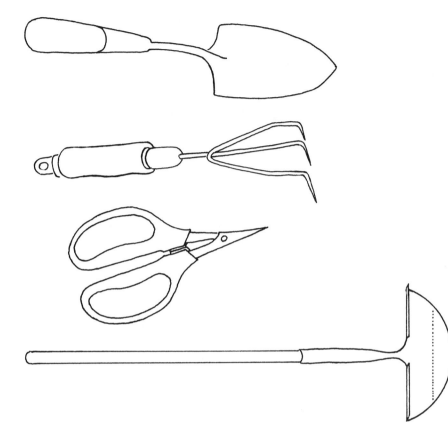

From top to bottom: trowel, hand cultivator, scissors, edger.

1. A hoe with a long or short handle or even hand-held (hoes have either diamond-shaped heads or flat-edged heads)

2. A cultivator, with either a long or short handle (cultivators have pronged heads for scratching the soil)

3. Gardening bags or sheets, buckets, or baskets for carrying weeds out of garden

4. A dandelion weeder

5. A hand fork with a long or short handle

Garden Talk
You'll find weeding tools listed under "cultivators" in most catalogs and garden centers.

225

The "Must-Have" Tools for Pruning and Cutting

1. A pair of pruners

2. A pair of garden scissors

3. And for later: a knife, sheep shears, long-handled pruners for roses and tall shrubs, a pruning saw, and hedge clippers

The "Must-Have" Tools for Mowing the Lawn

1. A lawn mower, with extra blades

2. An edger to edge the garden beds

3. A lawn rake (it doubles in the garden bed)

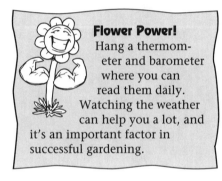

Flower Power!
Hang a thermometer and barometer where you can read them daily. Watching the weather can help you a lot, and it's an important factor in successful gardening.

The "Must-Have" Tools for You, the Gardener

1. A hat (do we need to tell you how bad the sun is for you?)

2. A wide-brimmed hat with a net around it if you have a lot of bugs

3. A pair of gloves, preferably two pairs, one in cowhide for heavy jobs, one in rubber or cloth for summer

4. And for later: a pair of knee pads or a kneeling pad; an apron with front pockets to hold your pruning shears, marking pen, gloves, and so on; a pair of clogs made of polyurethane that can be hosed off; maybe a new notebook for your gardening ideas; a gardening basket or bucket to carry tools; rain pants and coat to work in when it's raining or just after a rain shower; and gardening rubber boots

For the Garden

1. Supply of twine

2. Stakes for staking plants

3. Marker or pencils

4. Labels for your plants

5. Tape measure

What About the Wheelbarrow?

A good wheelbarrow will run you about $100, so it may not be your first investment. Eventually, though, you're going to want to have one.

Look for one with an 8-cubic-foot capacity in a seamless polyethylene tray. Polyethylene won't rust or corrode. Make sure your wheelbarrow has a heavy-duty steel undercarriage.

Green Meany

Caution: When you finish using your wheelbarrow, set it on its side, propped against a wall. Don't leave it upright—water will collect in it when it rains, creating a breeding ground for mosquito eggs. You'll also ruin the wheelbarrow even if it's rust-proof.

The Least You Need to Know

➤ Buy a steel-tempered spade, spading fork, and hoe, as well as a trowel, pruning shears, and a hat. The rest you can pick up later.

➤ Keep all your tools clean; keep sharp-edged tools both clean and sharp.

➤ Bring tools indoors when not in use.

➤ Drain water from hoses and store them indoors for winter.

Part 6
Making the Bed

There's no way to get around digging the garden bed, and it's strenuous work. Take solace in the fact that you only have to do it once! In years to come, your plants will enjoy the benefits of your hard work.

We'll talk in Part 6 about fertilizers—organic and inorganic—and how they are applied to the soil, then give you precise instructions on preparing the bed. One of the best things you can do for your garden is start a compost pile. Collect lawn clippings, fallen leaves, even coffee grounds and egg shells and put them together so they can decompose. The result is rich, luxurious compost that you didn't have to run to the store to buy.

Chapter 16

Don't Shoot the Messenger

In This Chapter

➤ Digging the garden bed

➤ Tools you'll need

➤ Dress for success: light clothing, hats, sun block, etc.

➤ Proper digging techniques

Now you're ready to start digging your garden. You've marked the garden out, you've purchased your garden necessities, and you've made choices about which plants to grow. The hard part's over, right? Well, not quite. Digging the garden bed is the hardest, on body and soul. Read on to learn how to cope with this most difficult of jobs, and keep in mind that once you've created your new garden bed, you won't have to do it again. And you'll be well on your way to successfully growing the garden of your dreams.

Flower Power!

Now's the time to enlist the aid of strong, able-bodied, friends and family members. The work will go twice as quickly!

Take a Moment to Look Over Your Potential Garden Bed

Your new garden bed may be, in the best of all possible worlds, in a part of your lawn where all you have to do is remove the sod and till the ground. But it may also be where tall weeds grow, and maybe even brambles with who knows what lurking around. The following is not meant to scare you off but to make you aware of what you want to avoid.

Check Out the Plot for Signs of Poison Sumac, Oak, or Ivy

The worst thing that happens to ambitious beginner gardeners is that they have so much enthusiasm they start working the land without noticing they're ripping out poison ivy with their bare hands. Don't do it! If you don't know what poison oak or ivy is, you probably will make the mistake of touching it. If you know what it looks like, you can avoid it.

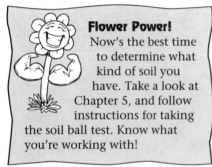

Flower Power!
Now's the best time to determine what kind of soil you have. Take a look at Chapter 5, and follow instructions for taking the soil ball test. Know what you're working with!

Poison sumac is a shrub or small tree with feather-shaped leaves and reddish berries. It's often found growing in swamps. You'll recognize poison ivy by its three shiny leaflets. It usually grows on fences, rocks, and trees. Poison oak is native to the Southeastern U.S. and also has three leaflets.

Beware of Ticks!

If you live in a part of the United States where ticks are a problem, you know how important it is to keep them from getting on your skin.

Ticks are most commonly found in tall grass, around evergreens, and near wood or rock piles. Tick awareness is high where Lyme disease has made inroads, so you can easily get information on how to avoid them and what to do if you find one on you. If you don't know where to get information, you might ask your local garden center—they probably have a pamphlet you can review before you start digging your garden bed.

Always wear shoes, and it's a good idea to tuck your pants hems in your socks. Don't expose your legs where ticks are likely to attach themselves. Also, wear lightly colored clothes so you can easily spot any ticks and get rid of them before you go back in the house.

Dress for Success

Even if you're a sun worshipper, and getting out in the garden is your way of getting a tan, don't forget this part of gardening, digging the bed, is strenuous exercise, and you can easily overtax yourself. Treat your first day out in the garden the way you would your first day on the beach. Don't overdo it!

The following sections give you information on how you should dress and what you should bring with you into the garden.

Wear Light-Colored Clothing

Ever notice that professional gardeners are always dressed in khakis and light-colored shirts? Working in the sun all day is hard enough without making conditions harder on yourself. So keep it light.

If you think you might be exposing yourself to poison sumac or ivy, you must wear a long-sleeved shirt and gloves. Also, tuck your pants into your socks to protect your ankles.

Hats and Gloves Are Not for Sissies

Be sure to wear a hat. If you're in your garden at the optimum time, when the average daily temperature is about 50 degrees, you'll still be thankful for the shade your hat provides when you begin to perspire.

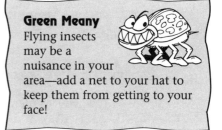

Green Meany
Flying insects may be a nuisance in your area—add a net to your hat to keep them from getting to your face!

Hats with broad brims are best, but in a pinch, use a baseball cap. Hats not only keep the sun from ravaging your skin, but also help keep the bugs from getting to your face. You can encounter lots of bugs and unsavory critters out in the garden wilds.

Sun Block, Handkerchief, and Water

You should bring sun block, a clean handkerchief (it won't be clean for long), and a bottle or pitcher of water into the garden with you. Your body will be losing lots of salt and water, so periodically sit in the shade and drink some water. Heat stress and sun stroke are more common than you may think, so be wise and be aware of your body's signals.

Get Out Your Garden Tools

You've got your garden tools, right? Whether you went all out and purchased everything from a hand trowel to a wheelbarrow, or bought only the bare necessities, you're now ready to dig in and get your hands dirty.

The following sections give you information on the tools you'll need to dig the garden, as well as a brief description of each tool you may buy.

Spade

A straight-edged spade has a long or short handle and an iron blade that you press into the ground with your foot. The blade itself is straight and sharp for cutting into the ground.

Fork

A fork has three or four prongs for lifting objects and for loosening soil.

Wheelbarrow, Gardening Bag, or Sheet

You'll need your wheelbarrow (if you have one), a gardening bag, or even an old sheet to haul things to the garden like compost, peat, superphosphate, and tools. You'll also use the wheelbarrow, bag, or old sheet as a receptacle for weeds and grass and anything else you come across in your digging and don't want in your garden.

Rake

You'll need a rake, preferably one with a level head and a long handle. Rakes are used for final grading and leveling the soil. A lawn rake can be used in a pinch.

Be Prepared: Have Soil Amendments on Hand

When you dig your garden bed, you'll be digging deeply into the soil, so now is a good time to improve the soil. A topsoil is only about 3 to 5 inches deep, and under that is the subsoil, which may be hard-pan: thick, clay soil. At any rate, the subsoil has been untouched for hundreds of years.

Of course, some gardeners will have to contend with extreme conditions, like an extremely thin topsoil with hard clay and rock beneath, or sand, which is also just as difficult to work with. For gardeners with these difficulties, you'll find some suggestions at the end of this chapter.

The following sections give you a list of some of the amendments you'll want on hand to add to your garden soil.

Peat Moss

Peat moss, also called "sphagnum peat" or simply "peat," is found naturally in wet bogs. But you can easily purchase it in bags. Peat, which you learned about in Chapter 5, helps soil by improving the soil structure, making it easier for water, air, and roots to penetrate. When peat is dry, water beads up on the surface of it, but once it's wet it retains moisture. Adding peat to the soil allows more water to be absorbed in the soil.

Compost

Composted manure enriches the soil with organic elements. There are many kinds of organic materials. Aged manure will benefit the soil immediately.

Flower Power!

Get your compost cheaply. If you live near a local horse, dairy, or chicken farm, see if you can purchase some agricultural waste, such as aged cow, horse, or chicken manure from the farm for a low price. Make sure, though, that the manure is aged—fresh manure will burn the roots of the plants in the garden (not to mention the fact that working with fresh manure is very unpleasant!).

Superphosphate

Superphosphate is a fertilizer that's imperative to the overall health of the plant. It helps the roots to develop properly and also helps plants to be disease-resistant. You can purchase superphosphate by the bag at your local garden center. You'll be adding it, according to the instructions on the bag, to the soil once you've tilled it. You're working with a chemical compound, so remember you're better off erring on the side of too little fertilizer than too much.

Garden Talk
Superphosphate is, according to Webster's, "a soluble mixture of phosphates used as fertilizer and made from insoluble mineral phosphates by treatment with sulfuric acid."

Before You Do Anything: Lessons in the Proper Use of Tools

You've come too far in your gardening education to let improper use of tools get in the way. It's also all too common to hear of beginner gardeners throwing out their backs by picking up heavy objects.

Bend and Lift When Carrying Heavy Objects

Whenever you're lifting heavy objects, you should always be aware of the strain you are putting on your back and your kidneys, and take all steps necessary to make it minimal.

Keep your back and shoulders straight and let your back bow slightly in the middle. Keep your legs bent with one foot in front of the other. Always keep your chin up when lifting the object (a great expression for these demanding tasks!). You want to keep in mind that you must let your legs do the work.

If you're picking up a heavy object, place one hand around the top of the bag and place the other on the bottom of the bag. If the object is heavy, like a bag of compost, empty some of the contents and carry the amount you can handle. Never bend at the waist, and never jerk your body when picking anything up.

Proper Use of Spades, Forks, and Shovels

Spades, forks, and shovels are tools you'll be using a lot as a gardener. You'll use spades to dig, make edges, and lift out plants; forks to lift out rocks and plants in rocky soils and to till the soil; and shovels to pick up and move materials. The same principles apply when using these long or short-handled tools: Let your legs do the work by lifting properly.

Once you've placed the tool on the ground, put your foot on the top of the spade, fork, or shovel and ease the tool into the ground. Whenever you're digging or lifting weeds and sod, try to pick up as little soil as possible. You want to keep as much topsoil in the ground as you can.

Step One: Remove the Grass and Weeds

Green Meany
Don't till the soil until you have removed the sod or killed the weeds first! You'll only be cre-ating more weeds by cut-ting up the roots.

It can be tempting to make the mistake of not taking up the grass and weeds when planting for the first time. But removing the grass and weeds is one of the most impor-tant elements in creating a useful and attractive garden bed. If you remove them properly, you may be less plagued down the road by persistent weeds (that should be incentive enough)!

If you have help at this stage of the game, great. If you're going it alone, take your time. Take small forkfuls at a time, and, at all costs, save your back!

The Effortless Way: Cover Your Garden with Black Plastic Sheets or Newspaper

If the weather in your area remains hot and sunny for a week or so, and you don't mind waiting a week for your weeds and grass to die, you can get rid of them by smothering the potential garden plot with sheets of black plastic or sections of newspaper. Lay the sheets or sections out, covering the garden plot entirely. Anchor the plastic or newspaper with rocks or whatever you have handy to keep the sheets in place.

In a couple of weeks, the grass or weeds should be dead, and you can remove the plastic or newspaper. Till and begin to amend your soil.

The Proper Way to Remove Sod: With a Jiggle and a Spade

Using the straight-edged spade, go into the marked-out garden at the edge. Cut into the ground about 4 inches deep, following the length of the garden. Once you have made the 4-inch deep cuts the length of the garden, go into the garden a foot, and do the same thing. When you've finished making these two parallel lines in the garden, make a vertical cut at every foot to connect the two lines together. This should look like you are cutting brownies into squares. You're making small squares that will be easy to lift out.

Now pick up your fork and slide it under the grass as far as you can. Without trying to lift the grass from the ground, jiggle the handle of the fork. Step to the sides of the sod and jiggle the handle from all four angles, trying to shake off as much soil as you can. When you've got the square of grass out of the ground with as little soil as possible, discard the sod in your wheelbarrow, garden bag, or sheet.

> **Flower Power!**
> In very rocky soil, you may do better by using a fork and forgetting about the spade. You can use the fork to lift out the bigger rocks, whereas the spade would just keep hitting them.

> **Green Meany**
> Caution: These squares of sod are heavy! Don't let your wheelbarrow get too full. Make frequent trips, if necessary, to your new compost pile.

Step Two: Till the Soil

To *till* means to work the soil for cultivation. You can till the soil with a tool, such as a fork or a spade, or you can till with the help of a machine made for tilling. The point is to break up the soil before you add organic matter, peat moss, or any other amending substance.

Breaking Up IS Hard to Do

Repeat what you did with the straight-edged spade, only this time you'll be using your fork or spade to turn over the soil. Go through the garden once, digging approximately 5 inches deep. After you've tilled the entire area once, go back over it one last time, this time adding to the broken-up soil, peat moss, compost, and superphosphate.

Bet You Didn't Know... Worms in the soil signal fertile soil.

Spread peat moss according to the instructions on the bag, usually at the rate of one cubic foot of peat moss per 30 square feet. The compost, which should also have adequate instructions on the bag, will suggest that you add enough to cover the top of the area with 1 or 2 inches of compost. The superphosphate, as we said earlier, should be used according to directions.

Step Three: Tamp Down the Soil

If you happen to have a large roller, the kind used for lawns, use the roller to run over the soil and tamp it down. If you don't have a roller, a rake with a level head works fine. Using the flat surface of the rake, tamp down the soil, then smooth and grade the soil, again using the flat surface of the rake.

You must then allow for the earth to settle, which takes about a week. If you're running out of time and need to settle the soil more quickly, water the newly prepared ground. At any rate, don't plant the same day because the soil must have time to settle. You risk exposing the crowns of the plants to the sun and air, which would cause the crown to dry out and die.

Final Words on Tilling the Garden

There are a few alternative ways to dig your garden bed. One is to rent a machine to help you (called a "Rototiller™").

The other is to prepare the bed by "double-digging." We've outlined below what you need to know about Rototilling and double-digging in the event that you opt to use one of these methods. If you don't use this information now, you can refer to it in case you decide to do things differently next time around.

Renting a Rotary Tiller

If you want to use a machine for tilling your new garden, you can rent a Rototiller™ from a nearby garden center. It has a long handle with rotary blades at the base of it, which break up the soil. You'll find Rototillers™ for rent at many hardware stores and garden centers. They do make easy work of breaking up the soil, and they are particularly helpful for gardeners with difficult soil.

Double-Digging (or Is It Double Trouble?)

Double-digging is a long, tiring, and physically demanding process. Heard enough? Actually, double-digging a garden bed is useful if you have a very poorly drained area and, in fact, is useful for any garden. You'll be rewarded for years to come with the best garden soil possible.

When you double-dig, you are creating 18 to 24 inches of good topsoil for a perennial bed. You'll need good digging tools (a shovel and a spade), a wheelbarrow, and at least one month between the time you double-dig the bed and when you plant. It's best to do this in the fall, let the soil settle over the winter, and plant in the spring.

Start by digging a trench about 1 foot deep down the long side of the bed. The topsoil you're removing should be deposited in the garden-to-be. When you've dug from one end to the other, start digging down another foot, this time taking out the subsoil and putting it into the wheelbarrow.

Subsoil doesn't have any fertile content, so you'll mix it with peat moss and compost before putting it back in the garden. Make a mixture of $1/3$ peat moss, $2/3$ compost, adding equal parts of subsoil to the mix. If you have very wet or moist soil, make the mix $1/3$ sand, $1/3$ peat, and $1/3$ compost.

Flower Power!
Make double-digging a three-man operation: One digs the top-soil, one makes the subsoil mixture, and one places the topsoil back into the trench.

Rake off the surface of the topsoil you've dug-up and put it back in the trench. Then add the amended subsoil back to the trench, on top of the topsoil. Begin digging another trench, repeating this process until you've double-dug the entire garden bed. Your soil level will be about 3 inches higher. Add super-phosphate as the icing on the cake, and tamp it in.

The Least You Need to Know

➤ Remove all weeds and grass before you do anything to your new garden bed.

➤ Invest in heavy-duty tools—they'll pay for themselves over time.

➤ Use tools properly and in accordance with what they were designed for.

➤ Pay attention to your body for signs of dehydration, fatigue, or sun poisoning.

➤ Don't hurt your back! Be careful when carrying heavy loads. And if it's too heavy, get some help.

➤ Even if you don't double-dig this garden, reread these instructions for further reference. You never know.

Chapter 17

Improving the Soil

In This Chapter

➤ What are fertilizers and how are they applied?

➤ The difference between organic and inorganic fertilizers

➤ How to make a compost pile

You learned exactly what good soil is in Chapter 5, and why it determines how well your garden will grow. Any soil—whether predominantly clay or sand, can be improved. You can also add organic fertilizers each year to replenish the soil and feed your plants during the growing season.

In this chapter, you'll learn what fertilizers are, both organic and inorganic, and when to use fertilizers for optimum benefits. You'll also read about different kinds of fertilizers (from alfalfa meal to zoo poop). And finally, you'll learn how to combine your fertilizer with your own compost pile.

Know Your Soil

By now you know what kind of soil you have—at least in a general way. Remember, soil is defined by its density or porosity. On the very dense side, you have clay soil, and on the very porous side, you have sandy soil. Even if your soil isn't one extreme or the other, you'll want to add organic matter to improve its structure and nutritional content.

Sandy Soils

As you know, soils with a sandy texture are generally not very fertile because nutrients drain through too quickly. A sandy soil will need more fertilizer than a clay soil. However, there are three important advantages to sandy soil: (1) Plant roots will spread easily through the light soil; (2) Drainage is good; and (3) A sandy soil warms up faster in the spring.

Clay Soils

Clay soils are heavy and dense with extremely fine-textured particles. Clay soil holds moisture in and takes all the air out of the soil. They usually have poor drainage, so roots may have a hard time establishing themselves. On the plus side, clay soils are often rich with nutrients.

Getting It Right

The best of all possible soil conditions is called "loam." Loam is well-structured and fertile soil that retains water, but allows it to drain freely as well. The texture of loam is very much like the topping of an apple crumb cake.

All About Fertilizers

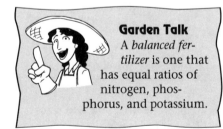

Garden Talk
A *balanced fertilizer* is one that has equal ratios of nitrogen, phosphorus, and potassium.

All fertilizers will contain some ratio of nitrogen, phosphorus, and potassium. You should always see three numbers listed on a bag of fertilizer, such as "10–10–10." These numbers refer to three elements: nitrogen (N), phosphorus (P), and potassium (K). This set tells you the fertilizer contains 10 percent nitrogen (N), 10 percent phosphorus (P), and 10 percent potassium (K). What about the other 70 percent? This percentage is made up of a mixing agent that will simply spread the fertilizer evenly throughout the soil.

What Nitrogen Does

Nitrogen develops the plant's green color in the foliage and stems. Nitrogen should only be applied in the spring when you want new growth to start.

What Phosphorus Does

Phosphorus is very important in developing flower, seed, and fruit production. It also helps in root development and aids the plant in resisting disease.

What Potassium Does

Potassium helps the plant in its overall development—its general health and durability. The stronger the plant, the better able it is to resist disease.

How Fertilizers Are Added to the Soil

Fertilizers come in three different forms: water-soluble, dry powder, and time-release. You can decide which one to use based on what works best for you.

Water-Soluble Fertilizers

Water-soluble fertilizers usually come in a granular form. You mix this with water to dissolve and then add it, in the dissolved form, to your plants. Read the directions carefully and use only one-half the recommended amount. Overfeeding will burn your plants' root systems. Water-soluble fertilizers tend to leach. Fertilize only during the growing season—every three weeks to a month is fine.

Flower Power!
Use water-soluble fertilizers for container plantings; they work best.

Dry Fertilizers

Dry fertilizers are applied directly to the ground by scattering the small, dry granules according to the directions on the package. Feeding plants this way is usually referred to as "top dressing" or "side dressing," because you're directly applying the fertilizer to the top of the soil or side of the plant.

The prime time for applying dry fertilizers is just before a rain. Be careful when using a dry fertilizer to keep the fertilizer off the foliage as it can burn it (water washes it off).

Dry fertilizers take a while to work into the soil, and as a result, they stay in the soil longer. You need to make only two applications per season, one in early spring when plants show 2 inches of growth, and one about a month later.

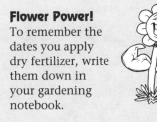

Flower Power!
To remember the dates you apply dry fertilizer, write them down in your gardening notebook.

Time-Release Fertilizers

Time-release fertilizer is the most expensive form of the three. You sprinkle the small, round balls of fertilizer in the soil, and each time the fertilizer comes in contact with water a bit of it will dissolve. There are three advantages to using time-release fertilizer:

1. It stops dissolving during the heat of the summer (when you don't want to fertilize anyway).

2. You only have to apply once and your plants continue to be fed.

3. It's easy to spread throughout the garden or in containers.

Go Organic

Organic food is derived from living organisms and provides plants and soil with necessary nutrients. In the same way, organic food also provides good nutrition for plants, as well as soil. Organic matter, on the whole, increases the availability of nutrients in soil. Peat moss and sawdust, for example, are added to clay soils to lighten up the heavy soil; organic matter in the form of peat moss and manure mix will help sandy soil by regulating the amount of moisture it receives.

There are many different kinds of organic fertilizers on the market. A list of the most common follows.

Alfalfa Meal

Alfalfa meal has lots of balanced nutrients and trace minerals. It helps the soil by enhancing its biological activity. This means fewer destructive organisms are present in the soil. Alfalfa is also high in nitrogen, so you might also want to add it to your compost pile.

Animal Manure (Cow, Elephant, Rhino...That Kind of Thing)

Green Meany
Never apply fresh cow or horse manure directly on the garden—always use manure that has aged at least one year because fresh manure can burn a plant's roots.

Traditional animal manure, like cow manure, can be purchased by the bagful at your local nursery. It's "composted," which means it has been decomposed, so you're not handling fresh manure —which isn't good for the plants anyway. There are other kinds of manure on the market too, such as fossilized seabird guano, desert bat guano, and chicken, armadillo, elephant, and rhinoceros manure. "Zoo poop," which is elephant and rhinoceros manure combined, has the added feature of deterring animals like deer and woodchucks from entering the garden.

Bone Meal

Bone meal is available in a dry powder form, which is applied directly to the soil. It's high in phosphorus and low in nitrogen, which means it's most helpful in producing flowers, seeds, and roots. Bone meal is slow reacting; it doesn't work overnight but takes a good season and it stays in the soil a long time. Farmers swear by bone meal. It's also popular among small critters, too. So if you already have a problem with chipmunks, you're better off using something else.

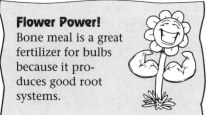

Flower Power!
Bone meal is a great fertilizer for bulbs because it produces good root systems.

Fish Emulsion

Fish emulsion comes in a liquid or a dry form. The liquid form is easier to work with since the dry form tends to clump if you add too much water. Roses, in particular, seem to love this fertilizer. If you buy fish emulsion, be sure to mix it outside because the smell is bad and will linger in the house.

Kelp Meal

Kelp meal fertilizer is made from seaweed. It's rich in minerals and has the advantage of increasing the water-holding capacity of the soil.

Peat Moss

While peat moss has no real nutritional value, it plays a huge role in creating good soil because it lightens heavy soil and helps more porous soil to retain water. It's usually sold in large cubic-foot bags. The fine, almost dusty consistency, works best if you moisten it before working it into the garden.

Green Meany
Don't work with peat moss on a windy day! It's so lightweight, it will blow around.

The Best Fertilizer: Your Own Compost Pile

The best fertilizer of all is your own compost pile. Compost piles are easy to make, especially if you can safely put together a 4 × 4-foot chicken-wire bin.

Returning Nature's Elements Back to the Soil

When you build a compost pile, you're using organic materials to create "humus," which is decomposed plant and animal matter. Humus is high in nitrogen and carbon and extremely nutritional for your garden.

What to Use

Materials high in nitrogen are usually fresh and green: grass clippings, sod, young weeds, and plant tops are all high in nitrogen. Kitchen scraps (also high in nitrogen) that can go in the compost bin include vegetable peelings, egg shells, coffee grounds, and even banana peels. Animal manure, like cow, horse, and chicken, is high in nitrogen and can be added to the pile.

High carbon materials, on the other hand, are dry and brown, like leaves, small prunings, straw, sawdust, wood ashes, and even shredded newspaper.

What Never to Use

Never use meat scraps and dairy products, which could attract rodents. Never add weeds that have been treated with a weed killer.

How to Make a Compost Bin

Now that you have a good list of ingredients, all you have to do is find a good spot for your compost bin. You could buy a compost bin or make one with chicken wire and six 4-foot-long stakes. Making a compost bin is easy and inexpensive.

A three-sided compost bin.

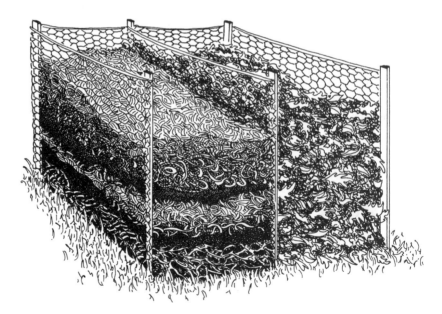

Where to Put Your Compost Bin

Find a hidden spot on level ground (not paved ground; your compost bin needs drainage) that will be easy for you to get to. Use stakes to hold the chicken wire in place. The bin in the diagram is three-sided with a divider in the middle. One side is for the compost, the other side is to put leaves so they can rot down for next year's winter mulch. Keep the front side open so you can get into it easily without having to lift anything.

Building Layers of Compost

The first layer in your compost bin should be some type of coarse material, such as small twigs, in order to allow air to circulate. For the next layer, add whatever you want: bags of leaves, grass clippings, sod, and so on. Try to alternately layer brown materials, then green materials. This will heat the bin more quickly. Use a hose to moisten the layers. After two weeks or so you'll see that your pile has shrunk. It's time to turn the pile over and mix it all up. If you can, add a pile of manure to the compost bin. The more you turn your pile, the quicker it will break down. In about six months your pile is ready to use—all the ingredients will have composted, leaving a rich, dark brown-colored humus.

If you plan to leave the compost pile untouched over the winter, turn the pile over at least once, just to mix it up.

Flower Power!
If space is hard to come by for your hidden compost bin, plant some shrubs to screen it. You'll be amazed at how beautifully the shrubs will grow with all the nutrients leaching into the soil.

Other Bins for Composting

Once you see how successful your compost is in establishing lush gardens, you may want to build more bins. Make one for leaf mulches, one for manure to top dress your garden in the fall, and save your original compost pile for adding to the individual holes you make when planting. While it may seem like a lot of work, you'll save a lot of money in the long run by not having to purchase bags of compost.

Inorganic Fertilizers

There *are* benefits to using inorganic or chemical fertilizers. Think of organic matter as a plant's meat and potatoes and inorganic matter as the quick pick-me-up candy bar. An inorganic fertilizer will give plants a needed burst of energy.

When Inorganic Fertilizers Are Beneficial

One of the advantages to chemical fertilizing is that the fertilizer is immediately absorbed by the plant, allowing you to put your plants on a regular feeding program. Roses, for instance, love being fed on a regular basis even when provided with the best soil balance of organic matter. They also benefit because feedings are timed to reach them when they most require it. Other plants that benefit are young plants.

Also, you may not have the luxury of a compost pile, so you can use chemical fertilizers as a low-cost alternative to buying more expensive organic matter.

Hazards of Chemical Fertilizing

You shouldn't think that because a little bit does a little good, a lot will do will a lot of good. If you give a lot of chemical fertilizers to your plants, you risk burning the plants' root systems and leaves. Basically, you will kill the plant with your kindness. To be on the safe side, use a diluted amount rather than the recommended amount on the package.

Use Care When Applying Chemical Fertilizers

Be very careful when you apply any chemical fertilizers, and always read labels and wear protective gloves. Wash up after using any chemical of any kind.

The Least You Need to Know

➤ Chemical fertilizers are good for the added burst of growth in spring and early summer.

➤ Organic fertilizers improve your soil's structure, as well as providing your plants with nutrients.

➤ Only use aged manure that's well rotted; fresh manure can burn a plant's roots.

➤ Make a compost pile—your plants will love you.

Part 7
Into the Garden

Part 7 includes guidelines for planting all kinds of plants: annuals, perennials, shrubs, and bulbs. Instructions are here for planting in the ground as well as in containers. We'll show you how to get the right container for your plant. You'll also learn how to create a good, clean edge to your garden bed that will give your garden the professional touch.

Chapter 18

Plants into Beds

In This Chapter

➤ Planting day checklist

➤ Planting annuals: Seeds and seedlings

➤ Planting perennials: Bare-root and container

➤ Planting shrubs: Bare-root and container

➤ Planting bulbs: Spring, summer, and fall blooming

Today's the day you plant your garden. You've got the garden plan, the plants, the prepared garden bed, and the tools you'll need.

Make sure you read this chapter before you plant your garden. You'll learn when you should plant and get some tips on how to properly space your plants in the garden. Most important, you'll learn how to correctly plant annuals, perennials, shrubs, and bulbs to ensure their health and vigor.

Checklist for Planting Day

Be sure you're ready for the big day. Have all your tools and plants on hand. Take a picture of your garden bed before you plant. Before and after photographs will be very useful.

Here's a checklist for you to look over before you head into the garden:

➤ *Is your garden ready?* Turn over the soil in your garden the day before you intend to plant. Grade it, level it, and water the soil to settle it.

➤ *Are your plants ready?* Keep all container and bare-root plants watered, standing upright, and cool in a shaded location. "Bare-root" plants are mail-order plants that are shipped soil-free in their dormant stages. They usually arrive in a lightweight packing material such as sawdust wrapped in plastic.

➤ *Is your garden plan ready?* Look it over one last time; make any last minute changes now.

➤ *Are your supplies on hand?* You have your trowel, gardening spade, wheelbarrow or gardening bag, rake, knife or scissors, tape measure and long stick, labels and pen, and something to water plants with—hose or watering can.

Plan Planting Day Around the Weather and Time of Day

Flower Power!
Take all your tools with you while you garden so you don't have to keep running inside for something you forgot.

An ideal planting day is cool and cloudy, when rainfall has recently soaked the soil, and perhaps, more rain is expected. It shouldn't be too windy. Spring weather is best for planting, when these conditions are seasonable, natural, and expected. Be sure to watch the weather and beware of a cold front or storm heading your way. Avoid planting when either is predicted.

Planting is best done before 11:00 a.m. or after 2:30 p.m. to avoid the hottest part of the day.

Where to Keep Your Plants Until You Plant

Keep your container plants in the shade until your garden is completely marked out and ready to plant. Any plant in a pot 6 inches or smaller should not be in direct sunlight, even if the plant is a sun lover. Check the soil each morning to be sure the soil is moist. Containers larger than 6 inches should stay moist—check to be on the safe side. If it's really hot, drape a lightweight shade cloth over the plants to keep them cool.

Your Bed's New Plants

To take the guesswork out of spacing your plants in the bed, mark out the bed. Take a stick and draw a line in the soil every foot. The first month after planting your garden you may look at it and wonder why there are all these big spaces between the plants, but by the second month you will see your garden begin to fill in.

"Staging" Your Plant

Another good technique for putting plants in exactly the right spot is to "stage" them, which means to turn your plant around from side to side to find how it looks best. You may want someone to work with you here—to either help you decide which side shows better or to hold the plant straight while you step back and think about it. Shrubs should always be staged since they can't be moved around like perennials.

Planting Annuals: Guidelines for Seeds and Seedlings

Annuals should only be planted outside after the frost date in your area. Starting seeds inside can be very challenging. We suggest purchasing annuals already started for you, called "seedlings."

Seeds

Seeds come in all different sizes and are planted a little differently depending on their sizes. In all cases, the soil should be raked evenly and moistened the night before. Make sure you water your seeds with care—a hard blast of water will wash your seeds away!

Small seeds, such as centaurea, cosmos, lobularis, myosotis, nigella, papaver, portulaca, and zinnias, need to be planted shallowly. The best way to plant small seeds is to create a shallow furrow one half inch deep (or the recommended depth on the package of seeds) and distribute the seeds with a handful of sand. Cover lightly with soil and gently water.

Larger seeds, like helianthus (sunflowers) or tropaeoleum (nasturtiums), should be planted more

Green Meany
Thinning out is the process of removing some seedlings when they are about 3 to 6 inches tall to encourage healthier growth of the seedlings that remain.

deeply—about twice as deeply as the size of the seed. Label each variety as you plant so you'll remember what's what.

Check the moisture of the soil, and if the temperature drops or rises fast, you may want to cover the soil with straw or a lightweight burlap until the seedlings emerge.

Seedlings

It's much easier to plant seedlings than seeds, because you don't have to provide germination conditions for them and you don't have to thin them. Seedlings also offer gardeners in the North a longer growing season.

You'll pick up most annuals in *flats,* which have four or six individual pockets. Look for healthy, green foliage and check the color the flowers so you get what you want. If any roots are showing through the bottom of the pot, trim them off with scissors first. Remove the seedlings from the flat and pull apart any roots that have grown together. Be careful not to hurt the seedling's young top growth or any of the flowers.

Flower Power!
If you have more than four flats of seedlings to plant, bring a few flats out to the garden and keep the others in the shade until you're ready to plant them.

Garden Talk
Pinching means pinching the stem to remove the top two leaves of a plant. It's done when the plant is under 6 inches.

Just before you plant your annual, cut off the flower that attracted you to the seedling in the first place. This will encourage new growth from the base of the plant and create more flowers. If the seedling doesn't have a flower, pinch back the plant for the same reason.

If the plant is taller than 6 inches, cut back the plant to half its size just above a leaf. Do this with all annuals except ageratum, wax begonias, tall sunflowers, and lobularis. Then cut off any dead leaves with scissors— don't pull or you may break the tender stems.

Plant seedlings at the same level or just a tad deeper than the original plant's level from the flat. Press the ground around the plant firmly to remove unwanted air pockets that could dry out the plant's roots. Place its label near the plant and water as you plant it. When all your plants are in the ground, water with a deep soak.

Planting Perennials: Guidelines for Bare-Root and Container

Perennial plants require about 1 to 2 feet of space between them. Planting them is basically the same as planting annuals—prepare your bed, water the plants in, mark the plants, and so on. The holes you dig for perennials will probably be deeper and wider to accommodate a larger root system, so you should use a spade instead of a trowel.

Perennials will need room to spread and fill out over the years. If you plant them close together the first year and space them out the next year, this will only set you back. Spacing also allows the plants to drink up the water and minerals without fighting against another plant. You will grow healthier, more disease-resistant plants when you space them out correctly.

Bare-Rooted Perennials

Bare-rooted plants are shipped in their dormant stage and usually arrive in packing material covered in a plastic bag. You can keep bare-rooted plants up to a week in their packing material, as long as they stay moist and are kept in a cool location so they don't break dormancy. If they do begin to grow, stand them upright, and in a few days time, they should begin to straighten out. If you have a shady section, you can plant them until you are able to replant in your new garden. If you see leaves that are turning yellow from the lack of light, you may want to trim them back.

Pick up the plant to check it out. Note where the crown is—it's often hard to detect with bare-root perennials. With some perennials, it's hard to know the top from the bottom. Plants like coreopsis have long shoots that can look like the root system.

Keep your plants cool with a moist towel or newspaper until you plant. Also, it's a good idea to take only two varieties with you out to the garden site, leaving the others in the shade.

Mail-order companies are usually very good at providing planting instructions for each plant. Be sure to read them. The main point is to dig a hole wide enough so you can spread out the roots and deep enough to cover the crown.

> **Flower Power!**
> Follow the garden plan you made or decided to use. It's not a good idea to make big changes on planting day.

> **Garden Talk**
> The *crown* of a plant is the top of the root system, between the roots and the new foliage.

Dig a good-size hole, make a mound of soil in the middle of the hole, and place the plant on top of the mound of soil. Spread out its root system and check the crown's level to be sure it's an inch below the soil level. Cover with remaining soil.

How to plant a hosta.

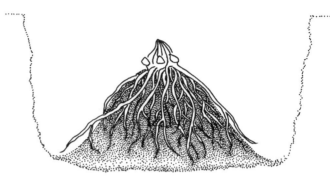

If you're planting a lot of plants at one time, pat the soil down firmly around each plant. After you have planted about a dozen or so, "walk them in," which means place your feet around a plant's crown (not on top of it!) and firm the soil down with your weight. Step around the plant a few times, water well, and label.

Flower Power!

Do the best you can to find any hint of which way's up and which way's down with bare-root perennials. If you can't tell, plant sideways, spreading the roots horizontally. The tops of the plants know naturally which way is up, and so they will grow upward toward the sun.

Planting Perennials from Containers

Flower Power!
Keep all receipts from the plants you bought in your notebook.

Keep all plants watered, whether they came from a mail-order company or if you purchased them from a local nursery.

Many perennials will still be in their dormant stages if they are bought early in the spring. Dormant plants adjust more quickly than those that have been growing in pots for too long—they'll have less risk of transplant shock.

Potted plants that are root-bound may need their root systems loosened up. The root systems may also be so tightly woven together that you'll need to take a knife and make a few slices on the sides, or cut off the bottom knotted roots to loosen them. Don't worry, this won't hurt the roots. Trimming up roots or making a few slices will encourage new roots to grow.

Be careful of the tops when you're planting or removing them from the containers. Try not to break off any stems. Trim up any broken stems or dead foliage, plant to soil level of container, firm in, label, and water.

Planting Shrubs: Guidelines for Bare-Root and Container

Shrubs can last a lifetime, and they aren't cheap, so take the time to plant these plants correctly.

Bare-Root Shrubs

These will be dormant when they are shipped to you. If their dormancy breaks, which means they've started to grow foliage, you should pot them up and keep them cool and watered. If they don't break, keep them in their packaging material, making sure they are moist, cool, and standing upright.

> **Garden Talk**
> A *node* is a visible bud on the stem, indicating future growth for a leaf or stem.

Soak your plants in a bucket of water for two hours before planting. Or soak them overnight if you will be planting the following day. Make clean cuts to remove any broken roots or stems. Remove any branches that cross each other. You may need to trim off the tips if they're damaged, always making a clean cut above a node on the outside of the stem. Trim up the plant while you're inside, taking the plants outside only when you're ready to plant. When you take them outdoors, keep them in the shade in their bucket of water until you are ready to plant.

Most shrub roots are brittle and stiff and should never be crammed into a hole or the root system will suffer. When the hole is dug out, stand the shrub in the hole to check if the hole is the right depth for the plant. Place a straight stick across the top of the hole to make sure the soil level is correct. A deeper hole is better—you can always raise the plant. Remove the shrub, and add a pile of soil to the center of the hole, making a mound with a peak. Place your shrub's root system on top of the mound and check the soil level again with the aid of the stick. The root system should be completely covered.

Fill in the hole with remaining soil and firm in by walking the plants in to remove any of the air pockets. The next step is to make a "water well" around the plant.

The "soil mound" or "ring" should be an inch high—this will act as a reservoir for your plant. It should be about a hand's distance from the stem of the plant. Water deeply two or three times.

If your shrubs came with a label attached to the stem, be sure to remove it. The label could hurt the plant if it stays on.

Making a water well around a shrub.

Planting Container Shrubs

Flower Power!
Don't forget to "stage" (defined earlier in this chapter) your shrub at this point. Adjust it so that it shows to its best advantage before planting it.

Check out your purchase: Examine the top, remove any broken or dead branches, crossed branches, and shape by removing any of the odd branches that are unsightly and sticking out. Keep the shrub in its container until just before you are ready to plant. You can also leave the shrub in the container while you're staging it.

Plant the shrubs at the same level as the pot level. Fill in with remaining soil and walk the plants in. Make the ring of soil for the reservoir.

Label As You Go

Always remember to label your plants. Labeling plants is very important, particularly for the beginner gardener. It's a good way to identify who's who in the garden, as well as a handy tool for learning plant names.

Planting Bulbs: Guidelines

Plant spring-flowering bulbs in the preceding fall, summer-flowering bulbs in the preceding spring, and fall-blooming bulbs in the same fall season. In the first two cases, the bulbs have a period underground of three to six months before you see them emerge.

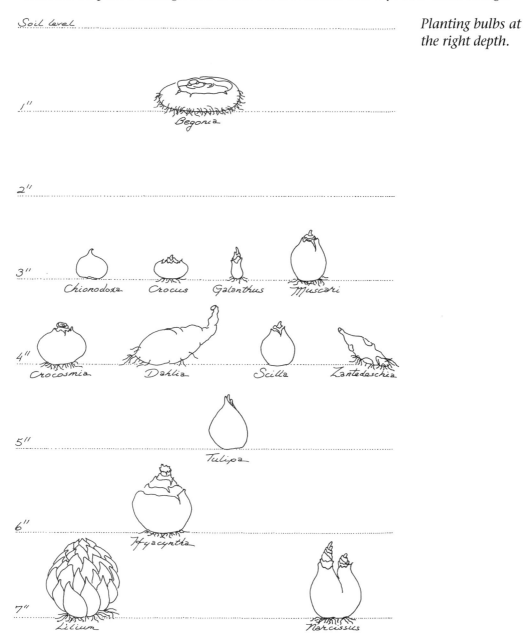

Planting bulbs at the right depth.

259

Before digging your holes, check out the bulbs. Make sure they aren't rotting—they shouldn't be moldy or soft. Next, look at the root system or *eyes*. A swollen eye, which is another term for a bud, is the sign of a healthy bulb.

Flower Power!
You may want to keep your notebook handy to record where you planted bulbs.

Dig your hole, adding a little bulb fertilizer or bone meal to each hole, before you place the bulb in it. Add the bulb with its growth tip—the narrow end of the bulb—facing up and cover with soil. Firm the ground well, label, and water. These planting instructions work for spring, summer, and fall bulbs.

The Least You Need to Know

➤ Keep plants and soil moist before and after the plants enter the ground so the plants retain moisture.

➤ Firm the soil around the newly planted plants to secure them and remove any air pockets in the soil that can dry out a plant's roots.

➤ Never plant in the heat of the day.

➤ Planting plants at their correct levels ensures active growth.

➤ Spacing plants correctly helps each plant receive proper amounts of sunlight, water, and nutrients.

➤ Check your plants daily for two weeks. Never allow them to dry out over a two-day span.

➤ Label your plants. Take notes of which varieties are doing better than others.

Chapter 19

Plants into Pots

In This Chapter

➤ Selecting the proper containers

➤ Selecting plants and quantities

➤ Planting day

➤ Watering and feeding program

Container gardening, putting plants in pots, is very popular these days. It's easy to see why: Many containers are very decorative, and if they aren't too heavy, can be moved around to show the pots and plants to their best advantage.

Be sure, however, that you pay attention to the needs of the plants themselves, and that means potting them up correctly, using the right potting medium for the plants, and giving the plants the conditions they need in terms of sun, space, and water.

Read on to learn how to get the best show from your potted annuals, perennials, bulbs, and even shrubs. There's virtually no plant than can't be potted up, as long as it's done right.

The Pots You Choose

Your first consideration in selecting a pot should be how you plan to use it. Will it remain outside year round? You'll need to be careful with clay or terra-cotta pots if you live where winter temperatures freeze. Will you put the pot by a swimming pool, on a high-rise terrace, or on the patio in direct sunlight? These areas get very hot, due to reflecting heat, and you'll have to make sure you provide enough water for the plants.

Follow Your Tastes

Selecting a container is easy enough—just follow your personal taste and use the containers you like. But not all pots are created equal, and there are some things you'll need to know beforehand about the differences in containers.

Porous Materials Need More Frequent Watering

Porous materials, such as clay or cement, drink up water and you'll need to allow for this when putting plants in these containers. Clay containers can be very decorative and tend to be more charming the older they are. If left outdoors all winter, clay will crack from the freezing and thawing weather conditions. You'll have to water more frequently with clay pots, unless the pots have a glaze on them.

Flower Power!

Here's a trick to using large clay pots: A huge clay pot doesn't need to be filled to the top with soil, making it unnecessarily heavy. Place a couple of flat boards across the middle of the huge clay pot, and put plants in several plastic pots. Put the pots on top of the boards. Drape the plants' foliage across the top or put enough soil on top of the plastic pots to conceal the smaller pots. In winter, remove the plants, extra soil, and boards. In the South, leave your clay containers outside all year round.

Plastic, Fiberglass, and Other Synthetics

Plastic pots have the advantage of being very lightweight and made of such durable materials that they can last a very long time. While they may not have the charm of an antique urn, they have plenty of advantages—especially that they are fairly inexpensive. There are plastic pots that closely resemble terra-cotta, so much so, that you have to look up close to see the plastic is fake. It's a winner.

Fiberglass is one of the newer materials to come on the market. These lightweight, nonporous pots come in every size, shape, and color to suit your needs. Fiberglass has the advantage of durability and can be kept outdoors all winter.

The best thing about these synthetic materials is you don't have to be as concerned about watering as you must be with clay, cement, or concrete containers.

Wooden Containers

Whether painted to match the rest of your house or left with a natural finish, wooden containers are often ideal planters for evergreen shrubs. Natural-looking and often lightweight, wooden planters come in all different shapes and sizes.

Whiskey barrels are very easy to find, and their depth makes them ideal for plants you want to winter over. Be sure when buying any wooden container to buy pressure-treated wood—it will last longer. Wooden planters also include window boxes, redwood planters, and large box-shaped planters for the terrace.

Wire Frames Lined with Moss

Wire frames lined with spaghum moss are also very attractive planters. They will need special watering care because it takes a long time for the moss to absorb the water. It's best to spray the moss with a fine spray of water before you water the plant.

Flower Power!
Raise large containers off flat surfaces with pieces of wood or rocks so the drainage hole remains exposed.

Bet You Didn't Know...
Here are some offbeat ideas for plant containers: an old shoe or boot that's missing its mate, an old coffee or tea pot you just can't throw out, an old watering can, a wheelbarrow, tire, or decorative tin can. Poke some holes in the bottom for drainage, and you've got a container for plants.

Flower Power!
If you're making these hanging baskets yourself, solve the watering problem by lining the wire frame with damp moss—it's easier to work with. Place a plastic pot filled with your hanging plant inside your wire frame. Fill with remaining soil to keep the plastic pot in place. This allows you to water the plant without worrying that the moss is taking all the moisture from the plant.

A Refresher Course on Potting Soil

Now that you have your container, you need potting soil. Remember, potting soil isn't garden soil, and garden soil doesn't belong in a pot for a number of reasons. Garden soil doesn't drain well, and pots with garden soil can't be brought indoors to winter over—the warm conditions in a house would create a haven for disease and insects. Potting soils (or potting mediums, as they're called), are a soilless mix. You can buy potting soil at the garden center, or if you're feeling ambitious, you can make your own potting soil.

Make Your Own Potting Soil

To make your own potting soil, follow this easy recipe: Use two parts peat moss, one part vermiculite, and one part perlite. Peat moss gives the soil its body, vermiculite holds the water in, and perlite aids in the drainage and keeps the mix lightweight. Remember that potting soils have no fertility; you must add fertilizers either in organic or inorganic form.

Other Mediums for Potting Soils

There are other mediums you can add to your mix, such as charcoal, lime, or composted bark. Charcoal in your soilless mix will help filter out any toxic elements in the soil. Lime will help regulate the soil's pH, and composted bark contributes to the composition of organic matter. If you do add composted bark, be sure the texture of the bark is a fine texture and smaller than the bark you use for mulch.

Add Organic Compost to Your Potting Mix

If you want to use organic compost in your mix, you'll have to sterilize it before putting it in a container. Unfortunately, sterilizing it yourself involves cooking the soil at 180 degrees for a half hour and enduring the disagreeable and lingering odor of strong manure in the kitchen. Store-bought sterilized mix is really the way to go.

Potting Soil for Outdoor Containers

You can use garden or top soil if you plan to leave your potted plants outside. Use two parts top soil, one part peat moss, and one part sand or perlite.

Weight the Bottom of the Container with Rocks

Remember that potting soil is very lightweight and, if your plant is top-heavy, or your plant's container is small, you'll need to add weight to the bottom of the container by adding a layer of crushed rocks or chips of broken clay pots. Add crushed rocks to large containers that are going to be staying outside for long periods of time. They add extra drainage and prevent the soil from passing through the drainage hole. Just don't let them block the drainage hole.

Sand is a wonderful drainage medium but it's heavy. Perlite, also a good drainage medium, is very light so you may prefer this. It's a good idea to add super-phosphate and lime (read the packages and remember, less is better) at the time you are making this potting soil. Mix well, water, and let it sit for a half an hour (take a break), then pot up the plant.

Flower Power!
If you're using a very large container, use Styrofoam™ peanuts instead of rocks and stones at the bottom of the pot so you can pick it up more easily.

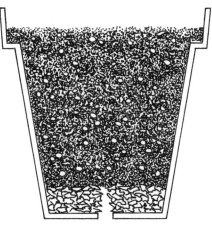

Potting Up

Anything goes into pots—there are no rules about what goes where. There are, of course, the plants' needs that must be met—sun, water, space, and fertilizer—as well as any chore the plant may need, like deadheading or pinching. Plant one plant per pot or mix three, four, or even five different types of plants together. Perennials, annuals, bulbs, herbs, vines, and even shrubs can grow happily together in containers.

Flower Power!
Always check a pot to be sure there are drainage holes in the bottom. If there aren't, don't use the pot or make the holes yourself.

All plants, annuals, perennials, tubers, and shrubs, must have their roots covered with soil. Never allow roots to stick out of the pot; they need protection from the drying winds and sun.

Annuals in Pots

Cram annuals into pots—they'll burst out over the sides of your container. Annuals that arrived in larger pots can have the soil knocked off to fit into a container. Don't forget to add a few trailing plants like nasturtiums and lobelia, to add to the effect, as well as annual seeds. Sprinkle some alyssum or poppy seed on top to give your pot the added touch it needs.

Flower Power!
Whiskey barrels are deep and make naturally good plant-ers for perennials and shrubs.

Perennials in Pots

Perennials and shrubs will do well in a deep container. You can keep them in this container for years if you give them the room they need to spread out their roots. The deeper the pot, the better the chances the plants will make it through a cold winter.

Bulbs in Pots

As a rule, large bulbs should be placed halfway into the pot, and smaller bulbs like crocosmia and gladiolus should be planted 2 inches deep. Never plant a bulb at the bottom of a pot. If you wish to add lilium bulbs to your pot, plant these first and cover with soil before adding any other plants. Some tubers, like tuberous begonias, *(Begonia x tuberosa)* will need special care in planting. The round, fleshy tuber must be planted close to the surface of the pot, with about half an inch of soil on top of the tuber. You can have wonderful bursts of color with summer-flowering bulbs.

Don't Forget Vines

Annual vines are great for containers. Add a wire trellis to any pot and let an annual vine, like hyacinth bean vine (*Dolichos lablab*), climb it. It's extremely vigorous, and by summer's end this vine may be well on its way to climbing anything and everything in sight.

Perennial vines are also at home in containers with trellises. Try bougainvillea, which seems to do fine on terraces. Use a deep container—it keeps the roots cool and it supports the trellis.

Care for Your Plants in Containers

Don't be afraid to move your containers around if you think your plants will be healthier in another location. If your shade-loving plant looks like it needs a little sun (its stems are growing tall reaching for sunlight), move it. Same goes for sun-loving plants. If your soil seems to dry out too fast or the plants seem to wilt during the heat of the day, move the container into a shadier spot.

Flower Power!
If you have back problems, use smaller containers so you can move them around easily.

Watering and Feeding Program

Don't overwater! More plants are killed this way than any other. The soil should be dry between each watering. Having a drip pan or saucer is a good idea, but it could cause problems if left unattended. If you leave an inch of water in a saucer for a week, it could damage the root system. Check your plants every other day to see if they need water or not, and check to see if the drip pan needs to be emptied.

Apply a Cool Mulch

Add a fine bark mulch or moss to the top of the soil to keep roots cool. In hot, humid areas you may want to add a thin layer of sand on top of the bark mixture to keep the bark mulch from growing mold.

Feeding Potted Plants

It's always better to underfeed than to overfeed. Feed with either a water-soluble fertilizer or dry fertilizer. A diluted solution of a balanced, water-soluble fertilizer should be used every three weeks. Remember that every time you water, you wash away fertilizer. An easier way to fertilize is with a time-release fertilizer that breaks down slowly throughout the growing season. However, remember that it is more expensive.

You should wait a few weeks before feeding if you've just potted your plants.

Caring for Your Potted Plants in Winter

If you live where temperatures dip to freezing, you'll have to provide special care for indoor or outdoor plants you wish to see survive the winter.

Wintering Over Plants Indoors

Flower Power!
The best indoor locations for your annuals and herbs are sunny windows.

When fall comes and you want to bring pots into the house, bring in any pots with annuals early enough in the fall so they can acclimate to indoor conditions. Check Part 3 for a list of plants that are known to "winter over" well (*wintering over* plants means caring for plants in containers in the hope that they'll survive the winter). Cut back to one-half any plants losing leaves to stimulate growth.

Perennials and Shrubs in Containers

Perennials and shrubs are meant to stay outside in winter and can be moved to a sheltered location, such as the corner of a terrace or against the south side of a house, when fall comes. Cut back perennials in containers as you would perennials in the garden, and add a winter mulch to help them winter over. Don't put perennials and bulbs in containers in a heated garage or basement. The heat will do them in.

Leaving Pots Outside

If you want to leave big, expensive clay or ceramic pots outside in winter, protect your investment by removing plants and soil and covering the pot with a plastic sheet. Also, put a board on top of it to keep any snow from caving it in.

The Least You Need to Know

➤ Clay or cement pots drink up water, and you'll need to allow for this when putting plants in these containers. If left outdoors all winter, clay will crack from the freezing and thawing weather conditions.

➤ Potting soils (or potting mediums, as they're called), are a soilless mix. You can buy potting soils at the garden center, or if you're feeling ambitious, you can make your own potting medium.

➤ If your plant is top-heavy, or your plant's container is small, you'll need to add weight to the bottom of the container by adding a layer of crushed rocks or chips of broken clay pots.

➤ All plants—annuals, perennials, tubers, and shrubs—must have their roots covered with soil. Never allow roots to stick out of the pot—they need protection from the drying winds and sun.

➤ Don't overwater! More plants are killed this way than any other. The soil should be dry between each watering.

Chapter 20

The Final Cut: Giving Your Garden an Edge

In This Chapter

➤ Stepping back to admire your work

➤ Making an edge around the garden

➤ Accessories in the garden

Now that your garden is finally planted, step back and take a good look at it. It probably still looks a little bare—newly planted perennials and shrubs will need time to fill in. But remember, you're much better off starting your garden with young or dormant plants that are properly spaced.

Check Your Garden Often

You should really check your garden every day for the first week. Make sure the plants are healthy, and straighten any plants that are not standing up straight; firm down the soil again if necessary. The second week you should at least go through a water check every other day. By the third week, just check the water every third day or so.

Check the Water Content

You need to check the water content in the soil. To do this, stick a trowel in the ground and push back and forth so you can see the soil an inch or so down. If it appears dark in color and is cool to the touch, it's moist. More often your plants will show you the signs of needing water before you need to do this.

Brush Up on Watering Techniques

As we've mentioned, it's better to water in the morning or afternoon and give the plants good deep soaks. The longer you soak an area, the less chance of the soil drying out quickly. Whether you'll have to water again will depend on your soil's capacity to retain water.

When Water Is Not the Problem

Green Meany
Muddy conditions are not good for any plants in their early stages unless they're bog plants.

If your plants have wilted even though you watered well the day before, it may be that the plants need a little shading from the afternoon heat and sun. Apply a lightweight shade cloth (found at your local nursery or through a garden-supply catalog company). You can still water easily enough through the cloth, but water lightly. The shade cloth will reduce the sun's rays, as well as keep the plants sheltered from strong winds. Remove the cloth after a week or so when the roots have anchored in.

Tidy Up the Garden

Now is a good time to remove any rocks, sticks, or old roots that you found while digging the holes for your plants. You may want to keep a rock or two in the garden as an accent if it has a nice shape to it. You can also use flat rocks as stepping stones within the garden. Rocks you find will look very natural in their setting, since they came right from your garden.

Scratch the Soil's Back

About a week or so after planting, you'll probably begin to see some weeds emerging. Don't add mulch yet: You want the little seedling weeds to come up so you can pull them out when young. "Scratch the soil's back," more commonly known as *hoeing,* which means cultivating the soil, will be your next assignment. You'll read about it in Chapter 21.

Give Your Garden an Edge

Whether you opted for a formal or informal look, you'll need to place an edge around your garden to keep lawn grass from infringing on it. Edges are useful in keeping the garden looking tidy and come in a variety of shapes and sizes—from the most natural to the man-made. A garden with an edge is much nicer than a garden without one. It's easier to maintain and easier to mow around.

Natural Solutions

Bricks, flat layers of stones, logs—anything works as an edging, as long as it provides a means of keeping your garden in and the lawn out.

Man-Made Alternatives

You can purchase a variety of different edging materials, from white metal edgings that are very showy to black plastic that doesn't (or shouldn't) show.

Edgings with a Spade

The most inexpensive edging is one's own edge, made with a flat-edged spade. To make a straight edge, you will need to use two sticks and a long string. Do a straight edge first to get the hang of it. Place two sticks at either end of the garden, about an inch from the garden's edge in the grass. Tie a string taut between the sticks and follow the string with your spade, cutting deeply into the sod. Try to make a clean line.

Make a proper edge to your garden.

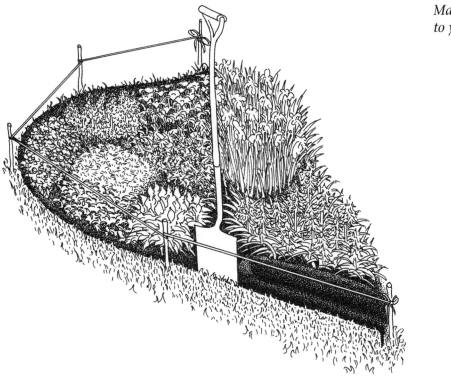

Flower Power!
Add the sod you take from your garden to your compost pile. It's high in nitrogen and will break down quickly, making it a good addition to the compost pile.

For a curve in the bed, you'll need about five sticks. Place a stick every couple of feet, and then wrap the string around each stick. Tie the string to the end sticks. Face your garden and place your spade straight down along the inside line of your string (that's nearest to your garden), and cut into the sod about 3 inches deep. Follow the string's edge along the grass. Remove the thin row of sod and shake the topsoil from the roots into the garden, about 2 inches from the new edge. This will make a small mound of soil. You can smooth out the mound or keep it to retain water in your garden.

Accessorizing the Garden

Gardening, like any hobby, can quickly become your new obsession, and you may find yourself spending a lot of time in the gardening sections of stores you never entered before. Look for garden accents, items of architectural interest, or just fun things you'll enjoy.

Flower Power!

Take a picture of your garden in its early stages of growth. Compare it with the picture you took of your empty garden. Then take another picture of the garden toward the end of the growing season. In other words, take *lots* of pictures!

Some Good Things to Have

Unlike an edge to a garden, these things are not absolutely necessary but they *are* fun. There are some pretty clay, cement, and ceramic accessories, such as bird baths and bird feeders, that make nice accents. A Victorian gazing ball makes an elegant focal point. Even a statue of an animal or little figurine can be a source of delight in a garden.

Staging Accents and Focal Points in the Garden

When you first place any of these things in your garden, they may seem to stand out a bit, at least until the plants mature and grow around them. At a later date, you may decide to rearrange them. Try half-hidden accents like a little turtle partially seen from beneath the leaves of a hosta. In a country garden, even a spading fork can look natural enough to stay in the garden (even though you shouldn't keep your tools outside). Other ideas might include an old gate you pick up at a flea market, which you could use to create a hidden entrance; an old bench; or even other garden furniture so you can relax by the garden.

The Least You Need to Know

➤ Physically check the soil's moisture content until you learn the signs from your plants and know your soil's capacity to retain water.

➤ Make an edge around your garden to keep it looking neater, to keep the grass out of the garden, and to make weeding easier.

➤ Keep your eyes open for new ideas: in books, garden centers, flea markets, and tag sales. You never know what you may find.

Part 8
Water, Weed, Feed, and Don't Forget to Mulch

Now it's payoff time: Your annuals and perennials are in full bloom! We'll show you how to keep the flowers coming with deadheading and proper plant maintenance.

But you may also see weeds cropping up in your garden. We'll also teach you how to weed for best effects. You don't want to weed more than you have to, and proper weeding can eliminate weeds.

Bugs and diseases may also rear their ugly heads. Maybe your tulips and lilies have been discovered by the larger critters. The key to plant disease and insect control is diagnosis, and we'll show you how to ID the culprits and deal with them.

Keeping Plants Healthy

The fruits of your labor are beginning to show—your well-tended garden has good, strong plants with attractive flowers. Now what?

You want to *keep* your plants flowering and lush, and you want to maintain the garden throughout the growing season so that it continues to produce flowers. In this chapter, you'll learn the basics to maintaining a garden—from thinning out the tiniest seedlings to pruning old overgrown shrubs. You'll also learn the answer to the big question: When can I start to cut flowers?

Pay-Off Time

You'll need to take good care of each plant so all your work pays off in beautiful flowers and healthy plants. It's important to keep paying attention to the garden at this point. Make a note of chores that need to be done and take the time to do them.

Assess the Success of Each Plant

Give yourself a certain amount of time each week to pass through the garden, looking at each plant to see how well it's growing. Note how each plant is doing. You'll see plants that have already bloomed and are now ready to be deadheaded; a shrub that flowered in the spring may now need to be deadheaded. Other plants will bloom later in the fall and now should be pinched; some annuals may now need pinching.

What All Plants Need

While the basic needs of plants are the same—food, water, sun—caring for them differs depending on whether they're annuals, perennials, vines, bulbs, or shrubs.

Get in the habit of doing certain gardening chores correctly right from the start. You'll be amazed at how successful your gardens will be.

Whenever You Cut a Stem

When cutting the stem of a plant or flower, make a good clean cut, always cutting at a slant just above a set of leaves. The tools you use are important: If you're trying to cut through a wooden stem with pruners and it's not working, use a pruning saw. And remember: Always work with sharp, clean tools.

Annuals and Their Care

Some annuals need less attention than others. In fact, some annuals require virtually no maintenance. Annuals that require little maintenance, portulaca, for instance, are best-suited to conditions where there is little water and no fertilizer.

However easy some annuals are to maintain, you'll always want to watch any growing plant to be sure it's healthy and doing well. You'll especially want to watch all plants, whether annuals or shrubs, when they are still young.

When You've Planted Annuals by Seed

You decide whether you want to plant seeds or seedlings. Seeds require more care than seedlings since you often have to be start them indoors, and giving them the right germination conditions can be a challenge. It's a little easier to sow seeds directly into the garden, but even then you must be careful to provide the right germination conditions.

Thinning Out Seedlings

Thinning out seedlings is the process of removing the weaker seedlings from the soil so the stronger seedlings have more room to grow. It can be as difficult as giving your baby his first hair cut! But you have to do it because, as discussed earlier, the seedlings have spacing requirements, and if you cram too many in to a small space, by two months time you'll have very leggy, unattractive plants.

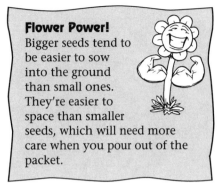

Flower Power!
Bigger seeds tend to be easier to sow into the ground than small ones. They're easier to space than smaller seeds, which will need more care when you pour out of the packet.

Thin out seedlings when the plant has two true leaves on it—it should be a few inches tall at this point. The best time to do this is on cool, cloudy days. Thin by either taking scissors and cutting the smaller seedlings at ground level, or gently removing the seedling from the ground. Be sure to pat the soil around the remaining seedlings, keeping it firm and in place.

Flower Power!
If you notice after thinning out seedlings that the remaining seedlings are flopping over, place a shade cloth over them for a few days so they can re-establish themselves. (A *shade cloth* is a lightweight netting that filters light but allows water to enter.)

What All Annuals Need

Whether you started with seedlings from a nursery or seeds sown yourself, you need to do the following chores to produce the healthiest plants and most flowers. These chores should be part of your weekly gardening, along with weeding and checking to be sure the plants have enough water.

Pinching Back Annuals

Pinching back is the act of removing the terminal growth (the growth at the tip of the stem) just above the next set of leaves. You can pinch back with your fingers, a pair of scissors, or a knife, whichever is easier.

Flower Power!
Don't forget to pinch annual herbs like basil to create a bushier plant. Continually cut from all herbs (using cuttings in the kitchen) to keep plants vigorous and healthy.

Pinch back one time when the plants are 3 to 6 inches tall. Pinching back will promote new growth by sending the energy down to the roots and creating a larger root system. New growth will then come back up through the plants' stems and give a big burst of energy to create side buds and a bushier plant. You'll get more stems and more flowers. If you don't pinch back a seedling, it will be a weak plant, with very few flowers.

While you'll pinch back most annuals, there are a few you won't need to pinch back. They are helianthus (sunflower), limonium (statice), lobularis (sweet alyssum), myosotis (Forget-me-Not), annual poppies (like California and Shirley poppies), and violas (pansies). For more information on a specific annual, check Chapter 7.

Feeding Your Annuals

Green Meany
Annuals aren't heavy feeders and should never be fed in the hot summer months. If you do feed them, you risk burning the plants' roots and/or leaves.

Feed annuals about a week after you've pinched them. You can use a granular fertilizer, a liquid fertilizer, or a time-release fertilizer, but begin by using one-half the recommended amount. After that, feeding depends on the kind of fertilizer you use. With a granular fertilizer, you'll fertilize twice: once in the beginning, and again in the early summer or beginning of June. With a liquid fertilizer, you'll fertilize every time or every other time you water during the spring months. With a time-release, you won't need to do any additional fertilizing: The capsules do it all for you.

Feeding Annuals in Containers

Feeding annuals in containers is slightly different because the soil is a soilless mixture and they don't have the advantage of minerals found in garden soil. Because of the lack of nutrients, fertilize with a diluted solution each time you water until the heat of the summer. Continue to water regularly throughout the summer, even when you stop fertilizing. Southern gardeners can pick the fertilizing program back up in the fall when the temperatures cool.

Deadheading

Deadheading is the act of removing spent flowers (flowers that have faded or passed). It promotes more flowers. If you cut flowers for the house, you'll have to deadhead less often.

Deadhead by cutting the stem with scissors or a sharp knife down to the next leaf. Put deadheading on your list of weekly chores, along with checking the water content and weeding. Deadheading is valuable in neatening up the appearance of the plants.

Flower Power!
The only time you might not want to deadhead is with plants that self-sow, in which case let the plant go to seed and enjoy the new plants when they come up the following year.

Perennials and Their Care

Perennials need somewhat less care than you may think. Of course they need to be tended when young, but in time you'll find caring for perennials to be second nature. Many of them have specific requirements, but as you learn to care for your plants year after year, each garden chore will come back to you easily.

Feeding

Perennials need minimal fertilizing. All the good organic matter you've added to your new garden bed will last at least four years, so your perennials will be getting most of their food from the rich soil as they grow. If you wish, you can add a chemical fertilizer for an instant boost when you first see growth.

Most perennials will require only two feedings: once in early spring when the temperature stays above 50 degrees, and then again in early summer.

Nitrogen should never be applied to perennials in the fall—doing so would promote new growth when the plant should be slowing down, getting ready to go dormant. Also, be very careful when you apply any chemical fertilizers: Always read labels, wear protective gloves, and wash up after using any chemical of any kind.

Pinching

Pinching will produce stronger stems, but there are just a few plants that will need pinching, such as fall-blooming asters and monarda. They should be pinched back early in the spring when they are about 2 to 3 inches tall. Pinching back will control their height and make for stronger stems. Fall chrysanthemums, on the other hand, should be pinched back (or disbudded) until July. This will encourage a strong root system and a much bushier, showier plant.

Flower Power!
When a flower has just bloomed, cut it and bring it indoors to enjoy as a cut flower. Just be sure to leave some foliage on the plant so it can make food.

Thinning

While thinning perennials isn't a big job, it should be done for many perennials, including, for instance, Tall phlox and monarda. Thin in early spring, cutting to ground level about one-quarter of the plant's stems.

Deadheading

Deadheading perennials neatens up the appearance of the plants and can often promote a second flush of bloom. This is true for achillea, ajuga, campanula, coreopsis, dianthus, digitalis, geranium, heuchera, iberis, nepeta, scabiosa, veronica, and violas. The second bloom may be less spectacular than the first, but who can say no to more flowers?

Flower Power!

Make a note of which perennials self-sow (echinacea, digitalis, or althaea, for instance) and wait a few weeks before deadheading these plants to give them time to self-sow.

Cutting Back

Cutting back a perennial during its growing season is done to neaten up the appearance of a plant that has turned brown from stress, perhaps because of too much heat or sun. Cut the plant back to about half its size and water at least twice in the next two weeks—this should bring the plant back to health.

Cutting back a perennial in the fall is a different story. You'll learn about this chore in Chapter 25.

Staking

Taller plants are staked to keep them from falling down. Peonies, for instance, have heavy flowers and should be staked using a "peony ring." The ring is slipped over the shrub in the spring while it's still growing. Other plants that should be staked include lilies (Lilium) and hollyhocks (Althaea), which have just one long, tall, stem that can break off in a bad wind. You don't need to worry about staking anything your first year—all this information is for later when the plants have grown to their full height.

Staking can be quite an art. Be creative; use sticks found in the yard to prop up fallen plants and bamboo sticks with twine to tie up long stems. You can purchase lots of different stakes; most of them will be painted green or brown to blend in with the garden as you don't want to let the supports show.

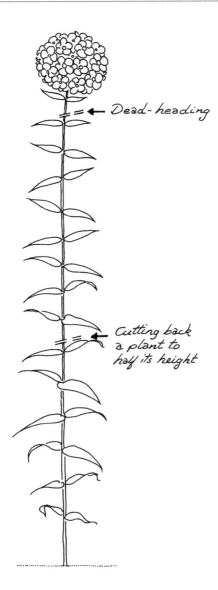

Cutting back versus deadheading.

← Dead-heading

Cutting back a plant to half its height

Flower Power!

Propping up plants the *au natural* way: One creative way to prop up plants is to let the surrounding plants support the plant that tends to fall over. For instance, a hard rain can knock baby's breath (*Gypsophila*) right over, but if you have plants in front and behind, it'll stay up with the help of the other plants. Try gypsophila with a woody wormwood (*Artemesia*) in front of it and a tall phlox or coneflower (*Echinacea*) behind it.

Trimming

Trimming up is done to shape a plant. Perhaps one stem grew much taller than the others, or a stem is infringing on another's space. Whenever you cut a plant, be sure to make a clean cut at a slight angle just above a leaf.

Dividing

In two or three years you may need to divide your perennials, either to increase your stock or rejuvenate the plants. To learn about dividing specific perennials, read about that particular perennial in Chapter 8. Basically, dividing a perennial is easier than getting a bundt cake out of a bundt pan.

Divide only in the spring or fall, when the soil temperature is cool. Lift out the perennial with a spade, (being careful not to disturb the roots), divide the roots' systems into as many as three or four segments, and replant. If the root center is difficult to break apart, you may want to take a sharp knife and cut it through the middle, or take your spade and wedge the roots apart.

Dividing Hostas

Hosta plants are easy to divide, and they provide a very economical way of starting a garden. You can start with 15 hosta plants and in two years time have four times that many!

Start with 15 hosta plants, three each of five different varieties (with two of the plants in a solid color). Work a shaded 25 square foot area, improving the soil with leaf and manure mixture and peat moss. Water deeply. Plant the hostas 2 feet apart and let them grow for two years. Prepare the rest of the area—about three times as large as the original bed for the following year's planting. In two years time, when you dig and divide your 15 plants, you will have four plants from each, giving you 60 plants. Group hostas of the same varieties together. If one variety seems stronger than another, use that variety to wind through the other clumps of plants. In less than three years you've created a huge, low-maintenance hosta garden.

Vines and Their Care

Vines are either annuals or perennials, and the basics, including fertilizing, are the same for both even if the plant is a vine.

Training

Many vines will need to be "trained," which simply means you'll have to help the vines move in the right direction. For instance, if you have clematis growing up a lattice, help the clematis along by placing any vines that have fallen reattach themselves to the lattice. Not all vines have to be trained, and training your vine will differ depending on whether it's an annual or perennial.

Perennials, on the other hand, are slow to start growing, but ought to be trained when they are young and pliable. Eventually, some perennials will create woody trunks over the years, so start the vine off right by training it to grow in the right direction.

Keep an eye on vines that grow by clinging to objects, so they don't start to grow where they shouldn't. Your house's foundation or chimney is fine; clapboard (or any wood structure) isn't. Know how a vine grows and you'll be better able to train it.

Flower Power!
Wisteria vines and morning glories shouldn't be fed fertilizers with too much nitrogen. Nitrogen will cause all foliage and no flowers.

Green Meany
Clematis stems are brittle and when bent will wilt away. Be careful not to bend the stems too hard when training them.

Feeding

What you feed your vines depends on whether the vine is an annual or a perennial. Follow the corresponding instructions.

Pruning

Pruning for vines is the same as for shrubs: Prune after the flowering period or prune an unwanted stem during the growing season to neaten up the vine. For specific information on a vine, see Chapter 10.

Bulbs and Their Care

Bulbs are some of the easiest plants you'll ever grow. Take the time in the fall or early spring to plant them (planting time depends on the bulb), and you'll have flowers when little else is flowering.

Feeding

As you know, bulbs store their own food in their root system, and sometimes their water supply, too. You may add a small amount of bulb fertilizer to each hole when planting bulbs, whether you plant in the spring or the fall. Top dress with a bulb fertilizer for next year's growth in the spring, and that's it.

Deadheading

If you don't plan to use the flower as a cut flower, it's a good idea to deadhead the larger flowering bulbs. When tulips are deadheaded, the dormant cycle speeds up, and when lilium are deadheaded (leaving all the foliage) you'll get a bigger and stronger bulb the following year. By deadheading tuberous begonias, you'll get more flowers throughout the season. As we've said before, deadheading neatens up the appearance of the plants in the garden.

Cutting Back

The spent foliage of spring-flowering bulbs can be pretty ugly, especially next to the new foliage of annuals and perennials. Cut back the foliage when at least one half has turned yellow. Summer bulbs like crocosmia should be cut back when the foliage just doesn't look good anymore.

Shrubs and Their Care

Shrubs require little care beyond watering well and checking the moisture content the first month. In a dry fall or during a drought, give your shrubs a good, long soak.

When cutting branches off shrubs, always cut above a lateral bud (a side bud) that's on the outside side of the shrub. This will create an open, fuller shrub.

Feeding

When you planted your shrub, you added organic matter to the soil, which is enough fertilizer to last the shrub a couple of years. You may want to fertilize the shrubs in a hedge, but be careful. You can also stimulate growth in shrubs by pruning. Flowering shrubs can use a balanced fertilizer every other spring or so after the third year, unless your shrub is an acid lover (rhododendron, azalea, and kalmia, for instance). Feed with an acid-tone fertilizer.

Deadheading

Flowering shrubs should be deadheaded to stimulate new growth and promote more flowers for the following year.

Trimming Up

Trim up any branches that were hurt during planting or broken by wind or rain. Any branch that grows at an odd angle or is taller than the rest of the shrub should be trimmed.

Flower Power!
Cut long stems of flowering shrubs like lilacs, forsythia, and hydrangea to enjoy as cut flowers in the house.

Pruning

Prune your shrub to maintain its shape and keep it growing strong. Check specific shrubs in Chapter 9 for pruning information on specific shrubs. Some shrubs will be pruned in late winter, like butterfly bush (Buddleia) and beauty bush (Callicarpa).

The first rule of pruning is to remove any dead wood. Second, remove any crossed branches. Third, prune to shape your shrub. Some shrubs like viburnum may need pruning every four years or so. Prune an older shrub to help it get back its vigor.

Thinning Out

Thin out a shrub by removing some of the branches in the center of the shrub. By removing the branches in the center, you allow more light in and improve air circulation.

The Least You Need to Know

➤ However easy some annuals are to grow, watch any growing plant to be sure it's healthy and doing well.

➤ Deadheading and pruning stimulates new growth.

➤ Taller perennials on single stems, and plants with heavy flowers, like peonies, need to be staked.

➤ Divide perennials only in the spring or fall, when the soil temperature is cool.

➤ Learn how your vine grows so you can train and support it properly.

➤ The more flowers you cut for bouquets, the less you'll have to deadhead.

Chapter 22

In the Weeds

> **In This Chapter**
>
> ➤ The most common weeds and how they grow
>
> ➤ Hoeing and pulling weeds by hand
>
> ➤ Reducing weeds with mulch

If you cringe at the sight of this chapter, don't worry—you're not alone. Just about everyone hates to weed.

But weeding is essential to maintaining your garden's good looks and keeping your plants healthy. If you don't weed, not only will your garden look awful but also your plants will most certainly be edged out by winning weeds. Weeds have a remarkable ability to compete with plants for water, nutrients, and sunlight.

In this chapter, you'll learn how to identify the most common weeds, how to practice weed control with hoeing and hand-pulling, and the best ways to keep weeds at a minimum with the help of various mulches.

What's in a Weed?

Weeds have the same overall characteristics as any other plant; that is, they are annuals or perennials. You'll become familiar with them as they crop up in your garden.

Garden Talk
If you didn't put it there and you don't want it there, it's a weed!

In a very general sense, a weed is no more than a misplaced plant. You may think golden rod *(Solidago)*, a tall plant with mustard-colored flowers and a familiar sight in meadows and along roadsides in many parts of the United States, is a weed. Actually this plant is a favorite in the English garden bed—although it's a weed to us. So there's no true definition for a weed—a plant's beauty really *is* in the eye of the beholder. If you find an unfamiliar plant, a potential weed, growing in your garden, and you like it, keep it!

About Annual Weeds

Annual weeds can get into your garden a number of ways. Most are carried into your garden by the wind, rain, birds, or animals. They could also be in your soil. In fact, when you first dig up the soil in your garden bed, any weed seeds that may have been in the soil for as long as seven years can now germinate and appear as weeds the following season.

About Perennial Weeds

Perennial weeds can be double trouble because unless you pull up the entire root system when you dig it out, you'll be creating more work for yourself by having to go at it again when it reemerges.

Bet You Didn't Know...
A runner can be as far as two feet away from the new top growth it produces.

Most perennial weeds grow in one of two ways. Underground *runners* grow horizontally through the soil. This means you have to follow and dig up the roots as far as they grow outward from the plant. *Tap roots* grow vertically into the soil, making it necessary for you for you to dig deeply into the soil in order to pull out the entire tap root. Dandelion roots, for instance, have long tap roots.

Proper Weeding Techniques

Weeding, like feeding and watering plants, is most effective when done properly. Sometimes shortcuts look appealing but unfortunately, with this particular chore, cutting corners, including not taking up the entire weed and letting weeds lie around after you've pulled them up, in which case they reroot back into the ground before you know it, will only create more work in the end.

Take the time to learn how to weed properly, and you'll have that much more time later on to smell the roses (and other flowers).

Eliminate Weeds When They Are Still Young

The first rule of thumb is dig out weeds when they are still young. If you wait for a dandelion to flower before pulling it up, not only will it have had time to produce its long, strong tap root but also the plant may have already gone to seed, which means baby dandelion plants will soon be sprouting up. All weeds grow stronger as they mature, and some will also set seeds, so make your life easier by eliminating them when they are still young.

Know Your Weeds

Get to know the most common weeds you see in your garden. Know a dandelion and get it out correctly by taking up its entire tap root before it flowers and goes to seed. You'll become familiar with lots of weeds as you gain experience gardening, and getting rid of them will be that much easier.

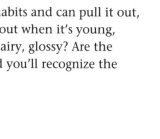

Flower Power!
Identify and pull up the weed when it's still young.

You're ahead of the game when you know your weed's growing habits and can pull it out, roots and all, before it's established or set seed. If you can't get it out when it's young, make a mental note of what it looks like. Is the foliage serrated, hairy, glossy? Are the leaves big or small? What color are the flowers? Next time around you'll recognize the weed as a seedling.

Hoe, Hoe, Hoe (the Tools You'll Need)

You can remove weeds with the help of a hand-held or long- or short-handled cultivator, or hoe. Cultivators have prongs, allowing you to loosen the soil and dig up weeds, roots and all, and hoes have either diamond-shaped heads or flat-edged heads, which allow you to dig down deeply, breaking up the soil. You'll also want to have a receptacle for the weeds—a big sheet to toss them on, a plastic bag, a basket, or a paper bag. All will work fine, but don't let them lie around!

Flower Power!
You can add weeds to your compost pile if you didn't spray them with a chemical.

The Weed List: The Ten Worst Offenders

The following sections tell you some of the most common weeds found in most parts of the United States. However, these lists are just the tip of the iceberg—you'll encounter many more kinds of weeds than we could possibly list here. It's a good idea to get a guide to weeds in your area. Call your local extension office and ask them about it; the number should be in the government pages of your phone book.

The following lists are organized according to how the weeds grow: by tap root, by seed, or by runner. Remember, to effectively remove the weed from your garden, you need to know how it grows.

Flower Power!
When dealing with tap roots, use a dandelion weeder to loosen the soil around the root, until you see the tapered end it. Gently tug out the root.

Weeds That Grow by Tap Roots

When you're digging out weeds with tap roots, be sure to dig deeply into the soil, removing as much of the weed as you can. These roots have the tapered shape of a carrot stick. If the root snaps while you're digging it out, keep digging to get out the very tip of it or you'll have to battle the same weed when it comes up later—bigger and stronger the second time around!

Here are ten common weeds that grow by tap roots:

1. Bindweed
2. Burdock
3. Wild Carrot
4. Chickory
5. Dandelion
6. Dock
7. Horse Nettle
8. Wild Parsnip
9. Pokeberry
10. Swallow-wort

Ten Weeds That Grow by Seed

Weeds that grow by seeds are going to come back each year, and you can't do anything to keep them from settling into your soil. The key to dealing with these weeds is to get rid of them early, before they set seed. Tackle these weeds when they're young or you'll be outnumbered in no time. Hoe and pull weeds weekly to remove newly emerged seedlings. Hand-pulling is best done when seedlings are small and the soil is moist.

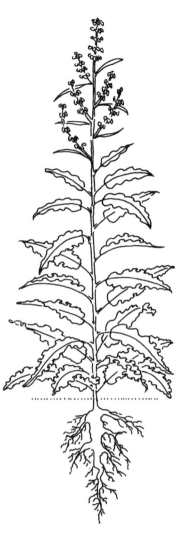

Dock with tap root.

Here are ten common weeds that grow by seeds:

1. Beggar's Tick

2. Chickweed

3. Crabgrass

4. Knotweed

5. Lamb's Quarters, Pigweed

6. Wild Mustard

295

7. Wild Oats

8. Purslane

9. Ragweed

10. Shepherd's Purse

*Purslane with seed
weeds.*

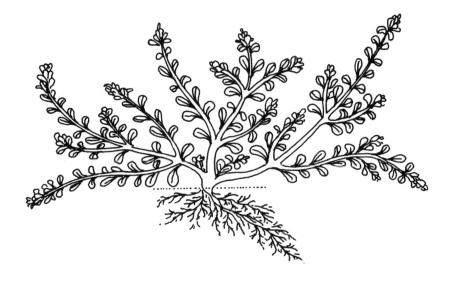

Weeds That Grow by Runners

Flower Power!
Making a good deep
edge around your
garden helps keep
out weeds that
grow by runners!

Weeds that grow by runners are some of the most aggra-
vating weeds you'll encounter. You think you've followed
the runner its entire length, but these pernicious runners
can be as far-reaching as 3 to 4 feet long! Any part of the
root still in the ground will eventually come up as a weed.
Do the best you can with these devils, knowing it'll be an
ongoing process.

Here are ten common weeds that grow by runners:

1. Creeping Buttercup

2. Devil's Painted Brush

3. Ground Ivy

4. Milkweed

5. Stinging Nettle

6. Plantain

7. Poison Ivy

8. Quack Grass

9. Thistles

10. Wild Vetch

Quack grass with runners.

Green Meany

Don't touch poison ivy with bare hands! You can identify poison ivy by its glossy, trifoliate leaves. Remove it safely by wearing rubber gloves and have a trash bag on hand in which to dispose of it. Wash immediately.

Flower Power!

If your neighbor complains of Wild Vetch running rampant through their garden or yard, go over and check it out so you know what it looks like. Weeds that grow by runners can eventually creep over to your garden, too.

The Chemical Alternative to Pulling Up Weeds

Chemicals that are used to remove weeds are called *herbicides*. Unfortunately, it's impossible to get herbicides that will kill plants selectively. Herbicides by their nature are nonselective; they kill all plants with which they come in contact.

How Herbicides Work

Herbicides kill plants by starving them to death. The active chemical is absorbed by the foliage and acts by interfering with the plant's ability to create food. The plant will begin to show signs of dying about a week after it comes in contact with the herbicide.

When to Use an Herbicide

If a weed is harmful to you or your family, such as Poison Ivy, you should use a herbicide like "Round Up"™ or "Kleen Up"™ to effectively remove it without injuring yourself. Be sure to use extreme caution when using herbicides and read the label on the container very carefully. Although these two chemicals don't harm the soil, you should wait at least three weeks after spraying before you replant in that area.

Bet You Didn't Know...
You might try dousing the weeds with vinegar first; it really works!

You may also decide to spray an herbicide where weeds appear in driveways or wide walkways. Remember, herbicides are nonselective killers, so you never want to use them where they may harm children, pets, or, obviously, plants you want to keep.

Green Meany

Never use chemicals as an easy way out for weed control. In the long term it's never the easy way (we learned the hard way about environmentally destructive chemicals like DDT).

Mulches in General and Mulches for Weed Control

Mulches, in general, help the soil to maintain an even temperature. Summer mulches keep the soil from getting too hot in the middle of the day, and likewise, winter mulches help the soil maintain an even temperature, keeping the soil cool even when temperatures rise on unseasonably warm winter days.

> ### Garden Talk
>
> *Mulch* is a covering on a garden, such as straw, leaves, manure, and bark chips that is left on the ground around the plants to prevent excessive evaporation or erosion. It can, depending on the materials in the mulch, enrich the soil. Mulch also stifles weeds from growing up around the plant.

You'll also want to add a summer mulch to your garden beds for other reasons. Mulches can add structure and fertility to the soil and can keep the soil on banks in place. However, one of the best reasons to mulch is for weed control. By placing about 2 inches of an organic mulch on the soil, you'll help stifle any weeds' chances of growing through. Be sure not to put mulch on top of your plants!

How Much Mulch and When?

Add about 2 inches of summer mulch to a well-weeded garden in the late spring. Brush away any extra mulch that accumulates around the bases of plants to give the plants room to breath. Mulches make it hard for weeds to grow, and would also make it hard for the plants you want to grow if you're not careful.

> **Bet You Didn't Know...**
> Not every garden needs mulch. If you regularly weed and cultivate, you can keep weeds to a minimum.

What Kind of Mulch?

Personal taste, as well as your pocketbook, can determine the mulch you use. Some mulches, like buckwheat hulls, are very expensive, while a man-made plastic sheeting can be inexpensive. Another factor in determining which mulch to use is purely aesthetic: In flower beds, for example, you want to be sure nothing detracts from the beauty of the flowers, so you would not want wood chips that are coarse, nuggetlike chips of bark that look out of place with more delicate flowers. This kind of mulch has its place, though, in a shrub border.

Some good mulches are discussed in the following sections. All of these mulches are available commercially, and many you can make yourself.

Green Meany
Buckwheat hulls are very expensive—as much as $12 for a 50-pound bag.

Buckwheat Hulls

Buckwheat hulls are tiny, disk-shaped hulls with a gray cast that are often used in stately garden beds and containers. They are light-weight and consequently blow away easily, so they don't work in windy areas. They do retain moisture well.

Cocoa Shells

Green Meany
Never apply more than 1 inch of cocoa shells as mulch—it's very high in potash. Don't use around lilacs and rhododendron.

Cocoa shells are similar to buckwheat hulls in that they are expensive. They smell like chocolate initially, but in a day or two the scent disappears. Cocoa shells will stay put in the garden, but if too much moisture hits them they sprout a crop of mushrooms. Great for flower beds—the dark-brown color is pretty beneath the plants.

Leaves

Leaf mulch is one of the best for adding nutrients and structure to the soil. It's wonderful for shade gardens; over the years it will add soil to those soilless areas. Leaf mulch keeps the soil moist and cool. Use only chopped leaves; whole leaves will mat, causing an area to remain wet. You can shred leaves with a home shredder or certain lawn mowers. Unfortunately, shredded leaves are not available commercially.

Pine Needles

Pine needles look pretty beneath evergreen trees and as paths through woodland gardens. Use in the shrub border, too. Pine needles won't retain moisture for the soil in drought periods, but they do allow water and fertilizer to pass through freely.

Shredded Bark

Shredded bark is one of the most commonly used mulches and is available in coarse grades and fine grades. Use the coarse grades under large shrubs and the finer grades in flower beds. You can get shredded bark by the bag at a reasonable price, or if you live in a rural area and have the outdoor space to store the bark, you can purchase it by the truckload to apply to garden beds throughout the summer.

Wood Chips and Shavings

These can be purchased by the bag. Use only aged wood chips and shavings because fresh wood chips robs nitrogen from the soil. Aged chips and shavings decompose, adding organic matter to the soil over time. They are great for keeping weeds down and temperatures cool.

Other Mulches You May Want to Try

If you want to use something other than organic mulch, try landscape fabric, black plastic, gravel, stones, or marble chips. Nothing can grow through these elements—certainly not weeds, but neither could plants, so use with discretion—don't put them to close to the plants. Desert plantings and Japanese gardens look great with marble chips or stones. Try to stick with the natural resources in your area to keep your landscape neatly tied together.

Flower Power!
Shop around for the best prices for mulch.

The Least You Need to Know

➤ Perennial weeds grow by runners, tap roots, or seeds. Know how the weed grows and pull it up right.

➤ Never apply more than 2 inches of mulch to a garden.

➤ Summer mulches are attractive, as well as useful for keeping weeds under control and helping the soil to stay cool.

Chapter 23

"What's for Dinner" by Unwanted Animals

In This Chapter

➤ The most famous garden critters

➤ They are creatures of habits—know their habits and you can deal with them

At some point everyone curses the small and large critters that damage their plants. Deer are famous (or infamous) for virtually chewing yew shrubs down to the bare stems. A single raccoon at the table of your daylilies *(Hemerocallis)* can dig up and destroy the whole lot over night. You vow to find a way to get rid of those critters. Thus the battle begins.

Battles against the critters—and the top of a "most wanted" list would certainly include deer, mice, moles, rabbits, and raccoons—are forever being waged by gardener against predator. The stakes rise when certain critters with good memories keep returning to the same restaurant—your garden! Soon you're battling tooth and nail (literally, and maybe using a bit of human hair in the garden, which is said to deter deer) to rid yourself of these destructive creatures.

But wait. There are other ways of approaching these unwanted animals.

The Most "Un" Wanted List

While none of us wants to see our plants destroyed by animals, neither do we want to hurt the animals by killing or trapping them.

A humane way of dealing with unwanted animals is to deter them. There are a number of ways to do this. We have tips for dealing with the unwanted animal population that will leave everyone feeling like they're on the winning side.

Dealing with Birds

Birds can be a problem, especially when they eat the sunflower seeds right out of your garden before they can grow into beautiful, seeded flower heads. Birds tend to eat any seeds.

First, try to get rid of them the fun way: Put up a scarecrow. Be sure to use the color red on the scarecrow—birds hate red—and make it big. Birds don't like big objects. If that doesn't work, try a wind chime. It may be music to our ears, but it isn't to theirs. Last resort: Put netting over your crop until the seeds have begun to sprout.

How Can I Hate Chipmunks as Much as I Do?

Every once in a while a certain population in the animal kingdom becomes unbalanced, and in the recent past, it's the chipmunk population. Chipmunks are a big problem today, and unfortunately, there seems to be no solution. The only good news on the horizon is that what goes up must comes down—and this should include the chipmunk population that will level off soon, or so we're told. Hang in there.

Flower Power!

Are the chipmunks (and moles, mice, and squirrels) getting to your bulbs? Protect your bulbs from rodent damage by placing ground oyster shells in the holes when you plant bulbs. The hard, sharp-edged crushed oyster shells make a barrier rodents don't want to cross.

Oh, Dear, the Deer

You can try to keep deer out of your garden with electrical fencing, which is expensive, or use shavings of Irish Spring™ soap, which is cheap (and pretty ineffective) but between the extremes are a lot of ideas, including a product with the trade name "Milorganite™," which is sewage from Cleveland! This can be effective when properly used, but if you have a lot of deer you're going to have a lot of deer problems.

Some gardeners have had success deterring deer by adding "zoo poop" to their garden beds. Zoo poop is an increasingly popular fertilizer that combines aged elephant and rhino manure. It does double duty fertilizing plants and keeping out animals.

If you live in a high-density deer population, avoid planting their favorite meals, like hostas, tulips, and yews. Instead, plant what they hate: daffodils, digitalis, and hydrangea.

Green Meany
Don't let the dogs ruin your flower beds. Teach your dogs to stay out of the garden.

Flower Power!
Need an excuse to get a dog? Preferably a big male that will mark his territory? While no cure is sure fire, deer tend not to come around when a dog is out (which could be a lot of the time).

Of Mice and Mint

If you have mice problems, think about planting a lot of spearmint (*Mentha spicata*). Mice hate the smell. Or you could try getting a cat. Or borrow your neighbor's cat: Bathe it, save the bath water, and sprinkle it on the garden bed. Or, if you don't want a cat and you don't want your neighbor's cat, try this: Place prickly briars or leaves of holly among the plants and seed beds. Mice don't like to run across these prickly plants and will soon avoid the area under threat. At any rate, steer clear of the obvious poisonous baits. You may harm a kitty, curious pup, or even a child.

Mice are cute, but can wreak havoc on your garden.

The Mole, the Vole

Moles and voles are destructive because of the tunnels they create throughout your lawn and garden. If you do have a mole or vole problem, try any of the following: Put moth balls in the tunnels—they hate the smell. Sink long-neck bottles upright into moles holes, digging them in as well as you can. The sound the wind makes in the bottles will drive them crazy. Be sure to have an inch or so of the bottle sticking up from the soil so you remember to remove it before you mow the lawn.

Another method for deterring moles, which has had great success, is drenching the soil around mole tunnels and mounds with castor oil. Moles won't cross a castor oil barrier. You can make the castor oil go farther and get the same results by diluting it with water. Use it year-round directly on the mole holes and tunnels or to create a barrier around your garden. It remains effective for about two months.

Run, Rabbit, Run

Those cute little furry animals aren't so cute when they are munching on your young plants. The first step is to make your yard less hospitable to rabbits by eliminating the living conditions they like: Tall grass, brush, and wood piles for raising their young are where you'll find them. Mow the perimeter of your garden and move your brush piles.

Flower Power!
If you're intent on a fence to keep out rabbits, be sure you dig it at least 6 inches into the ground. Otherwise the rabbits will burrow under it and into your garden.

Next, try planting the foods they hate, beginning with foxglove *(Digitalis)*. They also dislike any plant in the onion family, so plant tons of chives and ornamental flowering bulbs in the onion family.

Fox oil, also known as "stink oil," "animal oil," or "bone oil" is an organic product that is said to deter rabbits with its very pungent odor. You can pick it up in the pharmacy. Mix the oil with water and sprinkle it on the soil.

Raccoons

Raccoons are night-time creatures and very destructive. One day you plant a row of hemerocallis, the next day you return to find them entirely dug up. One of the biggest problems with raccoons is once they find you, they're not inclined to leave the party. They know where the food is, and they'll keep coming back for more.

Raccoons are good climbers and are especially adept with fruit trees. If you have a problem with raccoons and fruit trees, keep them from getting up the tree by wrapping a stove pipe around the trunk. Raccoons have all their weight behind them and won't be able to sink their claws into the tree.

Other ways to deter raccoons are the following: An electronic device that emits a sound they hate. You (and your dogs and cats) can't hear it. Other deterrents include dog poop (import a dog for the day if you have to), baby powder, dirty laundry, and red-pepper spray.

Green Meany
Never try to corner a raccoon. They can become very vicious when threatened.

Slugs and Snails

Yes, slugs and snails belong in the animal kingdom. Small as they are, they are part of the mollusk family. How are you going to keep these little critters from ravaging your hostas and any other leaf in sight?

While there are many commercially available chemical snail baits on the market, all are extremely harmful to animals and children. Avoid them, and try this effective solution: Diatomaceous earth, known as "DE" on the market. DE is an abrasive powder made from finely ground remains of single-celled aquatic plants. Dust it on the edges of your garden bed to keep slugs and snails out. DE kills by abrading and dehydrating the small critters and insects that crawl over it. Ouch!

Another popular remedy for ridding the garden of slugs is to place a dish of beer in the garden, buried up to soil level. They go for the brew, get drunk, and never leave. Check every few days for deceased slugs!

The Good Guys Get the Last Word

After all the talk about the bad guys, who are the good guys? A big round of applause for the animals and insects that help in a multitude of ways in the garden: the cats and dogs, bats and snakes, lizards, armadillos, frogs, praying mantises, fireflies, butterflies, and ladybugs.

Praying Mantises, Ladybugs, and Fireflies

These insects work overtime in the garden, eating harmful insects in the garden.

The Truth About Cats and Dogs

Dogs and cats are invaluable for keeping unwanted animals from coming into the yard and garden. They can scare away deer, rabbits, mice, and moles. Why not get your pets working for their keep?

Armadillos, Lizards, Frogs, Bats, and Snakes

Bet You Didn't Know... Skunks are good guys! You may think skunks belong on the most "Un" Wanted List, but they are actually valuable because they eat white-faced hornet nests. They don't eat or damage

These sound like animals little boys like, but so do we—they all help in different ways. Armadillos love to nibble on grubs, so even if they make some problems, they do some good. Lizards, of course, eat lots of unwanted insects, as do frogs, bats, and snakes. All these animals will find their way naturally into your garden. You can help the frogs get there by placing saucers of water to attract them, and you can attract bats by purchasing bat houses. You'd be amazed at the bat's appetite for flying insects.

Think of your garden in terms of your own ecosystem and keep it balanced. You start eliminating one thing and another problem, maybe a bigger one, will arise.

The Least You Need to Know

➤ A humane way of dealing with unwanted animals is to do your best to deter them.

➤ Try deterring deer with "zoo poop," an increasingly popular fertilizer that combines aged elephant and rhino manure. It does double duty fertilizing plants and keeping out animals.

➤ Dogs and cats are great for keeping unwanted animals out of the garden, from deer to rabbits to mice to moles.

➤ Deer and raccoons remember where their meals came from, and will return again and again. Avoid replanting their favorite meals.

Chapter 24

When Bad Things Happen to Good Plants

In This Chapter

➤ The most common plant diseases and pests

➤ What a sick plant's symptoms will tell you

➤ The bug: friend and foe?

➤ Pest and disease controls: Biological, cultural, and severe

---

The day may come when the stems of your poor, innocent Phlox are covered with a grayish-white powder. Or your beautiful Tulips are just sticks where the flowers used to be. Welcome to the world of plant diseases and pests.

Unfortunately, we can't simply point you in the direction of the nearest chemical sprays or dusts to get rid of pest and disease problems. We've learned the hard way that the powerful chemical sprays and dusts used liberally in the past did more harm than good. Treatments to battle pests in the past, even in the smallest amounts, contaminated water, destroyed fish and wildlife, and threatened the environment in a multitude of ways. Ironically, the pests became immune to even the strongest pesticides on the market. So today many gardeners and some farmers take simpler, safer steps to control pests, relying on the use of sprays and dusts only as a severe measure and last resort.

In order to grow healthy plants with natural disease resistance bred in, avoid the use of pesticides.

Diagnosis Is Key

The first step in dealing with damaged plants is to stop and ask yourself, "What exactly is the problem?" Correct diagnosis is extremely important and tricky, especially since all you often have to go on is the damage you see.

Don't Make a Mountain out of a Molehill

Don't worry about your plant if its overall health is good. But if more than one half your plant really looks sick, then worry. One bug here or there, a few missing, munched, yellow or otherwise stressed leaves, is okay—it happens.

Reasons for Problems in the Garden

Not every garden problem is caused by diseases or pests. Remember, damage may be the result of wind, heat, cold, even air pollution. Your plant may also be getting too much or too little water, too much or too little fertilizer, even too much or too little sun. Always consider these factors first and rule them out if they don't apply.

Look for the Culprit

Look for the culprit at the scene of the crime. Sometimes you'll find it right there: a Japanese beetle on your potentilla flowers, for example. However, other insects work under cover of night, making them difficult to find, and others may flee before you get there.

Consider the Remedies

In the following sections you'll find a list of remedies for diseased plants, ranging from the simplest (cut off the diseased portion of the plant), to the most drastic (remove the plant).

Flower Power!

Make this checklist your guide:

➤ Rule out too much or too little sun, water, or food. All of these can cause stress and make a plant sick.

➤ Is it a disease or a pest? What disease? What pest?

➤ Decide on a remedy. Consider carefully which measures to take to correct the problem.

Look at the Symptoms

Ailing plants are classified in the same way physicians classify our illnesses—by the symptoms. We get fevers, colds, blisters, etc. Plants get spots, wilts, blights, rots, cankers, or rusts, which are the names of the visible symptoms.

Where to Look

Take a good look at every plant, checking both the top and underside of leaves, stems, buds and flowers, as well as the bases of plants. You should also look for clues in the surrounding soil surface. Note the leaves that have any abnormality. Are they partially eaten, covered with webbing, or colored differently? Look for blackened, wilted or chewed stems, sticky exudate on branches, withered or brown flower buds or loose soil mounds near the plants.

Treat the Symptoms

Whether you've got a beetle or a blight, the symptom, black spots, white spots, whatever, can help you identify whodunit. You can take care of the damage early and remedy the problem before it gets out of hand.

Common Diseases

Diseases are viral, bacterial, or fungal in nature, the most common plant diseases being fungal. Viruses are generally the most destructive to plants (unlike the viruses we get, which are rarely so serious and can be dealt with easily), and once a plant is infected there is little that can be done to restore it. The following is a list of some of the most common plant diseases classified by symptoms.

Flower Power!
Fungal diseases are less likely to occur when growing conditions are right for the plant—not too wet, not too dry.

Blight

Blights cause leaves or flowers to wilt or to become brown and die.

Damping-Off Disease

Damping-off disease appears as blackened soil at the base of the plant and tends to attack seedlings when the soil remains wet for long periods of time.

Leaf Spot

Leaf spot is caused by various fungi and bacteria and appear as white, brown, yellow or black circles. Discard diseased foliage and spray remaining plant with a fungicide. Read the label and follow directions carefully!

Leaf spot.

Mildew

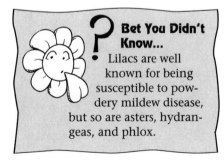

Bet You Didn't Know... Lilacs are well known for being susceptible to powdery mildew disease, but so are asters, hydrangeas, and phlox.

Powdery mildew is a fungus that appears as a gray or white powdery substance on foliage and stems. The first step is to dust sulfur on the affected parts of the plant in the morning when dew is still on the plant. If the problem persists, cut the plant to the ground (throwing away diseased tops), apply top dressing to the soil, and water to stimulate new growth. If the problems still persists, dig up and discard plant.

Powdery mildew.

Mosaic

Mosaic is caused by a virus, and the symptoms are yellow and green mottling of leaves, stems, and blossoms. Dig the plant up and throw it away.

Rot

Rotting caused by fungi or bacteria can cause decay of roots of the lower part of the stem. Cut back on watering (since rot is caused by too much water) and remove any mulch from around the plant in order to allow the soil to dry out. If the roots are rotted, discard the plant.

Rust

Rust is a fungus that appears as powdery, orange or brown pustules on leaves or stems. Cut off diseased portions of the plant and spray remaining plant with a fungicide.

Wilt

"Wilt" is a term used to describe a number of fungus and bacterial diseases that cause plants to wilt. If the entire plant has wilted, discard it.

313

Don't Spread the Disease

Don't risk spreading the disease by using the same shears on other plants. Take a tin of denatured alcohol and dip your shears or scissors in it before using them on another plant. Also, never compost any diseased foliage. This would spread the infection.

Dealing with Insects

You can imagine how impossible it would be for us to list every insect out there, but there are some notorious garden bugs you should know about—you're bound to meet up with them or the damage they do sooner or later.

Hand Picking

Hand picking, the first choice, means simply removing and crushing the insects. Wear gloves to avoid an allergic reaction. If enough insects are hand-picked in the spring and early summer, succeeding generations may be severely reduced. Early morning is often the best time to hand-pick the insects from garden plants. They are least active at this time.

Using Natural Predators

Natural predators of insects like toads, earwigs, lacewings, ladybugs, praying mantises, and stink bugs eat the insects whole. They are extremely useful in any garden. Buy adult ladybugs and praying mantis eggs, through garden-supply catalogs or a good garden-supply center.

A praying mantis.

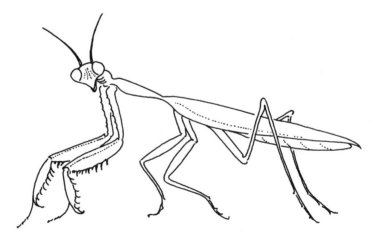

Using Parasites

Parasites, such as wasps (braconids) and insects (trichogramma), which are sold commercially as eggs, eat the pests from the inside.

Using Microbials

"Microbials" are microscopic organisms that make the pests sick when ingested. These include the commercially available Basillus thuringiensis ("BT"), which controls caterpillars; Bacillus popillae ("milky spore disease"), which controls the grubs of Japanese beetles and kills gypsy moth caterpillars; and nuclear-polyhedrons virus ("NPV") which also kills the grubs of Japanese beetles and gypsy moth caterpillars. Microbials are selective and don't harm good insects.

Insecticidal Soaps

Insecticidal soaps are widely used to control soft-bodied pests like aphids, spider mites, and whiteflies. A ground or powdered limestone and soap mixture, effective with leafminers and Japanese beetles, among other insects, is recommended for use only in cases of severe infestation.

Make a lime and soap mixture by combining 3 to 4 tablespoons of liquid dish soap and $1/4$ cup of lime per gallon of water.

Companion Planting

Companion planting is the practice of planting different plants near one another for beneficial effects, such as repelling insects. Marigolds, for example, are said to deter ants.

Natural Scents Repellents

This is closely related to companion planting. Natural scents and tastes confuse, lure, or trap insects. Some gardeners like to use Japanese beetle traps, which lure the beetles with the scent of a sex hormone.

Know Your Bugs

You're in the strongest position to go up against bugs when you know their habits. You'll know the bugs not necessarily by their looks, but by the damage they cause.

Check out the Damage

The following is a list of some common damage caused by certain pests:

➤ Leaves with holes in them are the work of chewing insects, such as caterpillars, grasshoppers, and beetles, leaving a kind of leaf skeleton. They also may chew away the surface leaf tissue.

Flower Power!

Record observations of plants in your garden notebook, noting the date you first observed the damage, and how it changes over time. Your notes will help you discover correlations between pest and disease problems and gardening or environmental practices.

➤ Seedlings cut off at ground level are the sign of cut worms.

➤ White pathways on leaves are left by leaf miners.

➤ Oozing, sticky sap is the sign of borers, which burrow into stems and branches, leaving oozing, sticky sap or sawdust.

➤ Wilted, twisted, yellow, spotted, or curled leaves can mean insects such as aphids, mealy bugs, scale, or white flies came and sucked the sap from plants.

➤ A sticky, shiny substance called "honeydew" on the leaf surface is left by aphids or scale.

The Most Common Pests

While you may not recognize these pests' names now, you're bound, at some point, to come across an aphid or Japanese beetle, so here is a list of the most common bugs and ways of dealing with them.

Flower Power!

Collect samples of any insects or damage that you may want to later identify. Take them to a local nursery or look it up in an illustrated guide to pests and diseases.

The Problem: Ants

The most harmful ants are fire ants, which are mainly in the southern parts of the United States. Any attempts at ant control should be directed at the ant colony.

The Solution to Ants

To repel ants, interplant spearmint, lavender, marigolds, or chives in the garden. Also, try bone meal around the plants or the juice of hot pepper pods on the plants to act as repellents. Last, spread liberal amounts of cayenne pepper around threatened plants. Ants hate moving over cayenne.

The Problem: Aphids

Aphids are half an inch long, pear-shaped bugs with or without wings. They are soft-bodied and can be green, yellow, or black. They usually cluster on the undersides of young leaves and shoots, sucking the juices.

Flower Power!
Control your aphids, and you shouldn't have a big ant problem. Ants like the gooey substance that aphids secrete, so they guard them from other insects.

Flower Power!
Recruit young gardeners: Many kids love bugs and science, so get them to be "Plant Detectives." Tell them to be on the lookout for bugs and to report any unusual behavior to you!

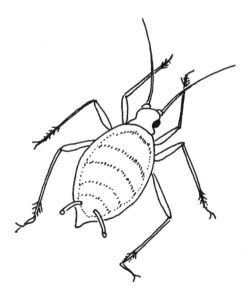

An aphid.

The Solution to Aphids

Pinch off and destroy leaves with aphids. Spray water with a little dishwashing liquid added to drown out aphids on the plants. Ladybug beetles and their larvae, as well as lacewings and their larvae, eat aphids and aphid eggs. Recruit them. Plant mint, garlic cloves, nasturtiums, lavender, sage, thyme, or dill to repel aphids.

The Problem: Chinch Bugs

These are about one-fifth of an inch long and black with white, red, or brown wings. They feed on grasses by sucking the juices.

The Solution to Chinch Bugs

Bring in ladybug beetles and lacewings. If that doesn't work, use soap spray to kill bugs or spray garlic, onion, or pepper extract.

The Problem: Harlequin Bugs

These shield-shaped, one-half-inch-long bugs are black and red or black and yellow. They suck plant juices. The winged adults lay tiny barrel-shaped eggs in rows or masses on the undersides of leaves. Harlequin bugs winter in trash or in leaves during both the adult or nymph stages. (A *nymph* is the stage of life-cycle of some insects between egg and adult.)

The Solution to Harlequin Bugs

Handle them by hand picking bugs and eggs. Control garden weeds and get praying mantises. In severe cases, use insecticidal soap.

The Problem: Japanese Beetles

Japanese beetles begin in their larval stages as white grubs, which are comma-shaped and two inches long. They feed on the tender roots of lawn grass. Adult beetles have metallic blue or green bodies and copper-colored wings.

Flower Power

Japanese beetle traps lure beetles to the trap and away from plants. Always hang a trap for Japanese beetles well away from sensitive plants, downwind at least 50 feet.

The Solution to Japanese Beetles

The first step in controlling Japanese beetles is to get rid of the white grubs by applying milky spore disease to lawns and grassy areas. Second, interplant garlic and larkspur as a natural repellent. Hand-pick the adults. In severe cases, spray garlic, onion, or pepper mixture on plants to deter feedings, or spray soap with lime added on the bugs themselves, which will irritate them.

The Problem: Leafminers

Leafminers are green or black and one-eighth of an inch long. They tunnel between the upper and lower leaf surface, leaving a white trail behind them.

The Solution to Leafminers

First, import ladybugs and lacewings to eat the eggs of leafminers. Remove and destroy the infested leaves and cover plants with a cheese cloth netting to prevent more egg laying. In severe cases, spray hot pepper juice or lime spray. Dust wet plants heavily with lime to repel flies and deter egg laying.

The Problem: Mealybugs

Elliptically-shaped mealybugs have a waxy, white covering. The females are immobile and wingless; the males have wings. You can recognize the presence of mealybugs by a sticky, honeydewlike substance they leave on the plant. Mealybugs damage plants by sucking juices from them.

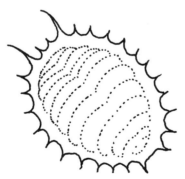

A mealybug.

The Solution to Mealybugs

In the early spring, spray the plant with a soap and water mixture. In severe cases, wash off the plant with high-pressure water, being careful not to damage the plant. Spray the soap and water mixture or touch individual insects with alcohol on a cotton swab. This may take repeated applications.

The Problem: Scale

Scale are noninsect pests similar to mealybugs. They also suck juices from plants, leaving a honeydewlike trail. Scale cause discolored leaves and stunt the plant's growth.

The Solution to Scale

Import ladybug beetles to prey upon the scale. Also, gently scrape scale off plants or touch with a cotton swab soaked in alcohol. Repeat this application every 3 to 4 days or until scale dies. In severe cases, use soap and lime spray in early spring before buds open.

The Problem: Spider Mites

These are also noninsect pests. These tiny, orange, brown, or green mites suck juices from plants, turning leaves yellow, silver, or speckled.

The Solution to Spider Mites

The most effective controls are ladybug beetles and lacewings. In severe cases, spray the plant with insecticidal soap, lime spray, or a combination of both. Dust wet plants heavily with lime to repel.

The Problem: Thrips

Thrips are minute yellow or black insects that rasp plants, sucking their juices and spreading plant diseases. When disturbed, they fly, hop short distances, and flick their abdomens over their heads like scorpions. Thrips can cause peony buds to turn brown. They also infest Japanese iris, daylily, lilium, and gladiolus.

The Solution to Thrips

Dragonflies prey on thrips and are a good biological control. Interplant with marigolds for cultural control, and in severe cases, spray insecticidal soap on plants in early morning when thrips are least active.

A Checklist of Preventative Care for Your Plants

You can minimize your disease and pest problems in a number of ways. Use the following as a checklist for keeping your plants healthy and minimizing your problems:

Choose Native Plants or Plants Adapted to Your Soil

Choose plants that are either native to your area or well-adapted to your soil and site. If you're using plants that aren't native, make sure you give them what they need in terms of soil and site.

Don't Crowd Your Plants

Don't overcrowd plants. Plants too close together make diseases spread more easily. Also, healthy plants are usually better able to tolerate the damage caused by pests and diseases.

Encourage Diversity

Encourage diversity in your garden by planting lots of different kinds of plants.

Build Healthy Soil

Build healthy soil. Every year when you add organic materials, compost, and peat moss, you improve soil texture and reduce pests.

Plant Only Healthy Plants

Plant only healthy plants and quality seeds.

Remove Old Plants

Remove and destroy old plants from the yard. Discard debris—don't let diseased plants linger.

The Least You Need to Know

➤ Always discard a plant that has lost its vigor or doesn't recover rapidly after treatment.

➤ Use biological and cultural controls first, before you try a severe measure.

➤ Wait until you see signs of bugs before you treat the plant.

➤ Know the difference between the good bugs and the bad bugs.

Part 9
Putting It All Together

In this part you'll learn how to put it all together, with guidelines for caring for your annuals, perennials, bulbs, and shrubs and planting instructions for the wonderful peonies, poppies, and irises that are best planted in the fall. Fall is a great time to plant spring-blooming bulbs and really pull your garden together.

You'll also learn about basic lawn maintenance. Every garden looks better when a green lawn enhances it, and you'll learn here how to choose the right lawn for your area. You'll learn how to install, repair, or renew your lawn, how to lay down sod, and how to maintain a healthy lawn.

Finally, we hope you'll want to keep learning about gardening (the next best thing to gardening is reading about gardening!) by reading the wonderful gardening catalogs that arrive in your mailbox each winter. We'll tell you about the good ones and provide you with a list of addresses so you can send off for them.

Chapter 25

Fall Chores: Clean Up and Plant Again

In This Chapter

➤ Cleaning up the garden

➤ Fall plantings: Spring-flowering bulbs, poppies, peonies, and tall-bearded irises

➤ Storing containers and wintering over plants

➤ Winter mulches

As the leaves on the trees begin to change color and drop, perennials, bulbs, and shrubs go through a similar change: Their leaves turn brown, and their stems may fall over. Their metabolism is slowing down, and any food being manufactured is going to the plants' roots, where it will be stored for the winter. This process is the same for all plants, whether perennials, trees, bulbs, or shrubs.

Everything is slowing down, and as the days get shorter and the nights cooler, chores in the garden will also slow down. But there are a few things you should do every fall to ensure the health of your plants and gardens. Fall gardening chores include raking leaves, cutting back perennials, cleaning up and storing plant containers, and planting spring-flowering bulbs, and it would be lovely if your fall garden chores also include planting the wonderful poppies, peonies, and tall-bearded irises.

Now you'll learn how to tackle the fall gardening chores like a pro, so the following year you'll have an abundance of healthy plants and flowers and maybe even some poppies, peonies, and tall-bearded irises.

Fall Chores (Like Raking Leaves)

Every garden bed should be kept free of the fall leaves that blow or fall into the garden. These leaves can mat, creating just the wet, dark conditions conducive to disease and rot.

Flower Power!
Newly fallen leaves aren't a mulch for the gar-den, but you can save them and com-post them to make a great leaf mulch.

Get Leaves out of the Garden

You may have to rake or blow leaves from the garden a few times during the fall season. If you're raking, do it gently, being careful not to injure plants. Leaf blowers are great pieces of equipment but not something most of us own. Another means of ridding gardens of leaves is to simply put on a pair of gloves, grab a bag, and pick them up by hand.

Perennials and Their Fall Care

As fall progresses, you'll see the perennials in your garden begin to look as though they're dying—they'll turn brown and the taller ones will flop over. In fact, they are said to be "dying back" at this time.

When this happens, you'll want to cut back the foliage on most of the perennials, leaving about 1 to 2 inches above the crown of the plant. There are a lot of good reasons to cut back most perennials in the fall, but one is that it neatens up the garden.

To Cut or Not to Cut (Back), That Is the Question

So which perennials do you cut back? This is hard to answer. Most perennials will need to be cut back, if for no other reason than to neaten the appearance of the plant and the garden. However, some perennials, like astilbe, achillea, and some sedum, have attractive flowers and foliage that stay looking good all winter, so it's best for aesthetic reasons not to cut them back. Other perennials, like iberis and dianthus, should probably not be cut back because their foliage is evergreen or semi-evergreen.

If you're uncertain whether to cut back a specific perennial, look it up in Chapter 8. Instructions are given for fall cleanup for each perennial.

Don't Make a Winter Home for Disease and Rodents

One of the most important reasons to cut back perennials is to lessen the chance that diseases, insects, and rodents will take up residence. Big, wet leaves smothering your perennials look like attractive lodging to rodents and can create a multitude of disease problems.

Make Spring Cleanup Easier

If you take care of fall chores in the fall, you don't have to do them in the spring. Spring is a wonderful time to have your eye toward the future, thinking about new plants, new gardens, etc. If you don't cut back the perennials in the fall, that's just one more chore you'll have to do in the spring when you could be doing something more fun.

Winter Protection

If you'll cut back stems to about 1 to 2 inches above the ground, that inch or so will allow for autumn leaves to collect along the stems, thus giving the plants a form of winter protection. A few autumn leaves on top is okay; be sure not to let too many accumulate.

Annuals and Their Fall Care

Fall cleanup with annuals is easy—just pull them out of the soil after the first hard frost and discard them or add them to the compost pile. Fall is the time to plant spring-flowering bulbs, and it's also a good time to add another inch or so of organic matter to the soil for next year's garden.

Plant Spring-Flowering Bulbs

Planting bulbs is a nice fall chore, and one for which you should allow time. A day or two of hard labor in the fall pays off handsomely in the spring—in bright and cheerful daffodils, tulips, or whatever else you plant.

Planting Depths

The correct planting depth for a bulb is important—it ensures strong growing stems, like those necessary for tulips and lilies. Refer to Chapter 18 for an illustration about planting depth.

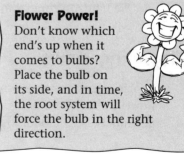

Flower Power!
Don't know which end's up when it comes to bulbs? Place the bulb on its side, and in time, the root system will force the bulb in the right direction.

When to Plant

Daffodils, hyacinths, and other minor bulbs like scilla and muscari will need time to root in the ground before winter comes, so plant these bulbs early in the fall. Tulips, on the other hand, need the assurance of a consistent cold period and shouldn't be planted until at least a month later.

Narcissus.

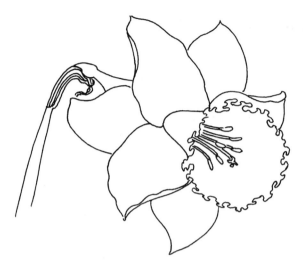

The Facts on Poppies, Peonies, and Tall-Bearded Irises

Poppies, peonies, and tall-bearded irises are three absolutely wonderful perennials you'll want to add to your garden in the fall. We've left these perennials for last, kind of like dessert. Although these are three very different perennials, they have a lot in common.

When to Plant Poppies, Peonies, and Tall-Bearded Irises

Each of these perennials should be planted in the late summer or early fall as they need a cool temperature during which to set their roots.

Hardiness Zones

Poppies, peonies, and tall-bearded irises are hardy in pretty much the same zones: poppies are hardy in zones 3 to 8; peonies are hardy in zones 4 to 8; and irises are hardy in zones 3 to 9.

Flowering Times

Poppies, peonies, and tall-bearded irises are some of the earlier flowering perennials. They flower in early June in zones 5 to 6 and even earlier in warmer climates. Like many perennials, their blooms don't last very long—two weeks at the most.

Soil Conditions

Poppies, peonies, and tall-bearded irises all need well-drained soil, and poppies like a fairly sandy soil. Peonies, on the other hand, like a rich soil.

All About Poppies

The Oriental poppy (*Papaver)* genus has more than a hundred different varieties of poppies, including flowers with single and double petals in every shade and hue of white, pink, and red. Depending on the variety, papavers will grow from 2 to 4 feet. The flowers are often quite elegant-looking, particularly the papavers with ruffled edges.

How to Plant Poppies

Plant poppies in very well-drained soil that's on the sandy side, and be sure to plant deeply. Dig a hole 3 inches deep, loosening the soil around it, and plant the poppies' crown about an inch below the soil surface.

Flower Power!
The hairy foliage on papavers turns brown in summer, after they bloom, and isn't attractive. Plant a leafy perennial in front of it or an annual to hide the foliage.

About Digging and Dividing in the Fall

Divide clumps of poppies late in the summer, if you wish, but it's not necessary unless you want to create more stock. When digging up the roots, use a spade because poppy roots are fleshy and brittle, and if you use a fork, you risk breaking the roots.

All About Peonies

Herbaceous peonies are some of the most satisfying plants you'll grow. The large-petaled flowers come in pure whites, deep reds, fiery reds, and pinks, as well as single and double forms. The double forms are extremely fragrant—*Paeonia* 'Vivid Rose' really smells like a rose, and the single forms often have showy stamens that dance in the center of the large petals.

Flower Power!
Don't confuse herbaceous peonies with tree peonies. Tree peonies are more expensive, harder to grow, and don't have herbaceous stems—they stay above ground all year.

As if peonies weren't great enough, the foliage stays a deep green all summer, turning the peony plant into a tidy little shrub.

Caring for Your Peonies

Peonies should be staked to keep the heavy flowers from falling over. Use a "peony ring" (available at garden centers) to slip over the peony when it's about one-half its height. Stakes support the ring, but be careful not to pierce the peony roots with the stakes. After the plant flowers, deadhead the seed pods and take the time to shape your peony. If a stem with foliage is a few inches taller than another, cut it even with the others.

Care in the Fall

Cut the peony to the ground when the foliage has turned yellow and is starting to fall down. You can dig and divide if you wish in the fall, or leave your peonies undisturbed for years. If you want to divide for more stock, do so in the early fall, around September in the North, October in the South.

Digging and Dividing Your Peonies

To dig and divide your peonies, you need to dig a big hole around the plant to take out all the roots. Make a circle in the soil around the plant, following the leaf line. Cut back the foliage, leaving about 3 inches of stem. Now make a new circle around the plant that is halfway between the stem and the circle in the soil.

Take a straight-edged spade and cut into the soil, following the lines of the new circle. Gently place the spade under the peony and loosen the soil with the spade. Walk around the plant, doing this in a couple of spots. When you can feel the roots are completely detached, lift the plant out. Try to remove all the soil from around the roots.

The pink buds you see around the stems are the "eyes," next year's flowering stems. You'll see the old stems, eyes, and a core where they attach to the roots. The roots are large—some may be an inch and a half in diameter. From a standing position, looking down on the plant, cut between the center of the old stems with a clean, sharp knife. Be careful not to hit an eye. Cut into the core of the plant, stopping at the roots. Twist gently to pull the roots apart. The goal is to get a plant with 3 to 5 eyes on it and at least one large root. Trim the roots to 6 inches and replant.

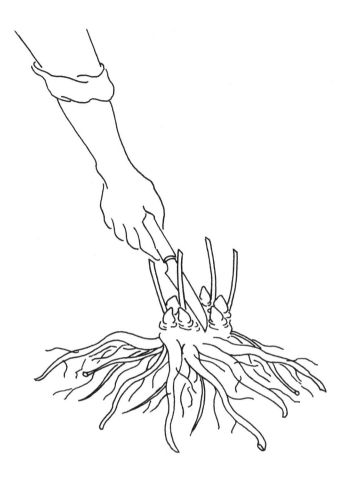

Dividing a peony.

All About Tall-Bearded Irises

Tall-bearded iris, or German iris, are very colorful plants that grow about 40 inches tall with flowers up to 6 inches in diameter. Many of them have a wonderful fragrance, almost like grapes. The colors and bicolors range from blues, lavenders, and pinks to whites, yellows, and gold. All tall-bearded irises work well as a single genus garden, particularly since the swordlike foliage stays green all summer. There are also dwarf- and intermediate-bearded irises that work well in smaller areas.

Flower Power!
Don't confuse tall-bearded irises or German irises with the irises listed in Chapter 8.

331

Tall-bearded iris.

Planting Instructions

Early September in the North, or early October in the South, are the times to plant German iris. They have a rhizome root system that should stay above the ground in the North, and in the South the rhizomes should be planted slightly under the soil's surface. The roots beneath these rhizomes are planted in the soil to support the plants. Place the "fan" or cut-back foliage, upright when planting.

For gardeners in the North: Prevent your irises from heaving in the winter by placing about one-half inch of builders sand to weight the rhizomes down.

About Digging and Dividing in the Fall

It's a good practice to dig and divide German irises every three to four years in September in the North; and later in October in the South. This way the irises keep their vigor.

Dig and divide the plants on the morning of a dry, sunny day. Before digging up, cut the foliage into a fan shape to make them easier to work with. Divide the plants in large groups, making clean cuts. Place the rhizomes in the sun to dry out before replanting them. Any rotten pieces of the root system should be thrown away.

Caring for Your Potted Plants in Winter

You need to take care of plants in containers. Above the frost line, clay pots should be emptied of annuals and soil and stacked and stored in a cool, dry place.

Wintering over Plants Indoors

When fall comes, bring in any pots with annuals early enough so they can acclimate to indoor conditions. Check the annuals list and herb list for plants that are known to "winter over" well. To stimulate growth, cut back any plants that are losing leaves to one-half their size.

> **Garden Talk**
> *Wintering over*
> plants means to
> care for plants
> in containers in
> the hope that
> they'll survive the winter.

Perennials and Shrubs in Containers

Perennials and shrubs are meant to stay outside in winter and can be moved to a sheltered location, such as the corner of a terrace or against the south side of a house in the fall. Cut back perennials in containers as you would perennials in the garden, and add a winter mulch to help them winter over.

Putting the Bed to Bed for Winter

The last thing you'll do for your garden bed, if you live where the ground freezes in winter, is put a winter mulch on it. A winter mulch is applied after the ground has frozen to prevent it from freezing and thawing throughout the winter. Freezing and thawing can cause plants to "heave," or become loosened from the soil.

> **Garden Talk**
> *Heaving* is when
> a plant be-
> comes loosened
> from the ground
> as a result of
> freezing and thawing winter
> conditions.

Which Plants Need Winter Mulches

Flower Power!
A few perennials that really need winter protection are althaea, dian-thus, and iberis.

New plantings will certainly benefit from a winter mulch because they are more susceptible to heaving than established plants. They don't have the root system in place to anchor them into the ground. Many tender and semi-tender perennials would also benefit, and you should apply a winter mulch for any perennial you think may not be hardy—you can't go wrong as long as you follow a few simple guidelines.

Don't Mulch Too Heavily

First, don't mulch too heavily—a few inches will do the job. Use straw or salt marsh hay, and place a few pine boughs on top to keep the straw in place.

Don't Remove the Mulch Too Suddenly in Spring

In the spring, when it's time to remove the mulch, take the mulch off the crowns of the plants and allow the mulch over the roots to stay down. If you remove all of it at once, and there's a sudden cold snap, the tender new growth may become damaged. Remove the rest of the mulch later. Remember to save your winter mulch to add to the compost pile.

Some Kinds of Mulches

Green Meany
Be careful of rodents making homes in hay or straw in the garden.

One of the best winter mulches is evergreen boughs. The ground should be frozen by Christmas time, and what better way to recycle your tree than in the garden as winter mulch?

Another winter mulch is leaves—the same kind of chopped-up leaf mulch you used on the garden. Chopped-up leaves won't mat and will break down quickly into the soil, improving the soil. Salt-march hay and straw are also good for winter mulch. Both are available by the bale, but salt-marsh hay is often hard to find (it's seashore grasses). These are lightweight and will need pine boughs to hold them down.

The Least You Need to Know

➤ Cut back the foliage on most perennials in the fall, leaving about 1 to 2 inches above the crown of the plant.

➤ Fall cleanup with annuals is easy—just pull them out of the soil after the first hard frost and discard them or add them to the compost pile. Fall is the time to plant spring-flowering bulbs, and it's also a good time to add another inch or so of organic matter to the soil for next year's garden.

➤ The correct planting depths for bulbs is important—it ensures strong growing stems, like those necessary for tulips and lilies. Refer to the illustration in Chapter 18.

➤ Plant poppies, peonies, and tall-bearded irises in the fall. Each of these perennials should be planted in the late summer or early fall as they need a cool temperature to set their roots.

➤ The last thing you'll do for your garden bed, if you live where the ground freezes in winter, is put a winter mulch on it. A winter mulch is applied after the ground has frozen to prevent it from freezing and thawing.

Chapter 26

Lawn Repair and Renewal

In This Chapter

➤ Starting a new lawn

➤ Maintaining your lawn

➤ Improving lawn

➤ Types of grasses

It may seem odd that a chapter about lawns is included in a book on gardening, but actually no garden looks better than the one with a pretty green lawn to enhance it. A well-tended lawn can make the picture complete.

Water

Most grasses need a lot of water. Turf is like any other plant in that it needs water. The fact is that every 100 square feet of lawn contains about 100,000 turf plants, and each of those turf plants needs water (even if the turf plant is a single blade of grass). Fortunately for gardeners in arid parts of the country, there are newer grasses on the market that require less water than traditional grasses and are the ideal choices for these drier areas.

You'll get the best lawn possible by selecting the right grass for your region and assuring it has proper watering, feeding, and maintenance.

Select the Best Turf for Your Region

In order to maximize the water from rain and irrigation, select the turf best adapted for your area. Bermuda grass works well in many southern states. Hot and humid regions do well with St. Augustine grass, Zoysia grass. The more temperate climates can use mixtures of Kentucky bluegrass, Rye grasses, and Fescues. Tall Fescue is often chosen in mid-Atlantic states with very hot summers and cold winters. Check with your county extension agent or local nursery to find out which grasses perform best in your area. There's also a list of grasses at the end of this chapter.

How Much Water?

The amount of water a lawn needs will vary. Consider the quality of the lawn, use of the area, intensity and duration of sunlight, and rainfall. Sandier sites may not need more water, but they will need more frequent irrigation than sites on loam.

Provide Proper Irrigation

Irrigation can provide you with a near perfect lawn during most of the growing season. It allows you to maintain a healthy turf during drier weather, control growth and color, and apply lawn amendments that need to be watered into the soil. A simple irrigation system is a hose and sprinkler. These are actually very effective, as long as you remember to move the sprinkler around.

More Sophisticated Irrigation Equipment

Most home-supply stores carry irrigation time clocks that turn the water on and off automatically. More complex irrigation systems include in-ground plumbing and multiple valves for partitioning the lawn into irrigation zones. These systems, when properly designed, give you a lot of flexibility and control over your watering. Good management of an irrigation system saves water and produces a good lawn.

Your Soil and Your Turf

Your soil plays a big part since the turf gets its water from the soil. A good soil lets both water and air move easily in and out of it. It doesn't become waterlogged or dry out too easily. Ideal soils have enough sand to keep them open, but enough clay to let them hold on to some water and nutrients. Loams and sandy loams are best.

In cooler, more temperate climates, rain alone will meet the turf's water needs, except perhaps in the very hottest months. However, hot, dry climates will require irrigation for most grasses throughout the year to maintain a useful lawn surface.

Your Soil's Depth

A deep soil, at least 4 inches, will hold more water and have more turf roots to take up water and nutrients. This means fewer waterings and less fertilizing. Otherwise, most grasses will need weekly watering in the summer.

Watering Tips

Evenings and early mornings are usually the best time to irrigate.

When it's time to water, measure how much your lawn is getting with the help of a tin can and a ruler. Place a tin can in the area you want to water, turn on the sprinkler, and fill up the tin can to one-quarter inch. After the water has filled up, use a screwdriver in the lawn to see how far the water has moved into the soil. Water again if it hasn't wetted the soil down to 5 or 6 inches. The idea is to keep the soil moist, but not wet and sticky.

Flower Power!
Clay and silt soils will hold moisture in, thus requiring less watering. One slow, prolonged irrigation may be enough to keep a lawn green for two weeks or longer.

Green Meany
Frequent light waterings encourage more weeds than grass.

Watering by Eye

Observe the lawn. Does your lawn appear lush, but not wet? Do the turf leaves spring back up in a few minutes after they've been walked on? Can you push a screwdriver 5 to 6 inches into the soil easily? If you answered yes to these questions, the lawn does not need to be watered. Water when parts of the lawn change to a grayish color, the turf stays down after being walked on, or you can't push the screwdriver into the soil easily.

Fertilizing

Begin fertilizing your lawn when spring-flowering bulbs are blooming, and apply a second application a few months later—the end of June for Southerners and the beginning of July for Northerners. You can choose slow-release fertilizers, liquid fertilizers, high-nitrogen fertilizers—all of which can be found easily at your local garden center. Find the right size bag for your lawn area.

Ways to Fertilize

If you use a slow-release fertilizer, you'll need to fertilize less often. You may need a lawn spreader for a dry fertilizer so that it's evenly distributed. These spreaders can be rented or purchased.

Flower Power!
When it comes to fertilizing, remember less is best. If you feel nervous about applying fertilizer, apply it lightly the first year (half the recommended amount on the bag). See if you have any changes for the better.

Another way to fertilize is with a liquid fertilizer that hooks up to the end of a hose. The problem with liquid feeding is it can be difficult to control the amount of chemical being applied, and areas of lawn may burn from too much fertilizer. Flush out that area with water if you see signs that this happened. Choose a high-nitrogen percentage (that's the first number in the series of three, the second and third are phosphorus and potassium) to give your lawn a good green color. Lawn fertilizers high in nitrogen are 30–5–8, 22–8–4, and 17–4–4.

Planting and Mending Grass

A lot about caring for your lawn will depend on where you live. In cooler climates, it's better to start lawns in the fall and mend patches of lawn in the spring. In warmer climates, you should do both—start your lawns and mend them in the cool spring. There are different ways to plant grass in the two climates.

Northern Grass Planting

Northerners can plant directly with seed or sod. Sod is grass that is already grown and comes in large rolls or pieces about an inch thick. Sod is instant grass and is great for slopes, walkways, and high-erosion areas. It's more expensive than seed.

Southern Grass Planting

Southerners can also purchase grass as seed or sod, as well as by sprigs or plugs. "Sprigs" are pieces of roots, which are planted underground. "Plugs" are individual plants of grass you have chosen, planted in a zigzag pattern. If you plant with sprigs or plugs, you may want to sow an annual grass by seed that will grow quickly and will shade the new plants, keeping them cool.

Mending Lawns

If you have a lawn you want to mend, rake the area with a lawn rake, removing old grass, rocks, etc. You may need to add top soil if the area isn't level. Lay down sod, plant sprigs, plugs, or sow seed the same way you would for a new lawn. Mulch the area lightly with hay (unless you laid down sod) until active growth begins. Remove hay when roots take hold and growth begins. Keep area moist, cutting down on water when active growth begins.

Starting a New Lawn

Starting a lawn can be a big job if it involves grading the area, and it's probably best to hire a contractor if grading is involved. If your area doesn't need grading, follow these directions.

Your Lawn's pH

If your soil is on the acidic side, lime may have to be added to correct its pH level. On the other hand, soil that's alkaline will need sulfur. The best way to find out if your soil's pH needs correcting is to submit a soil test to an extension service. They'll give you the results and recommend the lime or sulfur needed to correct it.

Soil Amending

Once you know about your lawn's pH, the next step is to amend the soil if it's too dense or too porous. Determine if your soil will need amending. Too much clay, add organic matter like sand and manure; if it's too sandy, add peat moss and organic matter.

Rotary-Till the Soil

Rotary-till the soil (these machines can be rented from a local hardware or garden-supply store). Rake the soil level with a heavy metal, short-pronged rake, making sure to remove any foreign objects. Plant one of the following: plugs (avoid making straight rows), sprigs (in a shallow trench and cover with soil), or sod (laying it down seam to seam in a tight fashion).

Lay down sod in a brick pattern. Create a tight, seam-to-seam parallel line by laying the pieces side by side, but stagger each piece to avoid joining the tops and bottoms of the pieces.

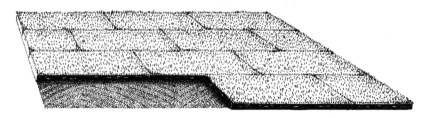

How to place sod.

341

Sowing Lawn Seed

Sow seed evenly in all directions by throwing seed out (like chicken feed) or use a "spreader," which will spread the seed for you (it has a hopper to hold the seed and an opening to distribute the seed).

The Same Day

After you seed, roll the area with a lawn roller once, if you're fortunate enough to have one. Sodded areas benefit from being rolled every day for a week to press the seams of the sod together. Rolling the sod cuts down on weeds growing through the spaces. You'll want to "walk-in" plugs and sprigs to firm the soil around lawn plants. To walk-in plugs and sprigs, simply place your feet around the plants and press the soil down firmly. The process will remove any air pockets that may have been created when you planted the sprig or plugs. Keep the area moist and cool until growth begins and roots take hold. Mulch seed and sprigs with hay or straw until growth begins and then remove.

Good Mowing Practices

Lawn mowers have blades that can be adjusted so you can cut the grass anywhere from 1 to 3 inches high. How high you mow will depend on the type or types of grass you grow, the season you're in, and the daily weather. If you feed and water a lot, you'll have to mow more often.

Mowing New Lawns

It's better to mow new lawns at a higher grass level for the first few cuts—until the grass takes over and starts to fill in. The taller the grass, the deeper the root system will grow.

Some General Rules of Thumb

Mow about an inch or so most of the year in southern areas—until the cool season, when the grass is under stress. Southern grasses love the warm temperatures. In northern climates, it's just the opposite: The grass is most under stress during drought periods and should be left taller, about $2^{1}/_{2}$ to 3 inches. The taller the grass level, the deeper the roots are. In the spring and fall, when the grass is actively growing again, change your level of mowing down to 2 or $2^{1}/_{2}$ inches. Any shaded areas are higher stress areas, and grass levels should be left a bit taller than grass grown in full sun.

Some Do's and Don'ts of Mowing the Lawn

Good lawns don't just happen, they are the result of good lawn care. Following are some tips on good mowing practices:

➤ *Do sharpen blades.* Do sharpen or replace your mower's blades every year. Most blades are under thirty dollars. If your blades aren't sharp, they can pull or make ragged cuts to the grass, which could cause disease problems. If you're buying a new mower it's better to buy a name brand that has guarantees.

➤ *Do mow regularly.* Mow regularly at least once a week during the grasses' growing season. This will cut down on any weeds in the lawn.

➤ *Do change the mowing direction.* Do change the direction you're mowing each week. Go north and south one week, then east and west the next. Lawns that are mowed in the same direction all the time won't get clean cuts.

➤ *Don't mow during drought periods.* Your lawn is under stress during drought and mowing creates more stress. Stressed lawns appear as brown patches

➤ *Don't mow grass when it's wet or still has dew on it.* You'll not only temporarily clog your mower's blades, the wet cut grass on the lawn could harm the grass it sits on.

➤ *Don't leave heavy grass clippings on the lawn for more than a day.* Clippings will hurt the lawn beneath it. Rake them up the same day or, at the latest, the following day.

> **Flower Power!**
> Rake up lawn clippings and use them in the compost pile.

What You Should Know About Thatch

If you overfeed, you could cause too much lush growth that will make the grass more prone to disease and thatch problems. Thatch is a problem if it becomes more than an inch thick, in which case you may be prone to insect and disease problems. Don't overwater, overfeed, mow when the grass is high, or leave many clippings on the lawn. These create thatch problems.

> **Garden Talk**
> *Thatch* is a layer of dead grass from clippings that form between the soil and the grass itself.

Dethatching for Good Lawn Health

Raking the lawn in the spring to remove brown fluff is called "dethatching." If you have a large area, you may need to hire a lawn service to come in for a day and dethatch for you. You can also rent a machine called a "vertical mower" which pulls thatch up and out of the lawn. This should be done early in the fall for cool weather climates.

Northern Grasses and Southern Grasses

Flower Power!
There are shade or sun grass-seed mixtures, choose the right one for your site.

Northern grasses are called "cool season grasses" and are hardy in zones 7 or cooler. There are usually a variety of grass types in one lawn. Cool season grasses are hardy for northern winters—they may turn brown during droughts or heat waves but will green up in the fall. Mow these grasses between 2 to 3 inches high.

Some cool season grasses include:

➤ *Bent grass* (very fine texture, likes cool, wet regions, sun or light shade)

➤ *Fine fescues or red fescues* (fine-textured, dark green, stiff, shade and drought-tolerant)

➤ *Kentucky bluegrass* (very hardy, dark-green color)

➤ *Perennial Rye grass* (holds soil in place but isn't a spreading grass)

Southern grasses or "warm season grasses," are hardy in zones 7 or higher and are usually planted by sod, sprigs, or plugs. They are coarser-textured grasses and will go dormant and turn brown in the cool weather. They will, however, keep their green color through long, hot summers and droughts. Best mowing level is 1 inch for most types of grasses.

Some warm season grasses include:

➤ *Bahiagrass* (coarse texture, sun, or moderate shade and grows in sandy and poor soils—one of the easiest to grow)

➤ *Bermuda grass* (coarse texture, deep-green color, needs sun, water, and feeding often, prone to thatch problem if not regularly mowed)

➤ *St. Augustine grass* (coarse-textured, shade-tolerate, dark-green color, difficult to mow)

➤ *Zoysia grass* (finer-textured, creates a dense, tough lawn, requires fewer mowings, prone to thatch problems)

The Least You Need to Know

➤ You'll get the best lawn possible by selecting the right grass for your region and assuring it has proper watering, feeding, and maintenance.

➤ Clay and silt soils will hold moisture in, thus requiring less watering. One slow, prolonged irrigation may be enough to keep a lawn green for two weeks or longer.

➤ If you feed and water a lot, you'll have to mow more often.

➤ Begin fertilizing your lawn when spring-flowering bulbs are blooming and apply a second application a few months later—the end of June for the South and the beginning of July for the North.

Chapter 27

Oooooh.....

Mail Order

Cruising the Mail-Order Gardening Catalogs

In This Chapter

➤ The learning annex: gardening catalogs

➤ What to look for and what to avoid in catalogs

➤ A few good catalogs

➤ Take notes in your gardening notebook

We hope that all the things you originally found daunting, intimidating, and overwhelming about gardening have found their way into the compost bin, and you can now wield a hoe like a pro and throw around big words like hemerocallis (let the sissies call them "daylilies"!). Kidding aside, it's no small feat to become a gardener—but you're a long way from where you started when you first picked up this book. Most important, you've got the tools now to create the garden of your dreams.

Get Your Great Ideas from the Catalogs

As you continue to build your gardening education, consider putting your name on lots of nursery, garden supply, and seed catalogs. They are great sources of inspiration for all gardeners, beginners and veterans alike—the beautiful pictures of enviable gardens make successful gardeners of us all. But more than an inspiration, the catalogs are a great education for the beginner gardener. There's a list at the end of the chapter of some excellent garden supply catalogs. Make use of these catalogs not only for the education but also for the good bargains!

You can learn a great deal about plants by browsing the catalogs. Many catalogs, like the ones from Wayside Gardens, Jackson & Perkins, White Flower Farm, and Thompson & Morgan, have very good photographs (in full color) of the plants they sell. While the plants' strange Latin names may not mean much to you now, it's worth looking at the pictures and getting an idea of what's out there in the big wide world of plants. You wouldn't know it, but as you cruise the catalogs you're actually building your gardening knowledge foundation, the first step in moving toward the garden of your dreams.

A Mail-Order Education

Browsing gardening and seed catalogs is a great alternative to purchasing a costly plant encyclopedia with a listing of a thousand North American perennials. You don't need to know about this many plants right now; you only need to learn about the ones that appeal to you and that you can grow in your area. Many of the gardening catalogs offer user-friendly descriptions of plants and gardens, information you can use while you're still just thinking about the garden you want to start.

Read Catalogs When You Can't Plant

? Bet You Didn't Know... If you want an idea of how popular gardening catalogs are, look at the famous Burpee Seeds catalog. It was established over 100 years ago, and it's still going strong today.

Gardening catalogs have always been popular reading for gardeners, especially during the winter when the ground is frozen or during the summer when it's too hot—or any time a gardener just wants to dream!

Catalogs, as you no doubt suspect, serve many more purposes than just occasional good reading. Later on, you may want to order plants or gardening supplies from gardening catalogs that you can't find at your local garden center. Some catalogs, like Van Bourgondien's, have bargains on a selected variety of plants, offered as plant collections.

Crash Course for Impatient Gardeners

Of course, you may not have time to peruse garden catalogs at your leisure, maybe next year. This year you want to get outside and start your garden! That's fine, but it won't hurt to order a few catalogs (or even one) for plants and supplies at a later time.

Every Picture Tells a Story

The catalogs chosen for this list are the ones that you can learn from, either because the photographs are good or the descriptions of the plants, or both. Some catalogs also provide good information about the plant's culture, as well as what you need to know about growing that plant.

Look for What Appeals to You Most

You'll want to pay attention to what appeals to you: colors, shapes, foliage. Get an idea of how the plant grows: Does it creep like a ground cover? Climb like vines? In other words, get an idea of the plant's habit of growth.

You may even realize, as you are looking at a picture of a shrub in the Jackson & Perkins' catalog, that this is exactly the plant you had in mind for that spot on the south side of the house. Be sure to make a note of

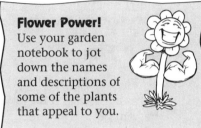

Flower Power!
Use your garden notebook to jot down the names and descriptions of some of the plants that appeal to you.

it in your gardening notebook. Or you may feel particularly drawn to a picture of a patch of herbs and think you want your first garden to be an herb garden. As you begin to know what you like and what you need, the idea for the right first garden will begin to take shape.

When You Don't Know What You Want, but You Know You Want Pink

It's particularly nice that some catalogs, like the Spring Hill Nurseries catalog, have sections with the plants organized by their color. This makes finding a plant easy when you don't know the name of the plant, but you know you want a certain color. Or you'll find, for instance, in the Wayside Gardens catalog, plants grouped together because they all do well in shade. All of this information can be extremely useful for you while thinking about the plants you like and the plants you don't like.

Don't Believe Everything You Read!

Just because the catalog says the plant is perfect, will grow wherever you plant it, and needs little or no attention, don't believe it. Some catalogs would have you think that every plant they sell fits this description. Don't dash to your telephone with your credit card in hand. You have to remember you are reading catalogs now to educate yourself.

Flower Power!
Just browse the catalogs at this time; don't order any plants. You need to be prepared for the day your plants arrive.

A New Garden Room?

Ready for a new challenge? Perhaps you'll want to spend the next winter, after you've put your garden to bed, thinking about next year's garden. Think about your property and your priorities. Have they changed since you first considered your new garden?

Put Your Garden Where You'll Most Enjoy It

If you planted a new foundation garden, and space is limited, consider using property lines for your next garden, perhaps by installing a shrub border. A shrub border, as you've learned, is very effective in cutting down street and traffic noises.

Make It Fun

Maybe your first garden was a garden of necessity—a shrub border, for instance, and you now want a garden for the sheer beauty of it. Put in a butterfly garden or a garden full of fragrant flowers.

Update Your Notebook

In addition to the things you've got in your gardening notebooks, such as the dimensions of your house, existing trees and shrubs, the sun's movement, green thoughts, and your favorite plants, be sure you have a plan of your first garden.

Make Your Own Lists

Finally, keep making lists in your gardening notebook. For example, you may be at a neighbor's barbecue and see a plant you fall in love with but can't find here in the guide. Write the name down (including genus and species) in your gardening book and gather facts about it. Eventually you'll have your own wish list of plants you like, and your garden will reflect your own personal taste. No gardener can do better than that—it's truly a garden of your own.

Continue to Use Plants That Work for You

Remember that it is always a good idea to stick to the plants that are easy and reliable and that you have used before. Keep a list of those plants in your notebook (also note the plants that fail on you).

The List of Gardening Catalogs

We've included catalogs that are useful to the beginner gardener. Catalogs are most useful when the copy tells you where or how a particular plant might work best.

Most of the catalogs are free, but some retailers do charge a fee. Write and request a catalog—in most cases you'll get one free, some will charge up to $5.

Antique Rose Emporium
Route 5, Box 143
Brenham, TX 77833
(409) 836-4293

Old garden roses from the Antique Rose Emporium are wonderful, and the full color catalog offers much of the cultural information you'll need to grow them. Antique Rose Emporium also offers perennials, books and supplies.

W. Atlee Burpee Company
300 Park Avenue
Warminster, PA 18974
(800) 888-1447

The oldest seed company in America (started in 1876) is still going strong. A great source for plants, seeds, books, supplies, tools, bulbs, each plant well described. Beautiful full-color catalogs arrive throughout the year, making shopping a breeze.

Carroll Gardens
PO Box 310
Westminster, MD 21158
(800) 638-6334

Carroll Gardens' informative catalog lists a huge selection of perennials, herbs, roses, vines, shrubs and bulbs.

The Cook's Garden
PO Box 535
Moffits Bridge
Londonderry, VT 05148
(802) 824-3400

A seed catalog that mostly specializes in vegetables and salad greens, the Cook's Garden also offers herbs, edible flowers and ornamental vegetables.

The Daffodil Mart
Route 3, Box 794
Gloucester, VA 23061
(804) 693-3966

The Daffodil Mart offers extensive catalogs of spring and summer blooming bulbs. They also offer supplies, tools and books. Buy in quantity for the best prices.

351

Farmer Seed & Nursery
P.O. Box 129
818 NW 4th St.
Faribault, MN 55021
(507) 334-1623

Order the Farmer Seed color catalog and peruse the pages for a broad selection of plants, seeds, supplies and tools.

Gurney's Seed & Nursery Co.
110 Capital Street
Yankton, SD 57079
(605) 665-1671

A color catalog chock-full of good advice and information, and a broad selection of plants and seeds, too.

The Herb Garden
P.O. Box 773
Pilot Mountain, NC 27014

The Herb Garden has it all for the herb garden: plants, books and supplies. Plants are all well described with cultural information. They also sell dried herbs, teas and seasonings!

Jackson & Perkins Co.
2518 S. Pacific Highway
Medford, OR 97501
(800) 292-4769

A favorite on everyone's list, the Jackson & Perkins color catalog offers a wide selection of roses as well as perennials and bulbs. A separate catalog each year offers beautiful garden ornaments and gifts.

Johnny's Selected Seeds
Foss Hill Road
Albion, ME 049010

Seeds, books and supplies are all offered here. Plants are well described with good cultural information.

Liberty Seed Company
P.O Box 806
128-1st Drive SE
New Philadelphia, OH 44663
(216) 364-1611

The color catalog offers a broad selection of annuals, perennials and garden supplies.

Mellinger's, Inc.
2310 W.South Range Road
North Lima, OH 44452
(216) 549-9861

Mellinger's offers a huge selection of plants, bulbs, seeds, books and gardening supplies. It's like walking through a huge department store!

Milaeger's Gardens
4838 Douglas Avenue
Racine, WI 53402-2498
(414) 639-2371

You'll find a good selection of perennials here, all very well described.

Nichols Garden Nursery, Inc.
110 N. Pacific Highway
Albany, OR 97321-8406
(503) 928-9280

Nichols offers a wide selection of herbs, all with good growing instructions. Also, books, seeds and supplies.

Park Seed Co.
P.O. Box 46
Highway 254 North
Greenwood, SC 29648-0046
(803) 223-7333

A big color catalog offering plants, seeds, books, supplies, tools and bulbs. One of the best!

Riverhead Perennials
5 Riverhead Lane
East Lyme, CT 06333
(203) 437-7828

A good selection of perennials, all well described.

Shepherd's Garden Seeds
6116 Highway 9
Felton, Ca 95018

These are some of the best seeds on the market, and the catalog offers good descriptions of all the plants and sound cultural instructions. Annuals, everlastings, edible flowers and growing supplies are all here.

Spring Hill Nurseries Co.
6523 North Galena Road
Peoria, IL 1632

Spring Hill offers just about everything that grows: perennials, shrubs, roses, bulbs, all in full color.

Stark Bros. Nurseries & Orchards Co.
P.O. Box 10
Louisiana, MO 63353-0010
(314) 754-5511

This color catalog offers shrubs and roses with descriptions and growing tips. Stark Bros. Nurseries is one of the largest sources for fruit trees, and the catalog is fun to have just for the pictures of scrumptious-looking fruit pies!

Surry Gardens
P.O. Box 145
Surry, ME 04684
(207) 667-4493

A good catalog to have for the selection of perennials and rock garden plants, all with very important cultural information.

Thompson & Morgan
P.O. Box 1308
Farraday & Gramme Avenues
Jackson, NJ 08527-0308
(800) 363-2225

Plants of all types are offered here with good descriptions and cultural information. One of the very best! You'll definitely want the Thompson & Morgan catalog to help you dream your new gardens.

Van Bourgondien Bros.
P.O. Box 1000
245 Farmingdale Road
Babylon, NY 11702
(516) 669-3500

These color catalogs offer beautiful photographs of spring- and summer-blooming bulbs and perennials, and each plant is well described. Cultural information is included.

Van Engelen, Inc.
313 Maple Street

Litchfield, CT 06759
(203) 567-5662

Van Engelen offers reduced prices on sales of Dutch bulbs bought in bulk, making them the ideal source for bulbs.

Wayside Gardens
P.O. Box 1
Hodges, SC 29695-0001
(800) 845-1124

This is on everyone's list of the best catalogs: the Wayside Gardens color catalog offers a wide selection of plants with very good descriptions and cultural instructions.

Weiss Brothers Nursery
11690 Colfax Highway
Grass Valley, CA 95945
(916) 272-7657

A good selection of perennials and herbs. Brief but good descriptions. Books, too.

White Flower Farm
Route 63
Litchfield, CT 06759-0050
(203) 496-9600

The White Flower Farm offers a broad selection of perennials, annuals, herbs, roses and shrubs, all with very good plants descriptions and detailed cultural instructions. They also offer bulbs in a separate fall catalog. Also here are supplies and tools: everything you need. This catalog is a definite must-have.

Yucca Do Nursery
PO Box 655
Waller, TX 77484

Perennials and shrubs that grow well in hot summer climates, Yucca Do is must-have for gardeners in zones 7 to 9. They also offer a good selection of native Texas and Mexican plants.

Quick Reference List of Gardening Catalogs

For Perennials:
Burpee
Carroll
Dutch Gardens
Gurney's Seed and Nursery
Jackson & Perkins

Milaegers
Spring Hill
Thompson Morgan
Wayside Gardens
White Flower Farm
Yucca Do Nursery

For Bulbs:
W. Atlee Burpee
Carroll Gardnens
Daffodil Mart
Dutch Gardens
Jackson & Perkins
Park Seed Co.
Spring Hill Nurseries Co.
Van Bourgondien Bros.
Van Engelen
Wayside Gardens
White Flower Farm

For Herbs:
The Cooks Garden
The Herb Garden
Nichols
Shepherds Garden Seeds
White Flower Farm

For Roses:
Antique Rose Emporium
Jackson & Perkins
Wayside Gardens
White Flower Farm

Mail-Order Catalogs for Garden Supplies

The following is a list of great sources of garden supplies. You can get just about any garden supply via mail-order—from tools and organic fertilizers (remember the power of bat guano!) to garden furniture, trellises, and ornaments.

Here are just a few of the many good garden-supply companies to order from:

Gardener's Eden
P.O. Box 7307
San Francisco, CA 94120-7307
(800) 822-9600

Garden Supply Company
128 Intervale Road
Burlington, VT 05401
(802) 660-3500
Fax: (802) 660-3501

Gardens Alive!
5100 Schenley Place
Lawrenceburg, IN 47025
(812) 537-8650
Fax: (812) 537-8660

Langenbach Fine Tool Co.
P.O. Box 453
Blairstown, NJ 07825
(800) 362-1991
Fax: (201) 383-0844

A.M. Leonard
P.O. Box 816
6665 Spiker Road
Piqua, OH 45356-0816
(800) 543-8955
(513) 773-2696

The Natural Gardening Company
217 San Anselmo Avenue
San Anselmo, CA 94960
(415) 456-5060
Fax: (415) 721-0642

Smith & Hawken
117 E. Strawberry Drive
Mill Valley, CA 94941
(800) 776-3336

The Least You Need to Know

➤ Gardening catalogs have always been popular reading for gardeners, especially during the winter when the ground is frozen, or during the summer when it's too hot, or when a gardener just wants to dream.

➤ Some catalogs also provide good information about the plant's culture, which you can read about and begin to learn about growing that plant.

➤ Be sure to take notes of the plants you like in your gardening notebook.

➤ Just because the catalog says the plant is perfect, don't believe it.

➤ Ready for a new challenge? Think about next year's garden!

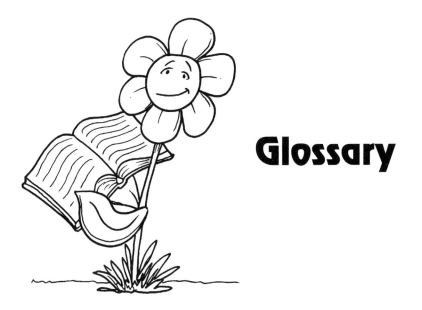

Glossary

Accents   Single plants used in a garden design. Accent plants draw attention to themselves with their dramatic or interesting foliage or flower color. Also called specimen plants.

Acidic soil   Soil with a pH value of less than 7.0.

Alkaline soil   Soil with a pH value of more than 7.0.

Annuals   Plants that live for one year or growing season.

Basal leaves   The term for leaves that grow from the base of a plant.

Beneficial insects   The term for insects, such as ladybugs, lacewings, dragonflies, and certain wasps and flies, that eat or parasitize the insects that damage plants.

Biennials   Plants that complete their life cycles within 2 years.

Bract   A modified leaf, either small and scaly or large and brilliantly colored.

Broadcast   To scatter seeds or fertilizer onto the soil by hand.

Bud   A flower bud develops into a flower; a growth bud on the tip of a stem or along the side of a stem will produce new leafy growth.

Bulb   A thick underground bud that acts as a food storage organ for the plant, with a stem from which roots grow. Often used as a generic term for related storage organs such as corms, rhizomes and tubers.

Clay soil   A type of soil with small, almost microscopic soil particles.

Compost   Decomposed organic matter that is added to the soil to improve its composition and fertility.

Corm   A solid bulb-like underground stem not separated into scales, e.g. crocus.

Corymb   A shape of a flower that is rounded or flat-topped.

Complete fertilizer   A plant food, either organic or synthetic, with all three of the essential nutrient elements: nitrogen, phosphorus and potassium.

Cotyledon   Seed leaves that are apparent upon germination of the seed. These first leaves are not "true leaves" and contain stored nutrients which aids growth of the new plant.

Cultivar   A plant variety that is selected from cultivation, not from the wild. When propogated, it retains its distinct identity.

Cultivate   The act of tilling or stirring the soil surface to eliminate weeds and aerate the soil.

Cultivation   Any habitat inhabited by humans—areas that are not wild.

Cutting   The piece of a plant, usually a stem, cut off from the plant and rooted to make a new plant.

Deadhead   The act of removing faded flowers to promote further flowering, prevent seeding, or improve the appearance of a plant.

Deciduous   Refers to plants (mostly trees and shrubs) that shed their leaves in the fall, and remain bare until the spring.

Divide   A way of propagating perennials to get more plants and keep plants vigorous and healthy.

Dormancy   A period of reduced activity in seeds, bulbs, buds, etc., in which growth does not occur.

Evergreen   A plant or tree that never loses all its leaves at the same time.

Dwarf   A plant variant that is small and/or very slow growing.

Diseases   Organisms (fungal, viral, or bacterial) that attack plants, hindering their development and producing mildews, rots, rusts and wilts on stems, leaves and flowers.

Direct sow   The act of planting seeds directly in the soil where they are to grow.

Family   A botanical division within the plant kingdom comprised of genera; *see also* Genus.

Fertilizer Any material, synthetic or organic, that supplies nutrients to a plant.

Foliage plants Plants used in gardens primarily for their attractive foliage rather than for flowers.

Genus A botanical division of plants within a family.

Germination The beginning of plant growth from a seed.

Ground cover A plant that spreads densely along the ground.

Habit The general appearance or growth patterns of a plant.

Harden off The process of introducing a plant to outdoor temperatures, by gradually acclimating the plant to the colder weather, in order to minimize the shock of the transition.

Hardy The term used to describe a plant's resistance to or tolerance of freezing temperatures. Hardy plants are those that survive cold winter temperatures.

Hardiness zone The climate in which a perennial is deemed hardy based on the plant's ability to tolerate the climatic conditions. The USDA plant hardiness map divides North America into 11 hardiness zones.

Heavy soil A term used interchangeably with clay soil to describe a soil made up of minutely fine particles packed closely together.

Herbaceous The term to describe plants with nonwoody stems.

Hip The fruit-like receptacles on a rose, high in vitamin C.

Humus Organic matter in its last stage of decay, usually brown or black.

Hybrid A plant that has been created by cross-pollinating different plants, hoping to create a new plant which is distinct from or superior to its parents.

Inflorescence The flower supporting structure of plants. Some inflorescences include umbels, corymbs, spikes and racemes.

Island bed The term for a garden bed that is set within a lawn. Its shape may be geometric or free-form.

Invasive Refers to a plant that spreads quickly, and if not checked, can take over a garden.

Leggy Refers to plants that are long, spindly, and weak-looking due to lack of sun or competition from other plants.

Loam A balance of sand and clay; the best type of soil.

Light soil   A term used interchangeably with sandy soil to describe a large-particled, loosely packed, free-draining soil.

Manure   Livestock dung, usually high in nutrients, used as an organic fertilizer and soil conditioner.

Mulch   The name for materials, synthetic and organic, spread on the soil surface to protect plants from excessive weather, stifle the growth of weeds, conserve moisture, or to enhance the look of a garden.

Native plant   A plant that is native to a particular region. Plants are often easiest to grow in their native habitats because they are adapted to the environment.

Naturalize   To plant out randomly, in a way that imitates nature and makes it appear as though the plants grew there naturally. Some plants will naturalize once planted, meaning they will continue to spread or re-seed themselves.

Neutral soil   Soil that is neither too alkaline nor too acidic; it has a pH value of 7.0. The broadest spectrum of nutrients reach plants in soils with a neutral pH.

Nitrogen   One of the three most important nutrients for a plant. Nitrogen helps plants to produce stems and leaves.

Organic matter   Any material that was once alive or that came from a living creature. Compost, sawdust and fish emulsion are examples of organic matter.

Pedicel   The individual stalk of a flower or fruit in a cluster.

Peduncle   The stalk of a flower cluster or a single flower.

Pests   The range of insects and animals that attack and damage plants, including aphids, mites, slugs, birds, rabbits and deer.

Perennials   Plants whose life cycles take more than two years to complete.

pH   The measure of acidity or alkalinity of a soil on a scale of 0 to 14, the lowest end being most acidic, the highest most alkaline; neutral is 7.0.

Phosphorus   One of the three most important nutrients for a plant. Phosphorus is important in developing flowers, seeds and roots.

Pinching   A process of pruning (with forefingers or scissors) to keep plants growing compactly and encourage the plant to become bushy.

Potassium   One of the three most important nutrients for a plant. Potassium helps in the overall growth of a plant and helps the plant to create strong stems.

Potbound   The condition of a container-grown plant whose root ball is thickly matted.

Raceme An unbranched flower cluster with many flowers borne singly along a main axis.

Rhizome A horizontal, underground root-like stem that serves as a food storage organ and from which spring true roots and stems of new plants, e.g. calla lily.

Root ball The entire root system of a plant in soil.

Runner *See* Stolon.

Sandy soil A type of soil that has large soil particles.

Seedling A young plant grown from seed (not cuttings).

Self-sowing Plants that sow themselves into the ground.

Shrub A multi-stemmed plant with woody branches.

Slug An invertebrate mammal in the mollusk family that often hides under stones and boards, feeding on leaves in the night. Slug damage is easy to detect by the chewed leaves on your plant.

Soil test An analysis of the soil to determine its pH level and the nutrients available.

Species A unit of plant classification within a genus. A genus may have one or more species within it.

Specimen plant *See* Accent plant.

Stake A structure to support plants that may otherwise flop over.

Stolon (runner) A stem that spreads horizontally along the soil which can root along its length. Many weeds grow by runners.

Succulent A plant with juicy, water-storing stems or leaves.

Suckers Secondary shoots that grow from buds on roots or stems.

Taproot The name of the main root of a plant that grows directly downward.

Tender The opposite of hardy; a plant that is sensitive to freezing temperatures and has a low tolerance for cold.

Thinning out The act of pulling up plants so remaining plants have enough room to grow.

Till To cultivate the soil.

Transplant The term for a plant newly moved; the act of moving a plant from one location to another.

Tree   A woody plant usually with a single truck and crowned at the top with spreading branches.

Tuber   A tuber resembles a bulb, but it has a swollen stem or branch with buds, usually underground, e.g. dahlia.

True leaves   The leaves that emerge from a seedling after the cotyledon leaves. The first leaves that are true to type.

Umbel   A rounded or flat-topped flower cluster; the flower stalks arise from a central point, like an umbrella.

Volunteer   A plant that has sown itself into the garden as a seedling of a mother plant.

Variegated foliage   Foliage that has more than one color, usually white or yellow, in spots, ribbons or some identifiable pattern.

Variety   A naturally occuring variant of a species.

Vermiculite   A mica-type rock expanded by heat that is lightweight, absorbent and used in seed-starting and -growing mediums.

Weed   An unwanted plant in the garden. Eliminating weeds improves the appearance of a garden and provides growing space for plants that are wanted.

Wilt   A disease that causes leaves to turn brown and often causes the plant to die.

Further Reading

People seem to love to talk about gardening (gardening talk is second only to talk of kids and pets, depending on those kids and pets) and there are, as you've no doubt discovered, a good many gardening books available. We hope the *The Complete Idiot's Guide to Gardening, Second Edition* has helped get you started, and that as you build your gardeners education, you'll make use of some of the wonderfully useful books and magazines on the market.

Books

Armitage, Allan, Maureen Heffernan, Chela Kleiber, and Holly H. Shimazu, Barbara W. Ellis, ed. *Burpee Complete Gardener*. New York: Macmillan, 1995.

Barton, Barbara. *Gardening by Mail,* 4th ed. Boston: Houghton Mifflin, 1994.

Breskend, Jean Spiro. *Backyard Design: Making the Most of the Space Around Your House.* New York: Bulfinch Press, 1991.

Clausen, Ruth R. and Nicolas H. Ekstrom. *Perennials for American Gardens*. New York: Random House, 1989.

Potterton, David, ed. *Culpepper's Color Herbal*. New York: Sterling Publishing Co., Inc., 1983.

Flower Garden Plans. San Ramon, CA: Ortho Books, 1991.

Green, Douglas. *Burpee Basics: Bulbs*. New York: Macmillan Publishing, 1998.

Herb Gardening. The American Garden Guides. New York: Pantheon, 1994.

Kingsbury, Noel, *The New Perennial Garden*. New York: Henry Holt & Co., Inc., 1996.

McGourty, Fred, and Pam Harper. *Perennials: How to Select, Grow and Enjoy*. Los Angeles: Price Stern Sloan, 1985.

Mercer, Cheryl and the Editors of Garden Design Magazine. *The Garden Design Book*. New York: HarperCollins, 1997.

Pavord, Anna. *The Border Book: An Illlustrated Practical Guide to Planting Borders, Beds and Out-of-the-Way Corners*. New York: Dorling Kindersley, 1994.

Pirone, Pascal. *Diseases and Pests of Ornamental Plants*, 5th ed. New York: John Wiley & Sons, 1978.

The Editors of Smith & Hawken. *The Book of Outdoor Gardening*. New York: Workman Publishing, 1996.

Sweeney, Emma. *Burpee Basics: Perennials*. New York: Macmillan Publishing, 1998.

Sweeney, Emma. *Burpee Basics: Annuals*. New York: Macmillan Publishing, 1998.

Sunset New Western Garden Book, 6th Ed. Menlo Park, Ca., 1981.

Taylor's Master Guide to Gardening. Boston, New York: Houghton Mifflin Co. 1994.

Weaver, Mary C. *Burpee Basics: Roses*. New York: Macmillan Publishing, 1998.

Magazines

American Homestyle & Gardening
G&J USA Publishing
375 Lexington Ave.
New York, NY 10017
(800) 627-3333

For home and garden, with good gardening information.

Country Living Gardener
Hearst Communications
250 W. 57th St.
New York, NY 10019
(800) 777-0102

A subsidiary of *Country Living* magazine, this colorful bimonthly publication is a very useful gardening and lifestyle magazine.

Fine Gardening
The Taunton Press
P.O. Box 5506
Newtown, CT 06470-9877
E-mail: fgservice@taunton.com
(800) 888-8286

An hands-on gardening magazine with informative articles written by expert gardeners.

Garden Design
Meigher Communications
100 Avenue of the Americas
New York, NY 10013
E-mail: GRDNDSGN@aol.com
(800) 234-5118

Beautiful photos and great ideas for garden designs in every part of the country.

Horticulture
P.O. Box 51455
Boulder, CO 80323-145
www.hortmag.com

The real thing. Has more information for the beginning gardener than beginners may realize. Not to be missed.

Organic Gardening
Rodale Press, Inc.
33 East Minor St.
Emmaus, PA 18098

This magazine is full of great tips and ideas for dealing with pests and diseases without resorting to dangerous chemicals. A great magazine for gardeners in all parts of the country.

Sunset Magazine
Sunset Publishing Co.
80 Willow Road
Menlo Park, CA 94025

Familiar to anyone who has gardened in the west. *Sunset* publishes four regional editions with customized information for each region.

The Gardener's Calendar

The following is a quick reference calendar to help you plan the chores each year in your garden. Information is included here for annuals, perennials, shrubs, vines, bulbs, herbs—everything! Use the plant hardiness zone map (located at the end of the color insert in the middle of the book) to find where you are, then use the calendar that corresponds to your region to learn which chores need to be done when. Do your best to get to these tasks on time.

Zones 2,3,4

Early Spring:

- ➤ Slowly begin to remove evergreen boughs as weather warms. Add to compost heap.
- ➤ Remove mulch from around spring-blooming perennials and bulbs as you see the shoots appear to help ground warm up.
- ➤ Place a peony ring around peonies.
- ➤ Prune shrubs that grow on old wood.

Late Spring:

- ➤ Clean up beds and borders.
- ➤ Plant and label new perennials.
- ➤ Dig and divide established perennials.
- ➤ Direct sow Shirley poppies and continue to sow every few weeks for a succession of color.
- ➤ Start checking leaves for telltale signs of pests and diseases.
- ➤ Begin weeding on a regular basis.
- ➤ Plant containers with annuals such as pansies and snapdragons. Add a trellis for a vine.
- ➤ Deadhead lilacs after they flower.
- ➤ Watch for last frost date: Direct sow annuals after last frost date.

Summer:

- ➤ Water deeply throughout summer.
- ➤ Continue weeding.
- ➤ Feed perennials and roses until the first of August.

> ➤ Put mulches in place in garden beds.

> ➤ Cut herbs and flowers all summer to enjoy indoors.

> ➤ Stake plants as they need it.

> ➤ Deadhead coreopsis, geraniums and other perennials for second flush of flowers.

> ➤ Pot up containers with heat-tolerant annuals such as celosia, portulaca and salvias.

> ➤ Continue pinching the annuals that need it for bushy growth.

> ➤ Shear annuals that have stopped blooming to encourage new growth.

Early Autumn:

> ➤ Divide daylilies and irises.

> ➤ After first hard frost, cut annuals to ground and add to compost heap.

> ➤ Cut back perennials to 6 inches above ground and add to compost heap. Leave perennials with ornamental seedheads such as sedum for winter interest.

> ➤ Plant bearded irises, peonies and Oriental poppies.

> ➤ Move perennials in containers to a sheltered space outdoors.

> ➤ Begin raking leaves.

> ➤ Plant flowering kales and cabbages.

> ➤ Dig up dahlia tubers and store in cool, dry place.

> ➤ Empty plants and soil from pots. Clean out terra cotta containers and store in cool place.

> ➤ Plant drifts of daffodils in the lawn early in the fall.

Late Autumn:

> ➤ Rake the last of the leaves; shred and add to leaf mold pile to use in the following spring as a mulch.

> ➤ Clean and store garden tools.

> ➤ Take down and store stakes for use next year.

> ➤ Cover heavy containers that are to stay outdoors with boards and a tarp.

> ➤ Plant tulips in the garden.

Winter:

> ➤ Add evergreen boughs to garden beds after ground is frozen.

> ➤ Peruse garden catalogs. Order seeds and bare-root perennials.

➤ Check stored dahlia tubers and remove any that have rotted.

➤ Walk around property. Think about where you want to plan new gardens, keeping in mind the angle of the winter sun and leafless trees.

Zones 5, 6, 7

Early Spring:

➤ Begin to remove evergreen boughs from garden...slowly! Add to compost pile.

➤ Fertilize bulbs when shoots are 2 inches high.

➤ Place a peony ring around peonies.

➤ Prune summer- and fall-flowering shrubs.

➤ Oil and sharpen pruning shears and other tools.

➤ Weed on a regular basis.

Late Spring:

➤ Clean up beds. When temperatures begin to stay above 65°F, add 1 inch compost to top of bed and till in.

➤ Direct sow Shirley poppies and continue to sow every few weeks for a succession of color.

➤ Watch for pests—it's easier to control them if caught early.

➤ Watch for last frost date; direct sow annuals accordingly.

➤ Pot up containers with annuals, adding trellises for vines.

➤ Deadhead perennials.

➤ Begin to pinch back mums and asters.

➤ Dig and divide perennials.

➤ Water when rainfall is scarce.

Summer:

➤ Renew mulch when the soil has warmed up.

➤ Deadhead annuals and perennials weekly.

➤ Fertilize perennials and roses until mid-July.

➤ Water deeply.

➤ Continue pinching annuals for bushy growth.

➤ Cut flowers to enjoy indoors.

➤ Harvest herbs for culinary uses.

➤ Water and feed plants in containers regularly.

➤ Stake plants as they need it.

➤ Shear annuals that have stopped blooming to encourage new growth.

➤ Keep plants mulched and watered all summer.

Early Autumn:

➤ Plant mums, flowering kales and cabbages.

➤ Dig up dahlia tubers after the first frost and store in cool, dry place.

➤ Empty plants and soil from pots. Clean out terra cotta containers and store in cool place.

➤ Divide daylilies and irises.

➤ Plant Oriental poppies, bearded irises and peonies.

➤ Dig and prepare new perennial beds.

➤ Remove leaves from beds and borders.

➤ Water all plants if rainfall is inadequate.

➤ Plant daffodils in drifts in the lawn.

Late Autumn:

➤ After first hard frost, cut annuals to ground level and add to compost heap.

➤ Rake up leaves on lawn and add to compost.

➤ Cut back perennials to 4–6 inches from the ground.

➤ Water during dry periods.

➤ Plant tulips.

Winter:

➤ Check stored dahlia tubers. Remove any that have rotted.

➤ Order seeds and bare-root perennials from mail order nurseries.

➤ Plan new gardens.

➤ Add evergreen boughs to beds.

➤ Begin making list of perennials to order.

➤ Plan new gardens on paper.

Zones 8, 9, 10

Early Spring:

> ➤ Deadhead faded annuals to keep them blooming through spring.

> ➤ Renew mulch in garden and shrub beds.

> ➤ Watch for insect and disease problems.

> ➤ Turn compost pile as needed.

> ➤ Dig and divide established summer- and fall-blooming perennials.

> ➤ Consider installing a soaker hose or other drip irrigation system in garden.

> ➤ Plant, feed, and deadhead pansies.

> ➤ Water when rainfall is insufficient.

Late Spring:

> ➤ Fertilize perennials and summer-flowering bulbs.

> ➤ Feed and water plants in containers.

> ➤ Put stakes in place.

> ➤ Water all plants when needed to prevent plant stress.

> ➤ Be on the lookout for aphids. Handpick them.

> ➤ Pinch back mums and asters.

> ➤ Prune spring-flowering shrubs after they finish blooming.

> ➤ Harvest perennial herbs like chives, French tarragon, oregano and rosemary.

Summer:

> ➤ Watch for insects—especially spider mites.

> ➤ Weed.

> ➤ Cut back plants as needed to rejuvenate.

> ➤ Continue deadheading throughout summer.

> ➤ Protect newly planted perennials from excessive heat with a shade cloth.

> ➤ Stop pinching mums and asters.

Early Autumn:

> ➤ Water shrubs, perennials and annuals as needed.

> ➤ Plant hardy annuals.

➤ Dig and divide perennials.

➤ Deadhead annual and perennial flowers frequently.

➤ Weed regularly.

➤ Continue looking out for pests.

Late Autumn:

➤ Cut perennials back to 4–6 inches.

➤ Remove debris from flower beds.

➤ Harvest flowers for drying.

➤ Continue monitoring garden for pests and diseases.

➤ Water as necessary; stake plants as necessary.

➤ Mulch garden bed.

➤ Deadhead and fertilize hardy annuals.

Winter:

➤ Water as needed when temperatures are above freezing.

➤ Deadhead as necessary.

➤ Remove fall garden debris, till soil deeply, and incorporate organic matter.

➤ Clean and sharpen garden tools.

➤ Protect half-hardy plants when frosts are predicted.

➤ Feed annuals as they begin to flower; deadhead perennials as necessary.

➤ Renew mulches.

➤ Order mail-order catalogs for seeds and bare-root perennials.

➤ Prune summer- and fall-flowering shrubs and roses.

Index

379

383